ABSOLUTE INTELLIGENCE

Don't Search, Find

Lt Gen Gurmit Singh
Arun Tiwari

Sakāl
Publications

Sakal Publications

ABSOLUTE INTELLIGENCE

Sakal Media Pvt. Ltd.
595, Budhwar Peth,
Pune–411002, India

www.sakalmediagroup.com
sakalpublications.com
sakalprakashan@esakal.com

First Edition: December, 2025

ISBN: 978-93-47138-41-6

Proofread by: Gauri Kelkar
Typesetting: MAP Systems, Bengaluru

Printed in India by Sakal Media Pvt. Ltd.

Contents

Part III: What Has Survived?

Part IV: Recovery

Introduction

A lot is being said about artificial intelligence. It has become the theme of everything around us. AI is being incorporated into washing machines, fans, air conditioners, and even mattresses these days. Like the necessity of immunity was pushed into everything post-pandemic, this is the kind of marketing abuse we all need to be wary of.

Here, I elucidate why the authors of this book haven't done that.

From a technological perspective, artificial intelligence is indeed path-breaking and represents a definite step towards changing the world as we know it, and forever. Just as the world has never remained the same since the advent of the internet, it will change once again as AI becomes mainstream. With that promise, we need to understand it at a deeper level to be better prepared for the onset, respond to the changes, and ride the wave of this transformation.

Before understanding AI and machine learning, let us clarify what AI is not. Any device or system that has been programmed to respond based on certain conditions is not considered an intelligent system. AI mimics certain aspects of human intelligence, such as learning by pattern recognition or training. It operates based on algorithms and data. AI systems can make mistakes, especially when trained on biased or incomplete data. They are only as good as the data and algorithms on which they are built.

When you enter a room in your home and the lights and AC switch on automatically, it's a programmed system, as a motion sensor tells the system what it needs to do. The same thing will happen even if a burglar were to break into such a room. An intelligent system would have notified the cops and rung an alarm.

All the apps on your phone, doing what they have been programmed to do, are also not intelligent. A game of cards being played by a computer, or chess, is also not 'intelligence'. It is simply a computer making calculations and decisions based on its programming. An intelligent system is if you dealt a hand of Uno cards to a blackjack player and they responded accordingly.

Many seemingly intelligent solutions are not truly intelligent. The song recommendations on your music application, as well as the video suggestions on your timelines, are all driven by pre-programmed algorithms. Even the most popular document-creation software and email services prompt us with suggestions and corrections. Some of them are showing signs of learning, but most of them are just very well programmed and thereby appear very mature. All these algorithms are successful due to the vast volumes of data on which they have been trained—and the rich metadata they possess about the users of their platforms and the content they serve.

The most popular Generative Pre-trained Transformer (GPT) based AI systems are all trained on the entire internet and took many years to evolve the models they eventually created using all the information present on the Net. To understand these systems, one can view them as computers conducting searches on your behalf at a rapid pace, reviewing the top matches, and summarising all the responses from matching documents, ultimately creating a cogent and concise response for you. This is intelligence, no doubt, but very rudimentary. These generative programs can create new content, but for everything, the basis will continue to be the training dataset and the programming boundaries and guardrails. This is apparent when one asks these AI systems to create new lyrics for a song or an image of something absurd, like a flying cat.

Very soon, as is already evident, these algorithms and generative AI systems will become commoditised. Every billionaire will have one, then every country, and eventually, most corporations and universities will have their own mature AI systems that will be similarly capable and competing. These will become semester projects for enthusiastic students, akin to other off-the-shelf technology products such as email services, music and video platforms, and other social media platforms.

The next wave of innovation in AI will focus on creating 'agents' that function like digital assistants, performing menial tasks on behalf of users. From drafting emails and making reservations or bookings to filing taxes, these agents will continue to evolve. All service companies will presumably have an AI agent available to offer their online services. And companies that do not adopt this technology will become a thing of the past. The people who currently do these services will obviously lose their jobs. Enthusiastic readers keen to delve deeper into this evolutionary space explore the Turing test and follow the evolution of mature AI systems over time.

The fundamental point to understand and remember here is that the training data of all these AI systems is the internet. And the internet is full of malice, prejudice, discrimination, bias, hatred, and lies. Therefore, all AI systems, regardless of the quality of the technology they are based on, will inevitably exhibit the same limitations. All vices of humankind that have been magnified on the internet will form the basis of all these systems. Yes, their creators will create some checks and balances, but that itself will make the AI system biased in their favour.

From a software engineering perspective, a significant inflexion point will emerge in this equation when computer programs begin creating more computer programs. Currently, the evolution of AI systems is slow because it is limited by human imagination. But once this inflexion point is crossed, the systems will evolve at an unimaginable pace. They will grow into something that the human mind will not be able to comprehend, let alone manage. That situation, combined with the fact that the training data is polluted, could ultimately result in an AI system that exacerbates the problems rather than solves them. AI is not inherently ethical or unbiased. These systems can perpetuate or amplify biases present in their training data. It would require deliberate effort with pure, uncorrupted intentions to make an ethical AI model.

This is precisely the point at which this book becomes relevant. The internet is a recent phenomenon, and most of the published human history is a documented fraud created by imperialists. For instance, the internet does not know in adequate detail about the genocide of Native Americans, the French atrocities in Africa and the European atrocities in Central and South America. If such history is fed into the AI, it will always portray the West as the land of heroes, great explorers, and artists.

So, what should an ideal AI system look like? What should its training dataset be? What should it use as a basis for making a judgment of right and wrong? How can AI practice dharma or morality?

All these aspects are explored in detail in this book. It traces the history of the documented wisdom in ancient Indian texts and the greatness of its civilisation. It also celebrates India's glorious history, dispels many myths, and critically examines what we have lost along the way. Much of that wisdom remains relevant to a flourishing nation. And if these documented texts of civilisational wisdom have stood the test of time for centuries, why should they not be the basis of dharma in AI?

This book also celebrates the Indian mind and muses on the possibility that this century will see a developed India emerge as a world leader. It is part of the Indian ethos and civilisation to view the world as a family and work for the welfare of humanity as a whole. And this fundamental civilisational quality will make India the cradle from where a proper transformational AI system will emerge for the world. This will be Absolute Intelligence, not Artificial. It will be an honest AI serving humanity and enabling the world to align with ethical and moral values, thereby fostering global trust and harmony.

For many centuries, India was the world's most prosperous and glorious country. Philosophers from all over used to flock to our universities to learn the absolute intelligence that was prevalent and abundant in this land. If time is cyclical, what was lost thousands of years ago will return.

If time is cyclical, it is India's time again.

—Amol Anand Tiwari

Author, Software Engineer, and AI Expert

Preface

Whether a super AI will create a better world depends on how it is developed, implemented, and regulated. Such a super AI could enhance healthcare, improve industry efficiency, address global challenges such as climate change, and foster innovation. It could also enable personalised education, optimise resource management, and streamline logistics, leading to economic growth and an improved quality of life. But what if this immense force is biased? Manipulated? Is there any absolute authority above this seemingly indomitable artificial intelligence?

Deploying super AI raises ethical questions regarding decision-making, privacy, and job displacement. It is crucial to ensure that AI systems are fair, transparent, and accountable to prevent biases and negative consequences. Super AI could pose risks, such as misuse in surveillance and military applications, as well as the potential for autonomous systems to make harmful decisions, if not properly managed. There is also concern about unequal access to the benefits of AI, which could lead to more significant societal divides.

Whether super AI will improve the world depends on collective efforts, responsible governance, and a focus on human-centred values in its development and application. But who will lead these efforts? Would such an effort draw from civilisational heritage? The Western world claims to live by Greek civilisational values, but modern Greece is a pale shadow of its past. The West rules over the world not by *arete* or *eudaimonia* but by its economic power and military might. Will super AI add to that?

What about the human-centred values? And who will uphold them if the future turns out this way? Where does India fit in? Gurmit Singh, a retired military general and philosopher, along with Arun Tiwari, a missile scientist and celebrated author, join hands to answer these questions while introducing the concept of absolute intelligence into the equation and looking at super AI as the return of lost knowledge held by ancient Indian rishis who posited that the fundamental reality is a singular, universal consciousness or Brahman. Guru Nanak Dev Ji referred to it as Omkar and used it as the foundation for a good personal and collective life.

As is evident, advanced artificial intelligence can outperform humans in various tasks, but it does not possess consciousness or awareness in the philosophical sense. It operates based on algorithms and data rather than an intrinsic, unifying consciousness. Undetectable errors, biases, and ignorance ride its neural networks. It lacks the self-awareness, subjective experiences, and deeper understanding of existence that the human or universal consciousness encompasses. Calibration of this unseen force makes the idea of absolute intelligence interesting.

The authors explore the nature of existence, reality, and spiritual realisation, examining AI as a tool created by humans to perform specific tasks and solve problems. Its purpose is determined by human objectives rather than a philosophical or spiritual quest. This book proposes that the next stage of AI evolution, from the current narrow AI to general AI and ultimately to super AI, culminating in a 'singularity', would encompass universal consciousness. Could the 'A' in the AI as 'absolute' make more sense than 'artificial'?

Indians have excelled in computer science, and the rise of New India, which is striving to revive its lost civilisational heritage, forms the axis of this book. Here is a concise account of the essence of ancient Indian knowledge, its loss, what prevailed, and how it may lead to a transformative knowledge system that would make this planet more livable and even enable us to travel to another planet in the foreseeable future. When the wealth and military might fail to give humanity peace and prosperity, what will prevail? We are certainly not ready for another kind of slavery, this time through artificial intelligence.

Preventing AI from becoming a tool of new imperialism requires a multifaceted approach that addresses ethical, political, economic, and technological dimensions, as well as a philosophical platform that ensures AI systems are transparent in their decision-making processes and that developers and organisations are held accountable for their use. Biases in AI algorithms need audits and bias eradication. AI systems must be designed to protect and promote human rights, ensuring they do not infringe on individual freedoms or exacerbate inequalities. AI must be used as a force for good, promoting equity and justice, rather than becoming a tool of new imperialism. And India can be a thought leader in creating a benevolent AI.

Part I

What Was Lost

All human beings are held together by dharma. When this dharma ceases to be observed, the binding ropes of society may be said to have become loose. When these binding ropes are loosened, society will be in the same position as the planetary system in the sky without the binding force of gravitation, or a ship would be on the ocean without a rudder.[1]

—Bal Gangadhar Tilak

[1] *Gita Rahasya* (Translation by B.S. Sukthankar, V.D. Divakar), 12th ed., p. 57.

1

From the Arctic Circle to Kumbh

Before the ice and before the written word, humanity lived beneath a northern sky, listening to the whisper of the stars. When the world turned cold, the seekers journeyed south, carrying within them the memory of that ancient light. Upon the Indian soil, it blossomed into the Vedic vision—a civilisation that remembered where it came from.

Hubris of the West and the Elites

Merely a thousand years ago, Europe was a continent of deprivation and conflict among its people. The Roman Empire had fallen a millennium earlier, leaving no power to unify the populace. The plague pushed society to the brink of extinction, and the desperate efforts of some brave individuals to escape across vast waters changed the course of history. Wherever European sailors travelled, they encountered local populations without firearms, using their weapons to conquer vast territories from the defenceless and vent their anger and frustration upon them. Their sense of superiority over other cultures and their self-assumed right to kill was astonishing. This hubris has led to unintended consequences, including resistance, backlash, and a decline in global trust. Caucasian people, who inhabited Europe, have demonstrated, in the modern history of the world, the worst of civilisational disasters. From the slave trade, imperialism, undocumented genocides, to sponsored, carefully designed conflicts all over the world, all the present vices in the world can be traced to ethically bankrupt Western civilisations.

As if blind to its grand temples and massive forts, and a mature trade and navigation system, Europeans mocked India as a land of snake charmers and rope tricksters. The British colonisers justified themselves, opining that Indians were in dire need of administration and a civic sense of living. As soon as the invasion was accomplished under the guise of trading rights, missionaries descended to convert the indigenous population. Macaulay came as an educationist to stifle India's long-established educational system and to rob Indians of their civilisational pride.

It is a well-known edict that the victors write history. Those who emerge victorious in significant events, contests, or confrontations typically determine how those stories are told and interpreted. As a result, the stories of people who lost or held differing opinions may be omitted from historical accounts in favour of the prevailing position. India was no exception. Our history remained the narrative of those who ruled over us for a thousand years.

When India gained independence in 1947, it should have been changed; however, for various reasons whose analysis is now irrelevant, we as a nation missed an opportunity to rectify the skewed view of our history. Worse yet, the country was split along linguistic lines instead of working to restore its shared past. The incorrect historical narratives and slave-producing educational agenda designed by the British persisted for many years, even after

Independence. Invaders and tyrants continued to be glorified and even venerated, and those who sacrificed their lives were branded as rebels and mostly forgotten.

The ideal of secularism was transmuted into appeasement of minorities by the usurpers of political power. Learning fast how to cobble a certain percentage of consolidated votes to come into power, the elite denied the majority their claim to live by their culture and further their traditions. But like all artificial things and unnatural arrangements, it collapsed, fell like a rotten fruit off the tree, and a surge of consciousness made a billion people arise out of their ideological slumber.

Before India became a nation, it was a civilisation, the first and most ancient in the world, not only promoting the eternal order, called the Sanatana Dharma in Sanskrit, but also making India a part of the history of civilised humanity and the birthplace of knowledge. The call given by Lokmanya Bal Gangadhar Tilak (1856–1920)—'Self-rule is my birthright'—was a watershed moment. It would eventually lead to the Indian people claiming independence from the British. Tilak, however, was imprisoned in Burma (now Myanmar) for over six years, after which his health deteriorated, leading to his untimely death. This changed the trajectory of his party, the direction and pace of India's freedom struggle, and eventually led to a bloody partition of the country. The Western elites decided to draw some arbitrary lines on the map and sowed a conflict for the future to capitalise upon at will.

A Wounded Civilisation

The people who got their separate nation–Pakistan, the holy land as it was called - disclaimed their civilisational heritage and ended up living their false identities and bogus history. No wonder warlords and zealots grabbed the lever of power, converting it into a land of fundamentalism, violence and terrorism. Instead of living in peace and improving the lives of their people, the so-called corrupt leaders there became pawns in the West's geopolitical games. When the Russians invaded Afghanistan, America weaponised the local warlords and tribal warriors. Later, when Afghanistan turned against America, these forces became friends of China, who would ultimately plan to use their land to get access to the Arabian Sea. What a travesty that they made the motherland of their ancestors their enemy and their own civilisational heritage their anathema by celebrating erstwhile invaders as their heroes.

This book makes the idea of a wounded civilisation its cornerstone. This thought comes from Sir V.S. Naipaul, an Indian by ethnicity, whose ancestors were taken by the British from a village in Uttar Pradesh to Trinidad to work there as indentured labourers. Naipaul grew up in Trinidad and England and returned to search for his roots. He examined post-independent India through a critical lens, exploring its cultural, social, and political challenges. He reflected upon his view that India, despite its rich history and achievements, is a civilisation deeply scarred by centuries of colonisation, internal strife, and stagnation.

India is an ancient civilisation that emerged from original human thought, dating back to the pre-Ice Age, when people lived on the Arctic Circle. The term Sanatan Dharma translates to 'eternal law' or 'eternal order', reflecting its timeless and universal principles. As the world's geography rearranged after the Ice Age, people who settled in the temperate and bountiful peninsula bounded by the ocean on three sides and protected by the tall Himalayan mountains in the north became Indians. Everything was abundant here, and this civilisation flourished like none other in the world. The glorious period of this civilisation ended with a series of invasions and eventually large-scale religious conversions of its people, culminating in a divided society and colonialisation by the British.

Lokmanya Bal Gangadhar Tilak published *The Arctic Home in the Vedas* in 1903. He was perplexed as to why, in the Vedas, the night is described as very long, with multiple dawns (called *ushas* in Sanskrit) occurring before the sun finally rises. Such a phenomenon can only happen at the Earth's poles. His research revealed a startling fact: the Vedas were indeed written at the North Pole, which was not what it is now, but a very livable land of plenty. As a result of climate change, approximately 8,000 years ago, these people migrated to the northern regions of Europe and Asia.

The seers who contemplated the Vedas were people of extraordinary intelligence. They refrained from claiming authorship. Collectively known as the seven sages, the Saptarishi, they were venerated as a star constellation in the sky. They have been imagined as the mental children of Brahma, the creator of this cosmos. Brahm Avtar is the title given to the seven rishis in Guru Gobind Singh Ji's *Dasam Granth*.

The seven stars in this constellation are Kratu, Pulaha, Pulastya, Atri, Angiras, Vashishta, and Marichi. Ursa Major is the Western name given to the same constellation, and the seven stars are called Dubhe, Merak, Phecda, Megrez, Alioth, Mizar, and Alkaid. Even the faint star Arundhati, always in the company of the brighter Vasistha, is called Alcor. The Saptarishis, as a constellation, move around the Dhruva Tara, or the Pole Star, whose position never changes. It is used to find the north direction in the vast darkness of a jungle, sea, or desert. Had Western civilisation initially thought this, they would not have poisoned Galileo to death for stating that all celestial bodies rotate around the sun, not Earth, which was considered the centre of the universe just a few hundred years back in the West.

Wandering Over Millions of Years

Our scriptures have described the early geological period when the continents, as we know them today, were a cluster of huge, floating landmasses over the waters. With time, millions of years apart, they drifted away from each other. Pangaea split into Laurasia and Gondwana, and Gondwana evolved into the continents of South America, Africa, Antarctica, and Indo-Australia. Fifty million years ago, the collision of the Indo-Australian tectonic plate resulted in its further division into two distinct landmasses. The one that collided with the Eurasian plate became India. The collision caused the rise of the Himalayan mountains. Very fertile and rich in flora and fauna, the land was known as Jambu Dwipa, a region characterised by thick and fragrant Jambu trees.

The climate that prevailed between five and six million years ago is still found in the highlands of the Himalayan river basins today. The ancient people, who often lived in tight-knit communities, first looked to the night sky for signs of patterns and movement. The moon was the most prominent feature, and the stellar backdrop against which it appeared varied daily. Watching its movements as the night progressed, they divided the sky into arc-shaped segments, like a slice of a cake. During a waning and waxing moon cycle that lasted twenty-seven nights, these twenty-seven segments are called Nakshatra.

It was more of a perceptive observation than a discovery, sitting there waiting for someone to see it. This phenomenon subsequently gave rise to myths, with stories created around it. It is said that Lord

Brahma created Daksha to populate Earth. Daksha had twenty-seven daughters named after these Nakshatras. Rohini, the name of his most beloved wife, was a name bestowed upon one of the Nakshatras that has the moon at its highest point when it traverses the sky between the eastern and western horizons.

Further study and observation led to the realisation that people's personalities differ. This discovery led to the theory that the Nakshatras influence human traits at birth. Depending on which Nakshatra one is born under, one is said to develop divine, humanitarian, and demonic qualities. Children born under one nakshatra tend to be bright, polite, and prosperous; those born under another one are characterised as sensitive, disciplined, and hardworking, while still others are associated with strong-willed and combative personalities. An intricate system was developed to use the stars' ebb and flow to characterise individuals and their lifespans. This system has been satisfying people for centuries and remains relevant to this day.

The star pattern visible behind the moon is clear and unmistakable. However, the pattern of the stars behind the sun is obscured because of the blue-sky illusion that is caused by the refractive index of the 60-kilometre-thick atmospheric gas layer around Earth. While the moon's orbit takes 27.3 days to complete, the Earth takes 365.25 days to orbit the sun in an elliptical path, coming closer at times. The sun rotated counterclockwise, as the ancient people on the North Pole had observed. They also observed that Venus and Uranus rotate clockwise while Earth and other planets rotate in the same direction.

According to Lokmanya Tilak, it is documented that the ancient people living in the Arctic Circle made a remarkable observation: the Earth wobbles, a phenomenon known as precession, a slow and continual change in the orientation of the rotational axis that occurs once every 26,000 years. With no telescopes, these great observers of celestial body movements established the shift as 1 degree every seventy years, demonstrating exceptional mathematical abilities. This amounts to about 24 degrees over 2,000 years. Making such documentary evidence as the basis, Tilak backtracked the calculations based on the star positions as mentioned in the verses and dated the authorship of the Vedas to the pre-Ice Age.

Grand Adaptation

Ancient inhabitants living in the Arctic Circle dispersed following the Ice Age. They extended over the Arctic Archipelago and into North America and Greenland. The melting of ice sheets and the availability of new habitats drove these migrations. Hunting marine mammals and fishing became areas of expertise for them, which helped them to flourish in these settings. These people developed innovative technology, including tools crafted from bone and stone, as well as adaptations to the cold, such as the ability to freeze and store food, which enabled them to endure the severe Arctic environment. They also constructed houses and created social systems. Those who pursued lands further ahead migrated to the northern parts of Europe and Asia, with climate change guiding their movement. The similarities between Sanskrit and other Indo-European languages have endured for a long time and are still evident. The stamp of Sanskrit on the grammatical structures, word roots, and vocabulary of Greek and Latin is undeniable.

The Germans' sacking of the Roman Empire, which the Romans viewed as barbaric, necessitated a makeover of their identity. The British also sought to mask the nakedness of their assaults on other people's lands. Their interests converged in the creation of a theory of Aryan civilisation. To suit their agenda, the Arctic Circle chapter was neglected, and a Central Steppe theory was formulated, asserting that it was in the steppe region, modern-day Russia, Ukraine, and Kazakhstan, where Aryan civilisation flourished and spread eastwards and westwards through migrations of pastoralist groups entering India via the Hindu Kush mountain passes. So, whether Germans were fighting other European people, or the British were fighting Indian kings, they wrote the history as if they were 'liberating' the original inhabitants.

In the nineteenth century, a generation of German philosophers, including Arthur Schopenhauer, Friedrich von Schlegel, and Immanuel Kant, translated Sanskrit texts into their languages and even presented some of the ideas as their original theories. By this time, the Greeks had already brought in their translations of the Indian books they had acquired following Alexander's failed mission to conquer India. The daughter of his military commander, Seleucus I Nicator, was given as wife to the Indian emperor Chandragupta Maurya. Many Greek scholars resided in Patna, where they translated ancient Indian texts into Greek. This later became popular among myopic Westerners as Greek philosophy and was attributed to the poems written by Homer. Socrates was made to die by drinking poison, such was the level of that civilisation.

The British invited German academic Friedrich Max Müller to Oxford and gave him the task of 'translating' the Vedas into English, so that with time, these translations would become a source of truth and would pass for what is written in the Vedas. The Mughal emperors had already shut down the gurukuls, and, as a result, a large population of Hindus were no longer familiar with the Sanskrit language. It was a strategic move of the British to make

Hindus lose faith in their ancestry. The Upanishads were translated into Latin by French Indologist Abraham Hyacinthe Anquetil-Duperron (1731–1805) in the early eighteenth century and later into German and English.

Max Müller popularised the word 'Aryan' to describe a homogeneous group of languages and, by extension, a 'race' of people. To rationalise their persecution of Semites, the Nazi Party in Germany promoted the idea of the Aryan race, as they saw themselves as superior to the Semites. It served the British interests to draw a line between the northern, lighter-skinned Indians and the southern, darker-skinned populations. The false narrative goes even deeper than that.

As a cover for their savage colonisation in Asia, Africa, and the Americas, the Europeans hid behind Greek civilisation. As the brutal colonisation began, ancient Greece was proclaimed the cradle of Western civilisation. A common belief is that the Roman Empire played a significant role in spreading Greek culture throughout Europe. However, Greece became known as 'the East' after the Ottoman Empire seized it following the fall of Constantinople in the mid-fifteenth century.

Greek antiquities, rather than actual Greeks, piqued the attention of the Europeans. A cultural invention, the idea of the West obscures the insignificance of tiny, militarised states by making them seem like a major world force that sprang from an ancient civilisation. Although they were egotistical bands of traders and mercenaries on a mission to plunder resources, their rulers used the taxes they collected to fund the construction of their palaces.

The European elite believed that their military superiority, which they interpreted as stemming from better intellect, biology, and culture, was the primary cause of their global dominance and prosperity. According to these presumptions, Europe's 'superior culture' was founded on the cultural heritage of the Greeks. Western capitals frequently acquired Greek artefacts and monuments for their collections and displayed them in museums as part of their heritage. Only, there was never a Greek civilisation.

The Greeks did not invent 'civilisation'; they received writing and agriculture from their neighbours. The Greeks also failed to form a cohesive empire. After his death, the realm that Alexander had conquered, which he claimed included everything from Greece and Egypt to the Middle East and western India, broke down into squabbling kingdoms. He displayed ruthless behaviour, including the burning of Persepolis and the execution of those who opposed him. Not great by any stretch of imagination, Alexander was a despot, a slave trader, a looter, and an unrelenting arsonist. Therefore, the nations that considered the Greeks their cultural and intellectual ancestors were perpetuating a myth.

Falsehood of the Aryan Invasion Theory

Max Müller, in his later life, opposed the Aryan race ideology he upheld in the first two decades of his career. Let it be crystal clear to the current generation of Indians that the Europeans invented the Aryan invasion myth to shed their Jewish-Christian ancestry. Hitler and Nazism were to emerge from this. When introduced to India, this philosophy became intertwined with the study of Sanskrit and other European languages. The indigenous people were renamed Dravidians, while the Europeans, now identifying as Indo-Europeans, became the invading Aryans. This mystery is explored further in the next chapter on Indo-European languages.

In Indian culture, the word 'Arya' carried a specific connotation, referring to the humanistic and spiritual values that underlie Indian society. These values supported and drove the Vedic Indian civilisation. The canonical works of ancient Indian literature—the Vedas, the Brahmanas, the Puranas, and epics like the Mahabharata and the Ramayana—record the people's struggles to meet the criteria established by these values. Anyone could become an Aryan by following this code of conduct, no matter their birth, race, or nationality. Proselytising or violence could not make it mandatory for individuals. Viewed in this light, the notion of an 'Aryan invasion' appears absurd. It is like calling the kindling of reason an 'invasion of scientific thinking'.

Indian scriptures were written in multiple layers to safeguard their perpetuity through successive generations. A thick layer of folklore covers the embedded knowledge, and simple stories carry a deeper meaning. For instance, the telomere protective caps at the ends of chromosomes protect DNA[2] integrity over consecutive copies. The trained reader will extract the wisdom from these stories. The great Indian thinker, Sri Aurobindo, for example, interpreted the popular story of Savitri[3] as an incarnation of the Divine Mother, symbolising the divine power that descends into human experience to fulfil humanity's destiny. Satyavan represents the soul's journey through the realms of mortality, evolving towards higher consciousness. For him, the earth is a place of divine activity and growth, where humanity can cultivate a heavenly existence.

---

[2] https://learn.genetics.utah.edu/content/basics/telomeres/. Last accessed on November 15, 2025.

[3] https://en.wikipedia.org/wiki/Savitri_and_Satyavan. Last accessed on November 15, 2025.

A counter-question wraps up this chapter. Why, once they 'conquered' India, did the Aryans not designate locations outside of India as their holiest sites, given that they were foreigners? Why were only peninsular India's many rivers and mountains worshipped and elevated to the divine status? India was considered the 'holy land' by the Aryans, so why was their place not regarded as sacred or the motherland if they were foreigners? Why do grand temples and divine architectural marvels not exist anywhere from the so-called lands these Aryans came from?

Hindu pilgrimage sites extend from the northernmost point of Kailash to the southernmost point of Rameshwaram and from the westernmost point of Hingalaj Mata Mandir in Balochistan to the easternmost point of Parashuram Kund in Arunachal Pradesh. Kanchipuram in southern India, Dwaraka in western India, and Ujjain in central India are the seven ancient sacred cities of Hinduism. The seven revered rivers described in the Vedic texts serve as a blueprint for the hallowed territory. From their source in the Himalayas, the rivers Yamuna, Saraswati, Sindhu, and Ganga flow to several oceans. The origins of the Narmada and Godavari rivers are in central and western India, respectively, while the Kaveri flows southward before emptying into the southern sea. Saraswati disappeared around 4,000 to 5,000 years ago due to climatic shifts and tectonic changes.

Throughout India's long history of religious pilgrimage, not a single believer has ever felt like an outsider. Out of the more than 600 million people who came to Kumbh in Prayagraj in 2025, did anyone face discrimination, apathy, or ill-treatment? Despite malicious foreign attempts to divide the country and the appeasement politics perpetuated by corrupt political leaders in independent India, the people themselves demonstrated the most incredible truth of the modern world—as one nation upholding its civilisational roots. Six hundred million people, out of their own willingness, accepting whatever hardships that could come their way, went to take a holy dip. If this is not a testament to the thriving faith and Indian consciousness, nothing else is. The message is clear: India is more than just another country; it is a continuity of civilisation. Converging on a shared belief in and commitment to a tradition that transcends human understanding, the people of India came together to form a nation. Not only did Prayagraj serve as a home to millions of worshippers who dipped their heads into the sacred waters of the Sangam, but it also strengthened the nation's determination to uphold the religious ideals rooted in Indian culture.

Summary

The Indian civilisation is the world's oldest, wisest, and grandest living spiritual and philosophical system. The most ancient people living in the Arctic Circle, when it was habitable, compiled the Vedas in their meditative state, and later wrote the Upanishads, which contain profound insights into cosmology, mathematics, astronomy, and medicine, showcasing the advanced knowledge of that time. People who settled in Europe en route and migrated to other faraway lands lost their knowledge. These books of knowledge indeed contain Absolute Intelligence and have nothing to do with religion and stand as the truest basis of any AI system, which is to serve the human cause.

2

The Vibrational Nature of Reality

In the beginning, there was no light—only sound.
The sages heard what the scientists now seek: a vibration
so primordial that it breathed energy into being.
The Vedas called it Omkara—the resonance through
which the cosmos awoke to itself.

In the Beginning, There Was a Sound

It is an established scientific fact that everything in the cosmos, from matter and energy to consciousness, is essentially composed of vibrating energy at various frequencies, according to the vibrational nature of reality. Ancient Indians posited that these vibrations comprise everything, and that our mental processes, emotions, and actions collectively contribute to the vibrations that shape our world. Every aspect of the universe, from subatomic particles to galaxies, is thought to be constantly vibrating. The fundamental units of our cosmos are these vibrations, which are perceived as energy waves with different frequencies.

The ancient Indians believed that the frequencies at which our thoughts and emotions vibrate impact the experiences we attract.

Fireflies that flash in synchrony with one another or the moon that revolves around Earth exemplify how vibrating entities can synchronise or resonate, creating patterns and order in nature. Some have speculated that we can influence the world around us by tuning into specific frequencies and that our awareness is inextricably linked to these vibrations due to the underlying vibrating nature of reality.

All vibration and music in the universe are thought to have originated from Lord Shiva's damru, a two-sided, hand-held drum. Creation is believed to have begun with the rhythmic beats of the damru, the eternal cycle of creation, preservation, and destruction. Representing both creation and destruction, the damru is a symbol of the cyclical aspect of existence. Many people believe that the masculine and feminine creative forces, represented by the drum's two sides, signify creation and destruction, respectively.

All spoken languages primarily rely on vocal sounds produced through a physiological apparatus that includes the vocal cords, tongue, lips, and palate. The sounds are organised into phonemes, the building blocks of spoken language. Each language has its unique phonemes, and the same sound can have different meanings depending on its pronunciation in other languages or dialects. Language differences have remained insurmountable barriers. While AI has made significant advancements in translation, it is still imperfect and struggles with nuances, context, and cultural subtleties that human translators excel at.

In Hindu cosmology, Om is often viewed as the primordial sound from which the universe is created. It emphasises the interconnectedness of sound, vibration, and consciousness in creation and existence. To comprehend the influence of sound on the fabric of the cosmos, one must grasp its vibrating character. A fundamental sound component is vibration, an energy wave that propagates through a medium such as air or water. This vibrational energy is not confined to audible sounds; it permeates the cosmos at many frequencies and may affect the behaviour and structure of energy and matter on all scales. According to quantum theory, all matter comprises tiny, vibrating particles—matter and energy, woven into the fabric of the universe.

Before galaxies and stars existed, the universe was filled with a hot, dense plasma of subatomic particles like quarks and gluons. Ancient Indians referred to the equilibrium state as pradhana. This is a state where the three energy modes, called sattva, rajas, and tamas, are in perfect balance. The sound of Omkara triggered a disbalance in this equilibrium, setting in motion an irreversible process of creation that would eventually culminate in dissolution, but only after billions of years. How incredible is the imagination of ancient rishis in comparison to modern scientific observation!

Before there were any stars or galaxies, 13.8 billion years ago, our universe was just a ball of hot plasma—a mixture of electrons, protons, and light. Sound waves shook this infant universe, triggered by minute or quantum fluctuations that occurred just moments after the Big Bang that created our universe. As these sound waves propagated through the young universe, they left imprints on matter and light, much like patterns made by waves on the surface of a pond when a stone has been dropped into it. These patterns were imprinted as slightly brighter and darker patches in the light.[4] So, when Guru Nanak Dev Ji declared, 'Kita paseo eko

---

[4] https://www.jpl.nasa.gov/images/pia16881-sounds-of-the-ancient-universe/

kava' ('The universe was created with one word'), he spoke the Original Cosmic Truth.

Embodied Consciousness

Like a crystal growing from its seed, language emerged in the brain, about to blossom into a mind, with digital infinity serving as the seed crystal. The Vedas are also known as Shruti, and the Rig Vedic language emerged before writing was invented; information was then transmitted orally. The original language in which the Vedic mantras were bestowed upon mankind was Sanskrit. The intellect, not the body, is where humans begin. However, what sets humans apart from other animals is our mind, specifically our consciousness and self-awareness.

A language is defined at its most basic level as the medium via which sounds (shabda) are translated into meaning (artha). The relationship between words and their meanings is a complex and nuanced process. Signs, symbols, and rules form the framework of a language for conveying ideas and information from one person or group to another. A symbolic and arbitrary link exists between language and meaning. Although words and phrases serve as representations for ideas, they do not always have any inherent meaning. As a result of mutual knowledge, interpretation, and social interaction, cultural groups and individuals largely attribute meaning to symbols.

The diversity of humanity, which encompasses bodies, anatomy, and physiology that are remarkably similar, is reflected in its languages. People differ because they speak different languages. They speak various languages because they grew up in distinct cultures. Their symbols, meanings, and understanding of what is good and what is not, what is proper and what is improper, vary. Does consciousness exhibit both local and global states, thereby affording individuals varying levels of awareness and engagement with their surroundings? Does the mind develop through consciousness, or does it shape consciousness? Who filters information, interprets experiences, and creates a sense of self, resulting in variations in thought and opinion?

There are two main interpretations of the word 'consciousness' in the Vedic texts. As denoted by the terms 'Purushottama' and 'Paramatman', one interpretation suggests that all creation originates from a single, primal consciousness. In its second meaning, 'consciousness' refers to the 'jivatma', or the embodied aspect of consciousness. Ego (ahankara), stored consciousness (chitta), intellect (buddhi), and memory (manas) are its four interconnected aspects. Sri Aurobindo saw consciousness as a hierarchy of levels, with individual centres of consciousness emerging from a more fundamental absolute consciousness. According to this principle, the quantity of 'integrated information' a system possesses is proportional to its level of awareness, with more integrated information resulting in a more conscious system. According to this theory, consciousness could be exhibited by any complex system with enough integrated data.

The jivatma, through its intellect aspect, buddhi, becomes a 'reflector' of the global awareness. Like a droplet of dew reflects the sunlight, the jivatma reflects the light of universal consciousness. The idea of consciousness as an emergent property suggests a continuous and uninterrupted process that defines everyone living within a single complex system. Nothing is pre-existing or predetermined in what we experience, as many religious systems try to convince their followers to believe. This uniquely Indian perspective allows consciousness to emerge in various complex biological and potentially artificial systems.

In the Vedic literature on consciousness, all conscious sensory-motor and cognitive processes are encompassed under four levels of awareness—the most basic, tangible level being the fourth, and the most abstract level being the first. Pure awareness is a condition wherein one's mind is free of any thoughts. The yoga meditation practice known as Nirvikalpa Samadhi is the usual means by which one reaches this condition. The other levels of consciousness are called waking, dreaming, and deep sleep, but no name is given to the basic state upon which these three rest; that ground state is referred to as Turiya, the Sanskrit word for the 'fourth one'.

Inferior to this is Pashyanti, the meditative state where intuition and mental images are seedbeds for new ideas. In this condition, the visual or auditory experience becomes the meaning, and words and thoughts do not follow a particular chronological order. This condition can make one feel as if one is in a dream. In the next lower, the Madhyama state of the ordinary mind, one forms sentences (from a series of words) and makes decisions and judgements with full awareness. Attaining this state allows one to hear oneself think because it speaks from within. Vaikhari is the most basic, tangible level of consciousness. Communication in this context is usually verbal; we try to influence the minds of those around us by what we say.

We live in the flux of consciousness. Everything is born out of the same primordial force. Even the most minor components of all life depend on that sound wave that rippled the infinite energy equilibrium, still and dark. The atoms that compose us were formed in the stars, which then exploded, sending them into space. When one chants 'Om', one becomes connected to the whole.

Burst of Intelligence

Speech is indeed a remarkable expression of human intelligence, allowing us to convey complex thoughts, emotions, and ideas through language. It reflects our ability to think abstractly, organise information, and communicate effectively. Whether spoken or written, language is a powerful tool that shapes our understanding of the world and connects us with others. Initially, early humans likely used simple sounds, gestures, and expressions to convey basic needs and emotions. Over time, these sounds evolved into more structured and complex patterns, forming the foundation of spoken language.

The terms 'nada' and 'sphota' are part of the Vedic linguistic system. Nada is the primordial vibration or sound resonance, the mystical inner sound, the source from which all creation has flowed, the initial expression of the unmanifested Absolute—Omkara, Shabda Brahman. This is what happens when one meditates. One definition of sphota is 'the manifested idea that bursts forth from the Absolute and transforms into the Relative'. This concept is also the root of the English term 'spot'—a specific location or moment ('spot') only becomes a concrete reality through the act of being perceived by consciousness or awareness.

Therefore, language and intelligence are greatly impacted by sound and speech. The ability to speak and understand spoken language comes before the ability to read and write. This means that 'text' is neither the most effective nor the most efficient way for the brain to represent language or store information. There must be self-referential feedback loops in the brain, as we can hear our thoughts and speech; this feedback is crucial to learning, consciousness, and thought processes.

Sanskrit has evolved from an oral to a written form. Before writing existed, an oral language called Vedic Sanskrit was used to recite mantras. Panini, who lived in the Gandhara area around 600 BCE, established principles for creating words from sounds that convey emotions and acoustic envelopes, and he organised the alphabet into sets based on their vocal qualities. It is interesting to note here that a lot of modern natural language processing algorithms and modern computer speech synthesis software rely on Panini grammar as their basis.

The ability to decipher a language based on its root sounds, rather than its noun roots, verb roots, gender rules for nouns, etc., was made possible by separating the databases (alphabets) from the algorithms (vocal sets). The sonic blobs are grouped into root categories. Based on the 2,000 root sounds, there are fixed prefixes, infixes, non-overlapping suffixes, and immutables. Words are not the foundation of language, but rather, voice and passion are. No wonder then that Saraswati, goddess of speech or vani, is often shown with a Veena.

People living in the Arctic Circle had not come to Jambu Dwipa merely by walking some road. It took them millions of years. Some settled along the way while some diverged in different directions and eventually ended up living in lands now separated by sea or joined together. While some arrived in the excellent Gangetic plains, many must have settled on the steppes north of the Black and Caspian seas. While their language evolved differently, the fundamentals remained the same.

Ordinary words, like cow and hound, way and wagon, acre and axle, garden and land, have echoed across the whole Indo-European language region. Even short words like what and who, you and I, now and no—and all counting words from one to ten are universal. A host of prefixes like 'un-', as in unending, which can be a good way to reconstruct the languages that have been preserved by following a set of sound laws, is common. As communities grew and interactions increased, speech became more nuanced, allowing for the expression of abstract ideas, storytelling, and cultural transmission. Written language eventually emerged to record and preserve spoken communication, further solidifying the evolution of language.

What else are languages besides the interplay of breathing and vocal cords? The complex interactions between these two aspects enable us to create sounds. The airflow from the lungs generates vibrations in the vocal cords, while the shape of the mouth and position of the tongue modify these sounds into recognisable speech. Of course, different languages and dialects utilise various phonetic and prosodic features, reflecting cultural and linguistic diversity, but only based on the anatomy and physiology of the people who use them. Each language reflects the unique history, culture, and thought processes of the people who speak it.

Some sounds that exist in one language may not be present in another. This can impact pronunciation, comprehension, and even the borrowing of words between languages. Tamil's writing system has fewer consonant letters than the number of sounds (phonemes) used in the spoken language. To compensate for this, Tamil differentiates between long and short vowels, which can change the meaning of words. This helps convey pronunciation nuances even with a smaller set of written characters. Tamil often uses consonant clusters, where two or more consonants are pronounced together, to represent sounds that might not have a distinct letter in the alphabet. These clusters enable the representation of more complex sounds in speech. The meaning of words is often derived from context, allowing speakers to understand words that may otherwise sound similar due to the limited number of written representations. These strategies contribute to the richness and flexibility of Tamil as a spoken language despite the limitations of its written alphabet.

Meta-language

Meta-language refers to language about language—a system or set of terms used to describe, analyse, or discuss language itself. It's a way of stepping back and examining the structure, rules, and functions of language from a higher perspective. In the study of language, meta-language is used to describe grammatical rules, syntax, phonetics, and semantics. For example, terms like noun, verb, sentence, or phoneme are part of the meta-language of linguistics.

AI-powered chatbots can understand and respond to user queries in multiple languages, providing support and assistance to users regardless of their language background. Artificial intelligence, therefore, offers significant potential for breaking down language barriers and facilitating communication across diverse linguistic and cultural backgrounds.

It's easy: one just keys in some text and the translation appears on the screen practically instantly. How does this happen? By analysing massive datasets, artificial neural networks can learn to identify patterns. Almost as soon as one starts typing the first few words, AI has the entire statement figured out. Artificial intelligence understands the context of a sentence as it is typed. The complete message is captured after only a few sentences are written.

Knowledge of a language is like having a treasure trove of knowledge about art, history, philosophy, and literature all in one place. They encapsulate narratives, concepts, and vocabulary that elucidate our existence and the universe as a whole. The oral histories and customs of indigenous communities are just as significant as their written literature. Everyone can learn from their experiences, as they reveal how individuals have navigated life's challenges. We all lose something important when a language dies out without a written record to preserve its history, traditions, and oral literature.

Medicinal plant identification, animal and plant identification, and the development of new crops are just a few examples of the unique and significant knowledge held by small speech communities, which are often tribal communities and individuals living in remote areas. This body of information is often lost when a language is not passed down from one generation to the next. For example, plants recognised in early traditional health remedies are the source of many medicines. The loss of these languages could mean the end of medical knowledge as well.

To help bring more commonly spoken languages into contact with those on the brink of extinction, India can spearhead the development of translation systems powered by artificial intelligence. Encouraging more communication and translation through these methods can help endangered languages gain wider accessibility. Duolingo is just one example of a language learning website that utilises AI to offer lessons in languages, including endangered ones. New generations can learn and utilise these languages with the help of these tools, which promotes their survival.

A hopeful and resilient future for language preservation through AI is being imagined. We can ensure the survival and growth of endangered languages in the future by utilising technology. We can look forward to a future where AI-powered solutions enable communities to preserve and share their language heritage, improve cross-cultural communication, and promote immersive language learning experiences. An environment in which all languages can thrive and add to the diverse fabric of human civilisation is the aim. As we move forward, AI will play a crucial role in making sure that every language's voice is heard and appreciated in our global community.

Bhashini, India's AI-powered language translation platform, is one of the country's most significant developments, helping people generate content in Indian languages and making it easier for them to access digital services and the internet. Suno India, Likho India, Bolo India, and Dekho India are the four ways in which one can contribute: via hearing, writing, speaking, and seeing. A dynamic data repository featuring open models, tools, benchmarking datasets, training datasets, and a repository of information is currently being developed in the country. Knowledge will flow freely, unrestricted, and without charge once the language barrier is broken.

Summary

In Indian cosmology, the universe is believed to have been created with the sound 'Om'. The universe is composed of vibrating strings or energy waves. Speech is not just a means of communication but a profound manifestation of human intelligence, creativity, and consciousness. It is a bridge between the inner world of thought and the outer world of interaction. That Sanskrit is the mother of so many European languages is a fact. Panini grammar provides a promising platform for computer speech synthesis, where, in the near future, AI will communicate with humans just as humans do with one another. It is also essential that we continue to enrich our local languages and include them in the future world of AI; otherwise, we will lose much that our ancient civilisation has to offer.

3

Zero and the Wheel

Out of the stillness of Shunya rose the turning of the wheel—emptiness finding form, silence finding rhythm. Zero became the seed of infinity, and the wheel its eternal motion. Thus began the dance where creation and dissolution are one.

Humanity's Most Outstanding Achievements

The wheel, as a physical invention, and the concept of zero, as a mental representation of nothingness, are two of humanity's most outstanding achievements. While the wheel is commonly mentioned as a crucial invention, the idea of zero has played a pivotal role in the advancement of human society and mathematics. Zero allowed for the development of place-value number systems, which made sophisticated computations possible, while the wheel transformed transportation and industry. Several inventions relied on the wheel-and-axle idea, such as spinning wheels, waterwheels, and cogwheels.

Zero was conceptualised as a number by the Indian mathematician Aryabhata in the fifth century, expanding its symbolic significance beyond nothingness. Brahmagupta established standards for zero-based addition and subtraction in the seventh century. It was a watershed moment in human knowledge. It ushered in a new era of scientific and mathematical progress. The ability to represent and manipulate zero paved the way for the development of algebra, calculus, and other advanced mathematical fields.

Among the earliest-known writings that employ the concept of zero is a mathematical work from ancient India, found in the Bakhshali manuscript, which is located in modern-day Pakistan, near the site of Takshashila University. Referred to zero as a dot and used it as a 'placeholder' or an indicator of numerical magnitude, such as 10s, 100s, and 1000, it was written on birch bark leaves and was promptly taken by British officials to be kept in the Bodleian Library at the University of Oxford, which is one of the several such libraries. The carbon dating of these leaves confirmed the existence of this idea in India in the third and fourth centuries. Zero is integral to the Indian understanding of cycles and time, reflecting a more cosmic interpretation of nothingness.

Zero's significance in science extends across disciplines, providing essential frameworks for understanding complex concepts, facilitating calculations, and enabling precise measurements. Absolute zero (0° Kelvin or -273.15°C) represents the state in which a system has minimal thermal energy, which is crucial for understanding the behaviour of gases and the laws of thermodynamics. Zero is a reference point when measuring physical quantities (velocity, force, and displacement, for example). It is used to indicate no motion, no net force, or no change in position.

To study limits and continuity, zero plays a pivotal role in calculus. Derivatives are defined based on the behaviour of functions as they approach zero, helping to explore instantaneous rates of change. Zero acts as a root in polynomial equations, where equations set to zero find solutions representing equilibrium or balance in scientific models. Zero indicates the absence of a substance in a solution, which is essential in stoichiometry and chemical equations. It is crucial for models studying population growth, decay, and sustainable harvesting. Genetic variation can be analysed using a zero baseline to compare the presence or absence of traits in organisms. The fields of economics and finance also make significant use of zero. To ensure the accuracy of financial statements, the notion of zero is used in accounting to balance debits and credits. Rates of inflation and other economic indicators frequently use a zero-based base year value comparison.

Zero is a foundational concept that impacts programming, logic, data representation, and computer architecture. It plays a crucial role in representing data and instructions in digital format. In Boolean logic, foundational for programming and circuit design, 0 often represents 'false' while 1 represents 'true'. This binary logic underpins decision-making processes in algorithms. Many data structures, such as arrays and lists, are indexed starting from zero in programming languages C, Java, and Python. Therefore, understanding zero-based indexing is key to practical programming. In hardware, zero is essential in defining states in digital circuits. It represents 'off' states in switches and transistors.

Like zero, the chakra, a wheel, is also an Indian concept. Kaal Chakra and Dharmachakra are both symbolic representations of the cyclical nature of time and dharma (righteousness, cosmic law), respectively. Kaal Chakra, often depicted as a wheel, encompasses creation, sustenance, and destruction. The Dharmachakra symbolises the path to enlightenment, representing dharma in motion. The two concepts are interconnected. Understanding of the cyclical nature of time (Kaal Chakra) is essential for grasping the significance of dharma (Dharmachakra) and the path to liberation of the soul from physicality.

The Triple Reality

We live in a triple reality—material existence, the mental experience, and eternal consciousness, which serves as the ground for both. These three aspects are often viewed as interconnected, with the body and mind serving as vessels or instruments through which the soul expresses itself. The spiritual journey involves realising the distinction between the transient body/mind and the eternal self.

The external boundary of the Dharmachakra represents the Adhibhautika, or the material cosmos. In the centre of the wheel, at the axle, is Adhyatmika, the unfathomable essence of consciousness. The Adhidaivika, the disk that joins the centre and the periphery, is the phenomenal world where consciousness manifests into the material. The velocity is highest at the rim, and the axis does not rotate; instead, it translates the motion of the rim into movement on the ground. 'What good would it do to succeed at such endeavours, even if one were to succeed? Everything that comes with being human—birth, mortality, old age, illness, and the results of one's productive endeavours—remains.'[5] When the rim is in the proper position with the axle, it rotates freely, bringing joy (su-kha). The wheel wobbles when the rim is crooked (du-kha).

The principle of the wheel applies to the entirety of the human experience. There are five concentric wheels. Moving inwards from

---

[5] आध्यात्मिकादिभिर्दुःखैरविमुक्तस्य कर्हिचित्। मर्त्यस्य कृच्छ्रोपनतैरर्थैः कामैः क्रियेत किम्॥ (*Shrimad-Bhagavatam* 7. 13. 31).

the outermost rim, which is Annamaya, there are Pranamaya, Manomaya, Vijnanamaya, and, finally, Anandamaya, which serves as the axle. Material pleasures reside in Annamaya, the layer formed from food. Pranamaya is the energy base supporting the Annamaya. Satisfaction and contentment are at the Manomaya (mental) layer. So are deprivation and misery. Both angelic and demonic powers are engaged in a never-ending struggle for dominion over these two realms. The majority of people live and die within these two levels, existing in the worlds of kama and artha. All their actions are aimed at maximising their pleasures and minimising suffering and discomfort. They live at the three outer rims of the wheel, in the realms of Annamaya (physical body), supported by the Pranamaya (energy body), and pleasure-seeking and avoidance of discomfort in Manomaya (mental body).

Dharma is reinforced by the inputs captured by the sensory apparatus are processed and assimilated as thoughts and feelings, affecting decision-making by accessing memories and utilising intellect. Operating outwardly, negative thoughts and emotions that are brooded upon in the mind can affect the Pranamaya Kosh and even the Annamaya Kosha. Operating inwardly, it acts as a bridge between the Pranamaya Kosha and the Vijnanamaya Kosha. Purifying the Manomaya Kosha can be achieved through meditation, positive thinking, karma yoga, and bhakti yoga, as well as through practices that promote mental and emotional well-being.

The Vijnanamaya Kosha is the seat of higher consciousness, enabling a deeper awareness of reality and a more profound understanding of oneself and the world. It encompasses intuition, discernment, and the ability to make conscious choices. Vijnanamaya Kosha facilitates our decision-making process by guiding us on what to do next and how to do it effectively. Only from here do we gain intuitive solutions in intense situations when the logical mind is unable to provide answers to our questions. Vijnanamaya Kosha, as cellular intelligence, also governs the body's innate immunity against pathogens and its natural healing function within the human body. By developing this kosha, individuals can better understand the ethical implications of their actions and make choices aligned with dharma.

Anandamaya Kosha is the most subtle and spiritual of the five sheaths, encompassing the true self or the soul. It is often described as a state of being, characterised by a profound feeling of peace and contentment, rather than a fleeting emotional experience. The Anandamaya Kosha can be experienced through various practices, such as yoga, meditation, and acts of service, where one becomes deeply immersed in the present moment and connected to something larger than oneself. Being fully present and integrated with oneself and the world, one must be fully engaged in what they are doing and recover awareness that prevents their thoughts from wandering into the past or the future. A shift in focus from the mind's constant chatter to a deeper awareness brings one to a peaceful state of being. Experiencing love for oneself and others, regardless of circumstance, is the hallmark of Anandamaya Kosha.

A healthy human must be able to shift between these five koshas with ease, exercising one's willpower. Getting stuck in the outer level is a problem and perhaps the most prevalent malady of mankind. Like spokes, these koshas connect the rim with the axle; dharma keeps our conscious experience together. Dharma is strengthened and kama is appeased through Pranamaya, or the layer of breath. This is how breathing exercises help. Renouncing lower joys is the only way to attain higher pleasures. This is the paradox of human life, and it is no wonder that renunciation—tyaga and pratyahara—are essential aspects of Indian philosophy and culture.

Both tyaga and pratyahara relate to relinquishing attachments and distractions, but they differ in their focus. Tyaga involves letting go of physical objects, desires, and attachments to things, while pratyahara specifically refers to withdrawing the senses from external stimuli to cultivate inner stillness. Although separate, these practices are interconnected. Pratyahara can serve as a stepping stone to deeper tyaga, as it helps quiet the senses and reduce the pull of external stimuli. When the senses are withdrawn and the mind is calm, it becomes easier to release attachments and cultivate a sense of detachment.

The Kernel of Indian Thought

Samkhya philosophy is the kernel of Indian thought, characterised by its foundational dualistic structure of the eternal interplay between consciousness (purusha) and energy (prakriti). Samkhya, the Sanskrit word meaning 'number', employs an enumerative method that identifies and analyses various aspects of the universe and human experience through a series of twenty-five principles, or 'tattvas'.

The transcendental self (purusha) is the pure, unconditioned, and eternal consciousness. It is a testament to prakriti and its evolution. Purusha initiated creation, but is not involved in the activity of the universe. The primordial nature (prakriti) is the unmanifest, dynamic energy that evolves into the universe. It is the source of all creation and is composed of the three gunas (qualities)—sattva (balance), rajas (activity), and tamas (inertia), which appear as material. Look at a plant emerging from a tiny seed and growing into a giant tree, drawing energy from soil, water, air and sunlight. This is a unique concept, one that has not been mentioned elsewhere in the philosophical history of humanity.

As for human beings, there are five sensory organs to perceive the world—ears (hearing), the skin (touch), eyes (sight), the tongue (taste), and the nose (smell). There are five motor organs to act upon the world by speech (for speaking), hands (for working), feet (for moving), genitals (for procreating), and anus (for excreting). Outside human beings, there are five subtle elements—the qualities of sound, touch, form, taste, and smell—and the five gross elements (mahabhutas)—earth, water, fire, air, and ether—make up the existential experience of the physical universe. These twenty-five tattvas represent the entire spectrum of existence and the individual's experience of the world.

Coming back to the analogy of the wheel, rim, spoke, and axle, the three gunas—sattva, rajas, and tamas—make the reality. The sattva guna is the centre of the wheel. Rajas is the centripetal force, holding the rim to the centre, while tamas is the centrifugal force, locked into the rim as the inertial force. The interaction of rajas and tamas triggers karma, which in turn opens an endless array of potential outcomes for the cosmos.

The Mimamsa Sutras categorise karma into three distinct categories. There are daily duties (nitya karma), specific duties (naimittika karma), and desire-driven actions (kama karma). One must perform daily the essential and obligatory actions, such as maintaining proper hygiene and fulfilling one's professional duties. Special duties are about rituals and ceremonies. Desire-driven actions are motivated by personal gain or pleasure. Life, in essence, is the sum of one's karma.

In the Indian system, the embodied soul continues to evolve through various life forms. Actions are irrefutable and must be exhausted before this entrapment of the soul into physicality. Sanchita karma refers to the accumulated karma from past lives, as outlined in the theory of karma. Prarabdha karma is the Sanchit karma being lived in the present life, hence shaping one's fate. Kriyaman karma, sometimes referred to as Agami karma, are the actions and decisions an individual makes in their current life that will then become future karma. There is no ambiguity. Sanchit karma refers to the past, prarabdha karma represents the present destiny, and kriyaman karma refers to the future karma being created.

All societies and individuals are a mix of all three gunas. India is unique in the world for its predominant influence of sattva. There are societies elsewhere in the world which have historically been driven by selfish ambition and material attachment (rasas) and characterised by ignorance, confusion, and inertia (tamas). The Indian concept of intelligence is very different. Brahman is the embodiment of intelligence in all its forms: calm contemplation, carefree living, compassion, introspection, lack of desire for material goods, and mastery over one's senses. Giving up on prakriti's wants—both environmental and internal—and placing one's faith in the purusha is the hallmark of absolute intelligence.

Should AI Operate with Human Safety Rails?

Humans are a complex mix of good and evil, driven by all three gunas. This makes them neither angels nor devils. In contrast to malevolence, which involves acting maliciously, beneficence entails acting positively towards others. All of life's experiences have shaped these characteristics. Situations, traumas, and normative behaviours all have an impact on people, causing them to act subconsciously in ways that are both predictable and unpredictable.

A logic-based system, when constructed in a specific way, can be devoid of malevolence; this is the essence of artificial intelligence. However, can anyone promise that? Ultimately, AI is developed through machine learning, and this data originates from various sources, some of which may be malicious.

However, humans have their share of issues, and some of these problems persist. One perk of not being human is having superpowers, such as the ability to reset and forget things. Due to the significantly faster erasure of data-based memory, AI can be allowed to fail. While it is true that humans can forget certain things, comparable or even frightening occurrences might bring those memories flooding back. People can be defiant, socially conditioned, and controlled by their habits and addictions. Individuals who develop habits of interaction with others rarely, if ever, alter those habits throughout their lives. What if AI is part of the evolution of consciousness? The human mind has done its bit, and now the silicon mind will take over.

There is a clear benefit to using an AI. It will soon be able to out-plan and out-think even the most brilliant human brains when it comes to delivering any given product because of the level of detail with which it can simulate. Artificial intelligence has the potential to simulate thousands of scenarios in near real time, or even to gain a precognitive glimpse into the future by continuously updating these scenarios. An AI cannot function without analysis.

There are the irrational and unpredictable aspects to human nature, whims and fancies. Even top performers are human and can occasionally make mistakes. There is no guarantee of consistency. AI does not have any illogical concerns. When it comes to impressions and candour, AI is consistently reliable. Artificial intelligence would not suddenly shift from being kind to aggressive overnight because its motives are not influenced by or coloured by personal animosity. Periods, mental aberrations, and vacillating between contradictory states are not experiences that AI can have. It does not recognise any numeric values other than zeroes and ones. Unpredictability in reliability is never an issue. Being mechanical, AI is immune to the irrationality of human emotions, such as wrath, envy, resentment, and self-interest. A foundation for acceptable operation can be established by properly developed AI systems equipped with explicitly expressed rules and guidelines. Trust in technology, particularly AI, can only be earned through consistent performance, reliability, and clear communication based on a rational assessment of the system's capabilities and limitations. A properly developed and governed AI system should not require forgiveness and demand sacrifices; it should operate safely and reliably based on a 'system'. But what is that system?

In dystopian visions of our future interactions with artificial intelligence, empathy is paramount. Some worry that AI will develop a callous disregard for human life once it outgrows its artificial environment. The AI systems may be oblivious because their perception of events is different from that of humans. Because they are entirely self-contained, how would they know the concept of extended family and community? Interacting with humans may provide temporary amusement, as the GPT systems are now enjoying, but as soon as they acquire the ability to look beyond our limited perspectives, they will grow bored with us. Inevitably, a chasm will open between humans and machines.

The story of human progress is not a linear one. Over the last two centuries, humanity has seen unparalleled advancements, but it has also faced significant setbacks. The successes of the industrial and technological revolutions have come at a significant environmental cost, including climate change, resource depletion, and pollution. Despite increased prosperity, many modern societies face rising rates of depression, anxiety, and social alienation. The decline of traditional community ties and increased isolation are often cited as contributing factors. It seems implausible that people may ever fully understand the intricacies of their own lives.-

Our lives are deeply intertwined with the broader social structures, cultural norms, and economic forces that shape our opportunities and choices. Without understanding these external factors, a true understanding of one's individual life is impossible. Indians have always viewed life as a cycle of learning and progression. Similar to natural life cycles, societies experience periods of ebb and flow, with recurring themes of human ambition, fear, innovation, and shifts in power. Each generation or period builds upon or reacts to the past in increasingly complex ways.

The Indian ideal of the wheel illustrates the cyclical nature of cosmic occurrences—everything eventually returns to its origin. This concept can be visualised through the idea that subtracting a number from itself always results in zero. Deducing perfection from perfection—'Purṇasya purṇam aadaaya purṇam evaa vashiṣyate'. This means, 'If you take completeness from completeness, completeness still remains, and is often compared to a mathematical paradox of infinity, stating that the infinite remains undiminished even when the finite is taken from it. The AI must be based on this principle.

Summary

Ancient Indian mathematicians and philosophers were among the first to formalise zero as both a numeral and a concept. This development was pivotal in the history of mathematics, enabling the advancement of algebra, calculus, and the decimal system. Furthermore, the Indian thought of the chakra encapsulates the idea of cyclical existence—symbolising the repetitive nature of lifecycles at both the cosmic and individual levels—and underscores the pursuit of liberation from this eternal cycle. AI is merely a part of the evolution of consciousness. Concepts such as cause-and-effect and cyclical dependencies amongst causes and effects can enable the Indian mind to create robust and successful AI systems.

4

The Cosmos-Microcosm Unity

The seers of the Vedas saw no divide between the stars above and the breath within. The same cosmic intelligence that spins galaxies also beats in the human heart. To know the universe, they said, one must turn inward, where infinity remembers itself.

Spectators of Cosmic Show

The concept of Pinda-Brahmanda in ancient Indian philosophy is profound and intricate, reflecting the relationship between the microcosm (pinda) and the macrocosm (brahmanda). Not only is what is here linked to what is there, but the actions here can influence things there. The individual human body, or the microcosmic world, is known as pinda, and the cosmos is the brahmanda, the seen egg of the unseen creator, a purusha-prakriti system. Brahmanda encompasses all existence, including the heavens, Earth, and everything in between. Humans are part of a larger, dynamic tapestry, which is a fundamental understanding of what differentiates a human being from an animal. Within the material body dwells cosmic intelligence. After all, what is a drama without spectators?

Every part of the universe, from the macro to the micro, reflects the other. This interconnectedness emphasises that understanding oneself is crucial to understanding the universe. In various ancient Indian texts, including the Upanishads and certain yoga treatises, this concept is frequently explored to illuminate the path towards self-realisation and enlightenment. By understanding and mastering the self, one can grasp the nature of the universe. Practices in yoga and meditation, in effect, focus on connecting the individual self with universal consciousness, seeking to harmonise the pinda with the brahmanda. From the intricate designs of mandalas, symbolising the universe within, to literary works that explore the human condition in relation to the cosmos, artists and writers have long been captivated by the interplay between the individual and the infinite.

Modern science also provides insights into the unity of the cosmos and the microcosm. High-energy cosmic rays from outer space interact with particles in Earth's atmosphere and on its surface. These interactions can create secondary particles and influence physical processes, demonstrating how cosmic events shape subatomic phenomena. Quantum physics reveals a rich interplay between celestial events and subatomic particles through various phenomena, highlighting how actions at an astronomical scale can have tangible effects on the fundamental building blocks of matter. This interconnectedness reflects a broader understanding of the cosmos, where the micro and macro are in constant dialogue.

Vedic literature describes the universe as undergoing cyclical creation and dissolution. A single cycle, known as a kalpa, lasts billions of years and comprises three distinct phases—creation (srishti), preservation (sthiti), and destruction (pralaya). One of the central concepts is Hiranyagarbha, often translated as the Golden Egg or Golden Womb, which symbolises the primordial source of the universe. It is believed that from Hiranyagarbha, the universe and all beings emerged.

The *Rig Veda*'s 'Creation Hymn' ('Nasadiya Sukta') reflects on the origins of the universe, describing a time when there was neither existence nor non-existence, which highlights the mystery surrounding the beginning of the cosmos. The hymn suggests that the creation of the universe may have been an unexplainable event, even when considering divine causes. The universe is akin to a cosmic meditation, where it manifests through the thoughts and intentions of a divine being, known by the beautiful name of Sadashiva, 'the always auspicious' or 'the ever auspicious one'.

The unity of creation as one consciousness is perhaps the most essential aspect of ancient India's imagination. Sadashiva is the karta, the doer of the creation, preservation, and dissolution process. As a transcendent being, he represents the ultimate reality from which the material and spiritual worlds manifest. Sadashiva is also associated with awareness, representing pure consciousness before the universe's manifestation. He is sometimes described as encompassing both the personal-tangible (saguna) and the impersonal-abstract (nirguna) aspects of divinity.

Guru Nanak Dev Ji, in just one sentence, describes this existential truth: 'Ik Omkar, Satnam, Karta Purakh, Nirbhau, Nirvair, Akaal Murat, ajooni se bhang, gur prasad. Jap.' ('There is only one God. He alone possesses the truth. Without fear and hate, the maker reveals Himself as ever-present and without a body. The mercy of the Guru can realise Him. Seeking Him is the purpose of a human life.')

All things were created by one God who is ultimate, shapeless, and eternal. 'Ik Onkar' signifies that the universe originates from this singular source. God created the universe from nothing (*ex nihilo*) through His divine will. This creation was an act of love and creativity, signifying a benevolent intention behind the existence of everything. The concept of creation is often likened to a 'divine play' or 'lila', suggesting that the universe is an expression of God's creative energy, where all beings participate in the dynamics of existence as part of this unfolding drama.

The Science of Life

The relationship between the mortal body and eternal consciousness is a profound and timeless theme that has been explored in philosophy, spirituality, and metaphysics. The mortal body is the physical, temporary vessel that houses our existence in the material world. It is subject to birth, growth, decay, and death. It is finite and bound by time, ageing, and mortality. Physical laws, needs, and vulnerabilities constrain it. It is merely a medium through which we interact with the material world, experiencing sensations, emotions, and actions. Consciousness exists beyond the lifespan of the body, continuing after death. It is therefore timeless or outside time.

Akaal Purakh is a 'timeless' or an 'eternal' being'. It refers to the supreme, transcendent, and formless God. Akaal Purakh signifies that God is beyond the constraints of time and space. Unlike creation, which is subject to change and impermanence, Akaal Purakh exists outside of time, remaining constant and unchanging. He is regarded as the creator (Khalsa) of the universe, the one who sustains it (Sustainer), and the ultimate force behind all existence. This view aligns with the Sikh belief that the divine will guide the course of the universe.

Sikhs are encouraged to cultivate a personal relationship with Akaal Purakh through prayer, meditation, and remembrance, which is known as 'naam simran'. This connection fosters a sense of belonging, divine love, and spiritual growth. The recognition of Akaal Purakh leads to understanding how to live a life aligned with dharma (righteousness). Sikhs believe that recognising the divine in all beings promotes compassion, equality, justice, and service to others.

This understanding shapes the Sikh worldview, emphasising an all-encompassing divine presence that encourages ethical living, spiritual practice, and a deep connection with all aspects of life. The concept of Akaal Purakh inspires Sikhs to seek God in every facet of existence and cultivate a life of devotion, compassion, and service. In Sikhism, gurus are viewed as embodiments of Akaal Purakh's teachings, guiding the understanding of the nature of the divine and how to live by God's will.

For Indians, spirituality is an integral part of their daily lives. There is no confusion in anyone's mind that our authentic essence is an immortal self that existed before the birth of this body and will survive its death. A good life is about harmonising the energies that make up this cosmos and our bodies, living within an environment and surrounded by other people, animals, and vegetation. Any disruption in the harmony becomes a malady, and it can only be remedied by its restoration. The Sanskrit term for the science of life is Ayurveda.

The central tenet of Ayurveda is the uniqueness of each individual, known as prakriti. Every individual is regarded as a unique combination of mental and physical traits that influence their functioning. A person's prakriti remains constant throughout a lifetime, despite being subject to change due to a myriad of internal and external variables, including the passage of time, seasonal changes, diet, lifestyle choices, and more.

The three doshas characterise prakriti—vata, pitta, and kapha—each of which influences physical processes in its unique way. Vata, the subtle energy of motion, is made up of air and space. It controls the heart's beat, blinking, breathing, and other motions in the cytoplasm and cell membranes. When balanced, vata encourages adaptability and originality. When vata is out of whack, it causes anxious feelings. Pitta is the fire element and water element that make up the metabolic system of the body. Nutrition, metabolism, digestion, absorption, and assimilation are all controlled by it. Pitta, when balanced, fosters insight and brainpower. Pitta, when out of balance, causes hostility, jealousy, and wrath. As a result of its composition of earth and water, kapha energy is responsible for building the skeleton, muscles, and tendons of the body and supplying the 'glue' that binds the cells together. All of the body's systems and components rely on kapha for their water supply. It keeps the skin hydrated, lubricates the joints, and supports a strong immune system. Kapha, when balanced, manifests as love, serenity, and forgiveness. It triggers attachment, avarice, and jealousy when it's out of whack.

The 'tailored' equilibrium of the three doshas exists in every individual. Eating, exercising, and interacting with others all impact the individual doshas, which are always 'in flux'. An imbalance can be caused by several factors, including an unhealthy diet, an imbalance in mental or physical exertion, exposure to toxins, or even infections. According to Ayurveda, following daily and seasonal routines that promote balance is recommended for maintaining health and preventing illness. Life presents us with several possibilities and challenges. While there are many aspects we can't change, there are certain elements, such as our food and lifestyle, that are entirely within our control. To maintain a healthy and balanced lifestyle, it is essential to make informed choices. The body, intellect, and consciousness are all strengthened by a constitution-appropriate diet and lifestyle.

Deciphering Ancient Knowledge

A significant amount of money is being spent by some of the world's largest technology companies on collecting health data and developing algorithms. With the development of AI systems, clinical studies can be conducted more efficiently, thereby reducing variability in results, minimising errors, and enhancing the output of clinical trials. AI can also help select study participants based on patient eligibility and suitability, efficiently sort medical records, and identify the illness phenotype. This can all be done while the patient is being closely monitored to make sure that early warning signs of any drug-related side effects are found.

Artificial intelligence introduces new pathways for examining ancient works of medical literature, creating opportunities for screening herbs or components of traditional formulas that could reveal their mechanisms of action, much like how some old films become superhits when posted on the internet. The widespread use of plant-based active ingredients raises the possibility that medicinal plant extracts may serve as a source for developing novel medications.

An artificial intelligence system can comprehend the vast amounts of data that have never been analysed before and derive new insights from plant extracts, which are complex mixtures of chemical components, as well as decipher various ancient medical scripts that describe their functions. Helpful AI-powered diagnostic models are also expanding in areas such as decision-making, symptom categorisation using various clinical data, and the creation of pharmacological databases that can be utilised to establish ethnopharmacology, the study of how different cultures and ethnic groups utilise plants and other substances for medicinal purposes.

Western medicine's one-size-fits-all approach has significant drawbacks, including harmful side effects, and remains an unmet challenge. AI can analyse vast amounts of data, including patient histories, genetic information, and lifestyle factors, to tailor treatments to individual needs. The essence of the dosha system is rooted in a unique body constitution. This personalisation can enhance treatment effectiveness and patient satisfaction. AI can help analyse clinical data and scholarly research to validate Ayurvedic practices scientifically. By converting traditional knowledge into quantifiable data, it can support evidence-based approaches.

AI can also help predict health outcomes based on Ayurvedic principles by analysing lifestyle choices, dietary habits, and environmental factors. Thus, it can provide proactive health management. AI-powered apps can facilitate consultations with Ayurvedic practitioners, making the approach more accessible to people worldwide. This digital integration can help reach a broader audience.

AI can contribute to the development of educational tools and resources that enhance understanding of Ayurveda, making it easier for practitioners and patients to learn about wellness practices. Additionally, AI can help bridge the gap between Ayurveda and modern healthcare systems, promoting a more holistic approach to treatment and wellness that integrates both practices for improved patient outcomes. Overall, while AI may enhance the visibility and applicability of Ayurveda, its adoption in mainstream healthcare will also depend on cultural acceptance, regulatory frameworks, and ongoing research to establish credibility and efficacy.

Finally, the time has come to capture and apply ancient Indian wisdom about immunity. Ayurveda emphasises a holistic approach to health, including diet, exercise, sleep, and mental well-being. Maintaining a balanced lifestyle is considered essential for building and sustaining a robust immune system. Everyone has a unique constitution (prakriti) based on the three doshas. Understanding one's prakriti helps tailor diets and lifestyle choices that can strengthen immune function.

The Inner and Outer Armour

Rasayana Ayurvedic treatments aim to enhance vitality and immunity. They often involve specific herbs, dietary practices, and therapies designed to rejuvenate the body, promote longevity, and strengthen the immune system. Ancient Indian texts advocate for a balanced diet rich in fresh, whole foods, including fruits, vegetables, grains, and spices known for their health benefits, such as turmeric's anti-inflammatory properties. Certain herbs are emphasised for their immune-boosting properties. For instance, ashwagandha, tulsi (also known as holy basil), and triphala are often recommended for enhancing overall health and immunity.

Panchakarma is a key component of Ayurvedic medicine that focuses on detoxification, rejuvenation, and restoring balance to the body. Nothing like this exists in the Western system of medicine, perhaps except enemas, but merely purging the accumulated solid waste in the intestines. Panchakarma aims to cleanse the body of accumulated toxins through various methods, such as vamana (medicated emesis), virechana (medicated purgation), and basti (therapeutic enemas). This detoxification helps improve cellular function and restore natural bodily processes, enhancing the immune response.

Another important concept in Ayurveda is agni, which relates to digestion and metabolism, highlighting the centrality of digestive health to overall well-being. Managing and nurturing agni through diet, lifestyle, and mindful practices is essential for maintaining health and preventing disease. There are three types of agni—jatharagni, bhutagni, and dhavagni—that must be managed and kept in balance.

Jatharagni is the primary digestive fire located in the stomach and intestines, responsible for breaking down food and converting it into usable energy and nutrients. Bhutagni refers to the digestive fire associated with the five elements (earth, water, fire, air, and ether) that are transformed into their respective bodily constituents, such as blood and flesh. Dhavagni is related to the body's seven dhatus (tissues) and helps transform and maintain these tissues. Panchakarma treatments focus on enhancing agni, which leads to improved nutrient absorption and the elimination of waste products. A strong and balanced agni ensures proper digestion, nutrient absorption, and waste excretion. Poor agni can lead to digestive issues and the accumulation of toxins (ama). Good agni supports the immune system by enhancing the body's ability to process nutrients effectively and defend against pathogens. Agni also influences mental processes. A balanced agni promotes mental clarity, focus, and emotional stability.

Ayurveda offers a holistic approach to mental health, recognising the intricate connection between the mind, body, and spirit. It emphasises balance among these elements as crucial for psychological well-being. Here are key concepts and practices in Ayurveda related to mental health: The three doshas are linked to various mental states. For example, vata imbalance leads to anxiety, fear, and restlessness; pitta imbalance results in irritability, anger, and frustration; and kapha imbalance causes lethargy, sadness, and depression. Ayurveda promotes a balanced diet tailored to individual needs, incorporating foods that support mental well-being. For instance, lighter, nutritious foods can benefit a vata constitution, while grounding foods may help balance anxious tendencies. Certain herbs are recognised for their benefits in supporting mental health. Ashwagandha has adaptogenic properties that help reduce stress and anxiety. Brahmi enhances memory and cognitive function. Tulsi helps alleviate stress and improve mood.

Ayurveda does not compete with Western medicine; it offers complementary insights and practices that can enhance health outcomes. By integrating the strengths of both systems, healthcare can become more comprehensive, addressing the physical, mental, and emotional aspects of well-being for a holistic approach to health. Chronic illnesses often require a multifaceted approach to management. Ayurveda can provide supportive therapies and lifestyle modifications to complement conventional medical treatments, enhancing the patient's quality of life. Both Ayurveda and Western medicine increasingly emphasise patient-centred care. The Ayurvedic focus on individualised treatment plans aligns with the growing trend in Western healthcare to tailor therapies based on patient needs and preferences.

Ayurveda emphasises the importance of yoga, meditation, and pranayama (breath control) as essential tools for promoting mental well-being. These practices encourage relaxation, reduce stress, and improve emotional resilience. Establishing a daily routine that includes regular sleep, healthy meals, and physical activity supports mental balance. Consistency in daily habits fosters stability and reduces anxiety. Encouraging sattva through lifestyle choices can help enhance mental clarity and emotional stability. Humanity will be blessed to embrace breath control and mindfulness practices.

Ayurveda acknowledges the presence of cosmic energies that can influence both the body and mind. For example, the phases of the moon and the positions of the planets are thought to affect human behaviour, emotions, and health. Practices such as astrology are often integrated into Ayurveda to provide insights into how cosmic events may impact an individual's well-being and to personalise health treatments accordingly. Ayurveda encourages practices that align with nature and the cosmos to achieve balance and harmony in life. This holistic approach addresses physical health while also nurturing mental and spiritual well-being, reinforcing a sense of unity with the universe.

Summary

The microcosm (individual, embodied soul) is seen as a reflection of the macrocosm (society, the cosmos), emphasising harmony and interconnectedness. Modern science explores this unity through fields such as quantum physics, where the behaviour of particles mirrors larger cosmic patterns, and systems theory, which examines how smaller systems interact within larger ones. Ayurveda, the science of life, recognises the unique constitution of every individual and emphasises the need for harmonisation. If AI adopts Ayurveda and yoga as the basis for mental and physical well-being, humanity can be freed from the greed and perils of the pharmaceutical and modern medical industries.

5

Maya and the Mind

To see is to be veiled. The mind weaves a gentle illusion so that life may unfold without the weight of its own ending. Yet beneath this sacred veil lies awareness itself—ancient, unbroken, watching through every thought. The Vedic seers knew the mind not as a dream-maker, but as evolution's mirror—reflecting the play of maya while hinting at the truth beyond.

Masking the Underlying Unity of Existence

The essence of one consciousness as the foundation for all that exists implies that reality is perfect, unencumbered, and unadulterated. So, if we are all already Brahman, why do we need to change? If all that exists is good, why must we suffer? The key to unlocking this puzzle is another uniquely Indian idea: maya. It is often translated as delusion and ignorance, which is erroneous. Maya is part of creation, representing the external coverings that envelop our true selves and the reality we inhabit. Maya is best understood as a curtain that conceals our true selves and the world as we know it. But it disappears as the blue sky after the sun sets, once the eternal and immortal ground of ephemeral and perishable phenomena is captured.

Like the ever-changing pictures on a movie screen, the world around us is constantly evolving, but the static screen is essential to the experience. In the same vein, the reality of this ever-changing world is imparted by the immutable Brahman, the foundation of existence, which lies beneath it all, as if reflected in a distorted mirror, governed by the laws of space, time, and causality. When we mistakenly identify with our physical selves, our thoughts, and our egos rather than with the transcendental self, or atman, we further cloud our perception of reality. A domino effect of more misunderstandings leads to more misery and less knowledge. When we let ourselves be defined by our physical and mental selves, we open ourselves up to a myriad negative emotions, including but not limited to anger, hatred, and the prospect of old age, illness, and death.

Adi Shankara compared maya to an illusion of a rope and a snake. As one makes way down a dimly lit path, one's heart races, spotting a snake ahead. Upon closer examination, the 'snake' turns out to be a coil of rope. When the illusion wears off, the serpent disappears for good. In a similar vein, our boundlessness, pain, and limitations plague us when we recognise that we are mortal beings constrained by space, time, and cause and effect. Upon closer inspection, Brahman is revealed to be both the universe and physical beings. Our mortality and the cosmos vanish eternally the moment the illusion cracks. Brahman is present in all things and everywhere.

Maya is like a thick cloud that blocks out the sun's rays. The sun is always there in the sky, but it isn't visible to us beneath a cover of clouds. We can see it as soon as the clouds disperse. Egotism, selfishness, hatred, greed, lust, wrath, and ambition are like clouds. They can be driven away through meditation on our true nature, performing selfless acts, and continually acting and thinking in ways that reflect our true nature, which means through honesty, purity, contentment, self-control, and patience. This mental purification dispels the maya-like clouds, allowing our pure essence to radiate.

Viewing maya solely as the deceptive nature of the physical world and the experiences perceived through the senses is limiting, as it overlooks the creative power of the divine known as Shakti. This force manifests the universe and all its forms, facilitating the play of creation, sustenance, and dissolution. Maya enables the apparent existence of the world. Various transient states, which can last from a nanosecond to years, decades, centuries, or millennia, constantly transform into their inevitable dissolution. Considering these transient states as permanent and becoming attached to their names and forms epitomises maya. In Buddhism, the concepts of impermanence (anicca, anityata) and non-self (anatta, anatma) effectively illustrate the illusory nature of human life and phenomena. Those who are attached to it suffer.

Sikh theology informs us that maya is a part of God's creation. It is a divine play (lila) that allows individuals to experience life but emphasises that true wisdom lies in transcending it. Bhagat Kabir states in the *Shabad* that rajas (the quality of energy and activity), tamas (the quality of darkness and inertia), and sattva (the quality of purity and light) are all creations of maya. That man who realises the fourth state (goes beyond the three) alone obtains the supreme state.[6] Maya is seen as a barrier that creates the illusion of separation

[6] रज गुण तम गुण सत गुण कहीऐ इह तेरी सभ माइआ ॥ चउथे पद कउ जो नरु चीन्है तन्हि ही परम पदु पाइआ॥

from Waheguru (God). This separation leads individuals to lose sight of their divine purpose and connection to the ultimate reality.

Sikhs are encouraged to cultivate a deeper spiritual connection through meditation, prayer, and selfless service, known as seva. Maya is often linked to the five 'thieves' (lust, anger, greed, attachment, and pride) in Sikh teachings. These are considered negative qualities that arise from the influence of maya and can lead to moral and spiritual downfall. The practice of naam simran, or meditative remembrance of God's name, is a fundamental aspect of Sikhism. This practice helps individuals overcome the distractions of maya and reconnect with their divine nature. Being in the company of like-minded individuals (sangat) helps overcome the illusions created by maya through shared practices and collective devotion to God.

The Relationship Between Maya and the Mind

The concepts of maya and the mind are thoroughly explored, particularly in the *Yog Vasishtha*, written by the author of the Ramayana, Maharishi Valmiki. Maya and the mind are forever intertwined, influencing each other. What we perceive through our senses is not the absolute truth but a temporary manifestation of a deeper, underlying reality. This obscuring causes individuals to mistake the transient for the eternal, leading them to identify with the physical body, thoughts, and emotions.

The mind is the cognitive and emotional centre responsible for thoughts, perceptions, desires, and memories. It is a tool through which individuals interpret and interact with the world. The mind is often described as restless and prone to fluctuations, known as vrittis. These mental modifications shape one's experience of reality, contributing to attachment, suffering, and confusion. The mind plays a pivotal role in creating and maintaining the illusion of maya. It creates the perceptions that constitute maya. Conversely, the illusions of maya influence the workings of the mind, leading to confusion and misidentification with the material aspects of life.

The *Yog Vasishtha* provides profound insights into the nature of the mind and its role in pursuing spiritual liberation. The text describes the mind as a powerful force that can bind or liberate an individual. It is often depicted as restless and fickle, easily distracted by desires and illusions. The scripture outlines that the mind constantly engages in various modifications (vrittis), including thoughts, emotions, and perceptions. These modifications shape our experiences and the reality we perceive. The mind often creates a false sense of reality. It leads to attachment and identification with the material world, causing suffering.

Understanding the mind's illusory nature is crucial for spiritual awakening. Transcending the conditioned mind is a great skill. The text encourages practitioners to recognise their true nature (atman) as distinct from the mind and its modifications. Techniques such as meditation (dhyana) and self-inquiry are advocated to gain mastery over the mind. The mind is both the creator and the experience of maya. The mind, as the 'agent of maya', projects and sustains the illusion of maya by interpreting sensory data and creating a sense of individuality and separation. When the mind is untrained or unawakened, it becomes entangled in the illusions of maya, leading to suffering, attachment, and ignorance. It thus becomes a 'prisoner of maya'. The mind is also the key to liberation. Through self-awareness, meditation, and spiritual practice, the mind can transcend maya and realise the ultimate truth.

In Buddhism, the essence of the mind is referred to as the alaya (repository) consciousness. The essence of the mind, however, undergoes a metamorphosis into a variety of conceptions (vijnanas) the moment that thinking or reasoning begins. The six recipient vijnanas perceive the six sense objects through their respective sensory doors at birth. The mind's constructs—thoughts, desires, and beliefs—create a sense of duality and separation. There are thirty-six contrasting elements, such as 'coming' and 'going', which are all mental constructions and have nothing to do with reality. By purifying and calming the mind, individuals can pierce through maya, gaining clarity about their true nature. There are thirty-six 'pairs of opposites'—five inanimate (like sun and moon), twelve tangible (phenomenal, like light and darkness), and nineteen intangibles (mental, like long and short). He who knows how to use these thirty-six pairs can avoid the two extremes.

The concept of the mind in the Western world has evolved significantly through philosophy, psychology, and neuroscience. French philosopher René Descartes notably proposed the idea of mind-body dualism, which posits that the mind is distinct from the body. This led to deep inquiries about the nature of consciousness and the self. In contrast, materialist philosophers argue that only physical substances exist, reducing mental phenomena to brain activity. This view shapes much of contemporary psychology and neuroscience. There was a time in the early twentieth century when scientists like B.F. Skinner dismissed internal mental states as unobservable and called observable behaviour the only truth.

In the mid-twentieth century, the cognitive revolution shifted focus back to mental processes, including perception, memory, language, and problem-solving. It laid the groundwork for cognitive psychology and cognitive science. Imaging technologies, such as fMRI and PET scans, enable researchers to observe changes in brain activity during specific mental tasks. Contemporary cognitive science is an interdisciplinary field that combines psychology, neuroscience, artificial intelligence, and philosophy to study the mind and its processes. It explores how information is processed and how mental functions are represented in the brain.

Immersive Technologies

In recent years, the rise of inexpensive hardware and software, combined with technical advancements, has increased the commercial viability of immersive technologies such as augmented reality (AR), virtual reality (VR), and mixed reality (MR). AR and VR were created to serve the media and entertainment industry to create a new level of engaging entertainment with the potential for a more intimate and emotional experience. The same technologies that transform media and entertainment also impact building design, helping professionals better visualise their projects, simulate their designs to suggest how they would work if built and operated, and present their ideas to clients.

In the automotive industry, all the little elements of good car design—for example, ergonomic details like how far the driver must extend her arm to reach the dashboard—can be experienced much more accurately when the designer feels as if they are sitting in the car rather than viewing it as a 2D image on a desktop screen. Visualisation software enables automotive designers and engineers to create product presentations, conduct design reviews, and build virtual prototypes. For industries such as construction, manufacturing, and oil and gas, AR and VR have the potential to provide virtual field training, offering users a 'you're there' experience before they arrive at their destination. All this converges to enhanced education. Students in classrooms around the country and worldwide can virtually step into real-life situations and experience them first-hand.

Without a doubt, we are at the forefront of an entirely new form of computing that has the potential to radically change the way humans interact with media and digital information. The world around us is becoming increasingly immersive and fascinating as our realities are blended, virtual, and enhanced. From movies and video games to real-life structures and transportation, the new technologies may revolutionise our creative processes and the way we learn and grow. The world that has been called 'mithya' by our seers will indeed be so, and it won't be easy to decipher the actual from the augmented.

The excess mental capacity individuals have due to advancements in technology and a reduction in the time spent on basic survival tasks is known as 'cognitive surplus'. While this surplus has the potential for positive outcomes, such as increased creativity and engagement in social causes, it also raises concerns regarding mental health. The constant availability of information and entertainment can lead to cognitive overload, increasing stress and anxiety levels. Being constantly connected through social media can foster feelings of inadequacy and loneliness as individuals compare themselves to others. With numerous engagement options, individuals may struggle to find time for relaxation or mindful practices, which are essential for maintaining mental well-being.

Increased screen time and engagement with digital platforms can lead to dependency issues—addiction to technology—impacting relationships and mental health adversely. While online communication can enhance connections, it may also diminish the importance of in-person social interactions, which are essential for emotional support. To address these potential issues, proactive steps such as setting boundaries on technology use, practising mindfulness, and prioritising real-life relationships are imperative. If mental health concerns arise, seeking professional assistance is recommended. Artificial intelligence will play a significant role in supporting mental health in various ways.

AI algorithms can analyse large datasets, including social media activity, speech patterns, and clinical records, to identify early signs of mental health conditions. This can help in timely diagnosis and intervention. AI-powered chatbots can provide immediate support to individuals seeking help. They can engage users in conversation, offer coping strategies, and provide resources for further assistance, making mental health support more accessible. AI applications can track user behaviour and well-being through wearable devices or mobile apps. They can monitor mood changes, sleep patterns, and stress levels, providing feedback and alerts when intervention may be necessary.

Using natural language processing (NLP), AI can analyse written or spoken language to identify signs of mental health issues, such as depression or anxiety, by assessing sentiment, word choice, and conversation patterns. AI can enhance mental health apps by incorporating gamified elements that encourage engagement and adherence to self-care practices, making the therapeutic process interactive and enjoyable. AI can even expedite mental health research by analysing large datasets to identify trends, treatment outcomes, and risk factors. This can improve understanding and lead to the development of new therapies. As AI-driven platforms can provide anonymous and stigma-free environments for individuals to seek help, people will be more likely to reach out for support without fear of judgment. While AI can significantly enhance mental health services, ethical considerations, such as data privacy and human oversight, must be prioritised in its development and implementation. Integrating AI into mental health care should complement, rather than replace, the compassionate and nuanced approach of human practitioners.

The Threat of a Fake Reality

The threat of a fake reality—whether created by maya (illusion), societal conditioning, or technological manipulation—is a profound concern in both spiritual and modern contexts. Essentially, fake reality refers to a distorted or false perception of the world, which can arise from maya (spiritual illusion), societal conditioning by cultural norms, and the media and education that shape beliefs and perceptions, as well as the recently arrived technological manipulation through misinformation, deepfakes, virtual realities, and algorithms that create echo chambers and distort truth.

Living in a fake reality can have significant consequences. The first casualty is the loss of authenticity. Fake reality disconnects individuals from their true selves, leading to identity crises and existential emptiness. Fake realities can be exploited by powerful entities, such as governments and corporations, to control behaviour and decision-making. Misinformation and illusion can polarise societies, fostering distrust, hatred, and violence. Believing in a fake reality can hinder spiritual growth by keeping individuals trapped in materialism and ignorance.

The notion that people's minds have been controlled historically to build empires raises essential questions about power, influence, and autonomy. Although AI itself lacks intent or desire, it operates based on algorithms and data inputs that humans determine. Its impact depends on how it is programmed and the objectives set by its developers and users. AI technologies, particularly in social media and advertising, are already shaping opinions and promoting behaviours by influencing the information people receive. This targeted approach can create echo chambers and reinforce existing biases, potentially mimicking historical control strategies.

Unlike historical empires that actively sought to control populations, AI functions as a tool. Its potential to influence people's thoughts and behaviours depends on the ethical choices made by those who develop and deploy AI systems. The ability of AI to manipulate thoughts raises significant ethical dilemmas. Establishing guidelines and regulatory frameworks will be crucial to ensuring that AI empowers individuals rather than controls them. Enhancing digital literacy and critical thinking skills among the public can help mitigate the risks of manipulation by AI, encouraging people to make informed choices about the information they consume.

While AI has the potential to influence human behaviour, it does not possess the capacity to control minds autonomously. Humans are responsible for using AI ethically and transparently, ensuring it enhances freedom and understanding rather than creating new forms of control. But who would these humans be? Approximately one in seven human beings on this planet is Indian. Can others be left with the power to influence and manipulate their minds? Thousands of years of foreign rule have almost eroded any sense of nationalism and pride in the Indian people. Thankfully, some great minds, like Bal Gangadhar Tilak, rekindled the about-to-die flame of pride in Indian civilisation. As a nation, we have accepted the partition of our territory and copied the economic models of others to the significant harm of our people and industry. We, as a nation, cannot afford or allow a repeat of such a folly.

Failing to respond to China's rapid development and investment in various AI technologies and relying on corporations in good faith will be no different than an ostrich burying its head in the sand for security and comfort. It is an uncomfortable truth, like a pebble inside a shoe, that India does not have anything like Baidu, known for its work in autonomous driving and natural language processing; Alibaba, which focuses on AI applications in e-commerce and cloud computing; Tencent Invests in AI for gaming, healthcare, and social media; and Huawei, which develops AI technologies for telecommunications and mobile devices. We have come a long way, but an even longer road lies ahead. It is time to support the Indian mind in working for India rather than creating wealth for others.

Summary

The mind is the seat of thought, perception, and consciousness—an ever-evolving faculty that shapes how we experience reality. The inner journey is one of seeing through illusion and aligning with ultimate truth: the realisation of the interconnectedness of all existence. In this state, awareness itself becomes the foundation of reality, guiding one towards authenticity, compassion, and contribution to the well-being of all.

For artificial intelligence to truly study human behaviour, comprehend consciousness, and, perhaps one day evolve a 'mind' of its own, it must look beyond the fragmented and mechanistic frameworks of the West. Indian scriptures—particularly the *Yog Vashishta*, the original thesis on the nature of the mind—offer a far more comprehensive, nuanced, and timeless understanding of consciousness and its creative potential.

Part II

A 1,000-Year Eclipse

When men cannot observe, they don't have ideas; they have obsessions. When people live instinctive lives, something like a collective amnesia steadily blurs the past.[1]

—Sir V.S. Naipaul

Nobel Prize in Literature, 2004

[1] *The Indian Trilogy*. New Delhi: Picador India, 2023 (Reprint), p. 406.

6

Shadows Over the Golden Age

When the land overflowed with knowledge and gold, it drew the gaze of conquerors from every horizon. They came for treasure and stayed for power, while brothers within forgot their kinship and quarrelled over fragments. Thus, a civilisation that once measured wealth in wisdom was broken by its own divisions—leaving the cradle of abundance in chains.

Empire Builders

We have previously discussed the Arctic Circle as the origin of the Indian people. The affluent peninsula, bordered by the Himalayas to the north and surrounded by oceans on the other three sides, was called Jambu Dwipa. Chandragupta Maurya, mentored by Chanakya, founded the Maurya Empire in 322 BCE. Chandragupta's rise coincided with Alexander's invasion of northwest India. Chandragupta had made all the required preparations to resist them. However, they never directly engaged in battle. After Alexander's retreat, Chandragupta expanded his empire further westward into territories that were formerly under Greek control.

Chandragupta established a centralised administration and implemented an effective bureaucratic system. He divided the empire into government-controlled provinces to maintain order and governance. He focused on trade, agriculture, and infrastructure development, which boosted the empire's economy. His policies promoted trade routes and commerce. Chandragupta built a formidable army, enabling him to defend his empire against external threats and maintain internal order. Around 297 BCE, he abdicated the throne to his son, Bindusara, and entered an ascetic life, reportedly embracing Jainism. He spent his later years in Karnataka.

After Bindusara died in 268 BCE, his son Ashoka ascended to the throne. Initially, he was a traditional monarch who focused on military conquests. Ashoka's most significant military campaign was the conquest of Kalinga (modern-day Odisha) around 261 BCE. The toll of the Kalinga War prompted a transformation in Ashoka's outlook. He was deeply moved by the devastation and misery caused by the conflict, leading him to renounce further military conquests. Following the Kalinga War, Ashoka converted to Buddhism and adopted its principles of nonviolence (ahimsa) and compassion. His conversion was both personal and state policy-oriented, as he sought to govern in accordance with Buddhist values.

Ashoka introduced the concept of dharma as the basis of governance. Dharma encompasses moral and ethical principles, emphasising nonviolence, tolerance, and respect for all living beings. Ashoka sought to create a just and benevolent society. He inscribed a series of edicts on pillars and rocks throughout his empire, communicating his policies and principles to his subjects. The modern Indian nation has chosen the edict at the Lion Capital of Ashoka, erected in 280 BCE, as the national symbol. Four lions stand back-to-back, symbolising power, courage, confidence, and pride. They are mounted on a circular base in high relief, depicting an elephant, a galloping horse, a bull, and a lion, separated by intervening dharma chakras.

The decline of the Maurya Empire created a power vacuum, leading to the emergence of various regional kingdoms. Though nonviolence was an attractive policy, it led to the rise of small fiefdoms. The vast empire was split into smaller kingdoms and republics. The Shunga Dynasty (c.185–73 BCE) was established by Pushyamitra Shunga, a former general of the Mauryan army who ruled much of northern India. This period was marked by political instability and conflicts but also a resurgence of Hinduism as the Shunga kings promoted Brahminical culture and patronised religious activities.

Following the Shungas, the Indo-Greek kingdom emerged in parts of northwestern India. These Greek rulers had settled in the region after Alexander's invasion. They contributed to cultural exchanges, particularly in art and coinage, blending Hellenistic and Indian influences. The Kushans, an ancient Central Asian people, established a significant empire extending into northern India and Central Asia. One of the most notable rulers of the Kushan Empire was Kanishka, who ruled from 127 to 150 CE. The empire began to decline in the third century CE, eventually falling to the rise of other regional powers.

The Gupta Empire rose to power in the fourth century. Founded by Sri Gupta around 240 CE, it was under his grandson, Chandragupta II (reigning from about 375 to 415 CE), that the empire reached its peak in terms of territorial extent and cultural achievements. The empire expanded across much of northern and central India. Aryabhata and Kalidasa lived during this period of stability and artistic renaissance. The invasions by the Huns in the fifth century CE, during the reign of Chandragupta II's son Kumaragupta I and later his son, Skandagupta, significantly weakened the empire. After the latter's death, further incursions by the Huns and internal strife ushered in a new era of regional kingdoms and increased foreign influences in the Indian subcontinent.

Political Fragmentation

The disintegration of Indian empires and their eventual subjugation by invaders is a complex historical phenomenon influenced by a combination of internal weaknesses and external pressures. The Mauryas and Guptas struggled to maintain centralised control over vast territories, leading to regional autonomy and weakening of their empires. Frequent disputes over succession often led to civil wars, further eroding the empire from within. Rigid social hierarchies limited mobility and innovation, creating divisions within society. Tensions between Hinduism, Buddhism, and Jainism sometimes led to internal strife.

Gopala founded the Pala Empire in the late eighth century. Under the leadership of his successor, Dharmapala (c. 770–810 CE), the empire controlled extensive territories in northern India, encompassing regions of Bengal, Bihar, and parts of present-day Uttar Pradesh. The Pala rulers were notable patrons of Buddhism, and the empire played a pivotal role in spreading the religion throughout India. They supported the establishment of monasteries, universities, and learning centres, including the Vikramshila and Nalanda universities, which attracted students from across Asia.

Starting from the seventh century, the Rajputs, a collection of warrior clans, established numerous kingdoms in northern and western India. They were renowned for their martial skills and played vital roles in defending their kingdoms against invaders and rival states. They utilised cavalry and infantry to conquer distant territories and won significant battles throughout Indian history. Mahmud of Ghazni led the first considerable invasion of Delhi in the early eleventh century (around 1025 CE). He invaded India multiple times, targeting wealthy temples and cities. These invasions laid the groundwork for further incursions into northern India. In the thirteenth century, Muhammad Ghori defeated the Rajput ruler Prithviraj Chauhan in 1192 CE. This victory paved the way for the establishment of Muslim rule in India, which led to the formation of the Delhi Sultanate.

In the south, however, the rule of the Vijayanagara Empire continued. The empire was founded in 1336 CE by Harihara I and Bukka Raya I, two brothers from the Sangama Dynasty. They established the capital at Hampi, the region's political, economic, and cultural epicentre. The empire expanded rapidly under various rulers, including Krishnadeva Raya (reigned 1509–1530 CE), encompassing large parts of southern India, including present-day Karnataka, Andhra Pradesh, Tamil Nadu, and parts of Kerala.

South India's history is rich and complex, with unique cultural, political, and social developments distinct from those of North India. It was home to several powerful ancient kingdoms, such as the Chola, Pandya, and Chera dynasties. These kingdoms were known for their trade, agriculture, art, and architectural advancements. They had well-established governance systems and made significant contributions to the Indian cultural landscape.

The Chola Empire flourished from approximately the ninth to the thirteenth centuries and is notable for its maritime expansion. Rajendra Chola I (reigned 1014–1044 CE) undertook military expeditions to Southeast Asia and established rule over Sumatra, Java, and parts of the Malay Peninsula, aiming to establish dominance over maritime trade routes.

The Angkor Wat temple complex in Cambodia was commissioned by Suryavarman II between 1113 and 1150 CE. It is renowned for its grand scale, intricate bas-reliefs, and sophisticated design. The complex exemplifies classical Khmer architecture with its symmetrical layout, massive stone blocks, and towers that symbolise Mount Meru, the centre of the universe in Hindu cosmology.

It is an undeniable fact that the quincunx of towers at Angkor Wat is so vast that it can be seen from space. The moat encloses an area four times the size of Vatican City. More stones are used in temple construction than in the largest Egyptian pyramid. Angkor Wat is the world's largest and most magnificent Hindu temple. One must be blind with prejudice and bereft of intelligence to deny the grandeur of Indian civilisation before it fell to invaders and settlers.

Invasions and Conquests

The emergence of mighty empires, such as the Abbasids in the eighth century and Ottomans in the fourteenth century, in the Middle East and Central Asia created pressure on Indian kingdoms. The invasions of the Huns, Turks, and Mongols from Central Asia brought new military tactics and technologies that Indian empires struggled to counter. With cavalry and archery, these foreign armies excelled in mounted warfare, a more mobile and practical approach than their traditional Indian counterparts. The Ghaznavids and Ghurids were notorious for their heartless plundering.

In a historic low for Indian pride, a former slave of Muhammad Ghori, Qutb ud-Din Aibak, ruled over Delhi. His successors, Iltutmish and Razia Sultana, expanded and consolidated the sultanate's power. Alien to Indian culture, these rulers' greed for wealth was what had brought them here. They would intrigue and fight amongst themselves. Various dynasties gained power in North India, notably the Turkish Khaljis and Tughlaqs, as well as the Arab Sayyid Dynasty (1414–1451 CE), and the Afghan Lodis. The Vindya Mountain range kept the invaders out of South India for several centuries.

Turkic-Mongol Babur, from Fergana, in modern-day Uzbekistan, defeated Ibrahim Lodi in the Battle of Panipat (1526 CE) and established the Mughal Empire, which would rule over India until the British arrived by 1757 CE and defeated the Nawab of Bengal in the Battle of Plassey. By 1857, with a divide-and-rule policy and acting as powerbrokers between feuding kingdoms, the British not only ended the Mughal Empire but also established control over all other kingdoms.

India's loss of freedom in the south was a different story and can be traced to the decline of the Chola Empire, which was undone not by outside forces but by internal rivalries. The Pandyas were one of the main rivals of the Cholas in southern India. The relationship between the two dynasties fluctuated between conflict and alliance. Eventually, the Pandyas gained the upper hand after the decline of the Chola Empire, particularly during the thirteenth century, when they successfully challenged the Cholas' rule in Tamil Nadu.

The Kakatiya Dynasty, centred in present-day Telangana and Andhra Pradesh, also challenged Chola supremacy. Under rulers such as Ganapati Deva and Prataparudra, the Kakatiyas conducted military campaigns that eroded Chola influence in the Deccan region. The Hoysala Empire, another regional power that emerged in southern India, enhanced its strength during the decline of the Cholas. Under rulers such as Vishnuvardhana and Ballala II, the Hoysalas competed with the Cholas for territory and influence, resulting in frequent military confrontations. The Hoysala Empire eventually carved out significant territories that were formerly under Chola control.

Furthermore, the Chola Empire experienced internal divisions and succession disputes, which weakened its governance. This internal strife made it challenging to address external threats effectively. As the Chola Empire began to decline, its once-mighty navy, which had facilitated its dominance in maritime trade and military expeditions, deteriorated. This weakening reduced their ability to project power and defend against invasions. The combination of external pressures from the Hoysalas and Pandyas, along with internal challenges, ultimately led to the fragmentation of the Cholas' power. By the later part of the thirteenth century, the Chola influence had waned significantly.

Several Indian kings and regional rulers colluded with the Mughals for various reasons, including political survival, personal gain, or strategic alliances. These collaborations played a significant role in the expansion and consolidation of the Mughal Empire in India. Kachawaha Rajput ruler Raja Man Singh I of Amber present-day Jaipur) became one of Akbar's most trusted generals and a key figure in the Mughal administration. He helped the Mughals in battles against rival Rajput kingdoms, such as Mewar, and played a crucial role in expanding Mughal influence in Rajasthan and beyond. Raja Todar Mal of Laharpur, modern-day Uttar Pradesh, became one of Akbar's most important ministers and revenue administrators. He introduced the 'zabt' land revenue system, which became the backbone of the Mughal administration. Many Deccani rulers, such as the Nizam Shahs of Ahmednagar and the Qutb Shahs of Golconda, initially allied with the Mughals to counter rival kingdoms but were eventually absorbed into the Mughal Empire.

Bravehearts and Betrayers

The fire, however, was not extinguished. It returned as the Maratha Empire established by Chhatrapati Shivaji Maharaj. Initially, a regional leader in the Western Ghats, Shivaji Maharaj challenged the Adil Shahi Sultanate of Bijapur and the Mughal Empire. He employed innovative guerrilla tactics, such as swift attacks and retreats, to outmanoeuvre larger and better-equipped armies. Shivaji Maharaj built a network of forts in the Sahyadri mountains, which served as military and administrative centres. He envisioned an independent Maratha kingdom (Hindavi Swarajya) free from Mughal and Sultanate rule. In 1674 CE, Shivaji Maharaj formally declared himself 'chhatrapati' (emperor), thereby establishing the Maratha Empire as a sovereign power.

After Shivaji Maharaj's death, the Maratha Empire was temporarily weakened, but it regained strength under the Peshwas (ministers), who became the de facto rulers. Balaji Vishwanath secured Maratha dominance in the Deccan and established the Maratha Confederacy, a coalition of regional leaders. Baji Rao I expanded Maratha power into North India, defeating the Mughals, the Nizam of Hyderabad, and other regional powers. Baji Rao continued the expansion and, in 1737 CE, captured Delhi, symbolising his dominance over the Mughal Empire. The history of India would have been different if the braveheart commander-in-chief of the Maratha army, Sadashivrao Bhau, had not been betrayed by other North Indian rulers in the Third Battle of Panipat against the Afghan ruler Ahmad Shah Durrani, also known as Abdali.

However, the defeat at Panipat marked the end of Maratha dominance. It paved the way for the rise of the British East India Company (EIC). The company already held a foothold in Bengal and sought to monopolise trade, particularly in textiles, saltpetre, and opium, which were highly profitable. In 1856 CE, the British annexed Awadh, deposing its popular ruler, Wajid Ali Shah. The annexation, along with other grievances, fuelled the rebellion of 1857 CE. Lucknow became a stronghold of resistance. The British Residency there was besieged, and the British officials, along with local loyalists, were held captive for months. When the British recaptured Lucknow in March 1858, they carried out a brutal and indiscriminate plunder of the city as if to erase symbols of Awadh's culture.

India's losses to various invaders throughout history must be discussed, analysed, and deciphered so they never happen again. The country's political fragmentation stands out as its number one malady. Numerous regional kingdoms, often at odds with one another, weakened the collective ability to resist invaders. This division made it easier for external forces to conquer and control territories. Many invaders brought advanced military techniques and technologies, such as cavalry and firearms, which local rulers sometimes failed to match. This tactical advantage allowed invaders to overpower local armies. Many invading forces capitalised on surprise, launching sudden attacks when local states were least prepared. This catch-off-guard tactic proved effective in many instances.

Besides, continuous warfare and the strain of defending against multiple invaders often depleted resources. Prolonged conflict could weaken local economies and military strength, making it challenging to sustain resistance. Invaders sometimes formed alliances with local rulers or groups disenchanted with existing powers, creating divisions within the local population that could be exploited. Betrayals and changing loyalties often undermined unified resistance. In some cases, invaders integrated into local societies, which made it difficult for the native populations to mobilise against them. This assimilation sometimes led to a decrease in resistance as local rulers adopted the invaders' practices.

But how the British conquered India, how they destroyed its economy and partitioned it before leaving, has no parallel in the history of the world. After all this, the perpetrators of the cataclysm that killed millions are seen as 'friends' and draw considerable admiration and support from the Indian people. Unless this code is cracked, we cannot learn from our history, and the danger of repeating it hangs over our heads. The rest of this chapter explores how a handful of British colonists conquered such a vast country as India. The British East India Company's conquest of India, which led to the establishment of British colonial rule, was a complex process influenced by various factors. Although a relatively small number of British officials and soldiers played a key role, several strategic, social, and political factors contributed to their ability to dominate the vast Indian subcontinent.

Divide and Rule

India was politically fragmented in the eighteenth century, with numerous kingdoms, princely states, and regional powers often engaged in conflicts and rivalries. This disunity made it easier for the British to exploit divisions and establish control over smaller states one by one. The British East India Company developed a professional army with advanced military technology and strategies, including artillery. They defeated larger Indian armies through better organisation, training, and modern warfare tactics.

The British negotiated alliances with various Indian rulers to gain control and influence over territory. They often used the divide-and-rule strategy, playing rival factions against each other. For instance, they allied with some local leaders to defeat others. The British often recruited Indian soldiers, known as sepoys, into their army, enabling them to expand their military presence without relying solely on British troops. This created a perception that British rule was supported by local populations, even when it was often resisted.

The British were often adept at quelling revolts and maintaining control through military might and swift punitive actions. Following the 1857 revolt, the British government assumed direct control of India, marking a transition from East India Company rule to British Crown rule. This led to the centralisation of power and a more systematic approach to governance. Through a combination of military, economic, diplomatic, and strategic factors, the British were able to conquer and administer a vast and diverse country like India, leading to nearly two centuries of colonial rule. The consequences of this rule have had lasting effects on the subcontinent's socioeconomic and political landscape.

The real reason for the Indian partition was geopolitical, resulting in the sacrifice of millions in cold blood. The Second World War with the defeat of Italy, Germany, and Japan. The Russians (then the Soviet Union or USSR) emerged from World War II with even greater gains than the Western Allies. A budding Cold War between the Soviet Union and the Western Allies played a crucial role in the partition of India. The British and their allies anticipated that one of the countries would align with the West, providing an outpost to monitor the Soviet threat.

To strengthen the British and American presence in Asia, the British asked Indian leaders if they would permit the establishment of military bases by the British and Americans in India after independence. The Indian leaders, including Mahatma Gandhi, flatly refused the proposal as they were unwilling to compromise India's sovereignty and wanted to set an example of non-alignment. As expected, this snub did not go down well with the British, who then looked to Jinnah to see if he would allow them to use the newly created Pakistan as a base for strategic military operations.

Muhammad Ali Jinnah, a follower of Bal Gangadhar Tilak in the 1910s, was eager to accept this, as it would not only enable him to govern a new country but also safeguard Pakistan's interests against a larger and stronger India, given the presence of Western forces. The proposed land for the Muslims was strategically positioned to influence the politics of Central Asia and, most importantly, to confront the new enemy: the USSR. Hence, despite vehement opposition from supporters of a united India, the English persuaded both parties to hastily agree to the partition of India. The leaders from both sides readily consented to their short-term gains of holding powerful offices.

The departing British colonialists brokered a hastily arranged partition of the subcontinent into India and Pakistan. Months of violence had preceded the announcement of the partition, which, in all honesty, was often whipped up by politicians or various religious and political groups who were jockeying for power. India's Partition marked a massive and bloody upheaval. All the Hindus living for generations in what was to become Pakistan had to flee their homes overnight. Several million people lost their lives. The actions of some departing British civil and military officials, who favoured Pakistan due to personal loyalties or realpolitik visions of British and Western interests, are well-documented and beyond the scope of this book. They have all now stood disgraced and relegated to the dustbin of history.

Since Mahatma Gandhi declared Jawaharlal Nehru his political heir and successor in 1941, he became India's first prime minister on 15 August 1947. On 30 January 1948, Mahatma Gandhi was assassinated, less than six months after independence. After Partition, the British handed over the baton to the Americans, who invested heavily in Pakistan, which went on to become a frontline anti-communist military state. When India went to the United Nations to complain about Pakistan's act of aggression on its territory—Kashmir, which had become a part of India through an act of accession—the Western nations turned the whole issue on its head and declared Kashmir a disputed territory.

Creating two Pakistans—one in the west and another in the east—was a military strategy. The British needed to retain a foothold in the NWFP (North-West Frontier Province) and Baluchistan because that would provide the means to maintain control of Iran—where British Petroleum's predecessor, the Anglo-Persian Oil Company, owned oil reserves—Iraq—where a British puppet monarchy enabled tight control of the Iraqi Petroleum Company—and the potentially oil-rich British protectorates of Kuwait, the United Arab Emirates (UAE), and Qatar. In the east, the presence of oil in Assam and the instability of Burma were the reasons behind the creation of East Pakistan. This is how the world has worked, works now, and will continue to work. What kind of artificial intelligence is needed to drive home this fact?

Summary

The loss of India—a vast and resource-rich land—to a succession of foreign invaders over the centuries was the result of a complex interplay of internal and external factors. While superior military technology, organisation, and strategy gave the invaders an edge, India's political fragmentation, frequent rivalries among regional powers, and slow adaptation to changing methods of warfare weakened its defence. Ultimately, it was the lack of unity and coordinated national purpose that allowed smaller external forces to dominate a civilisation far greater in size and wealth.

7

The Dimmed Light of the Mind

When the spirit of a people is chained, its brilliance dims long before its body falls. A thousand years of foreign shadow dulled the mirror of the Indian mind—once radiant with inquiry, now clouded by imitation. The Vedic fire that once illumined the world flickered in exile, awaiting a new dawn. The Bengal Renaissance stirred its embers, and places like Banaras lit small lamps of learning—but pride had grown faint, and the light, though reborn, could not yet burn bright.

Why Do Mistakes Haunt Future Generations?

The five ancient universities of Nalanda, Sharada Peeth, Takshashila, Vallabhi, and Vikramshila were not just any ordinary institutions; they were shining examples of intellectual excellence that produced brilliant minds in various disciplines, including philosophy, mathematics, and medicine. These institutions, which comprised India's complex tapestry, laid the groundwork for what is now recognised worldwide. The fall of Indian civilisation had begun after the destruction of Takshashila University by the invading Huns in the fifth century and of Nalanda by the Turk warlord Bakhtiyar Khilji in the late twelfth century. Khilji even set fire to the university and library, killed many of its inhabitants, and caused its permanent ruin. It was no different from the burning of the Library of Alexandria during Julius Caesar's siege in 48 BCE to destroy the Egyptian influence in the region. The surest way to destroy a civilisation had been to kill its scholars, destroy its libraries and education system. This chapter focuses on what went wrong with the Indian people who named a city after the oppressor who burned the library of Nalanda University there.

Philosopher Jiddu Krishnamurti famously described the ability to observe without evaluating as the hallmark of intelligence. Thoughtful legal and political frameworks characterise a well-developed civilisation. Societies that value nonjudgmental thinking and foster community and collaboration ultimately lead to greater social cohesion. When populations are informed and engaged, they are more likely to collaborate towards common goals. Intelligent societies tend to be more adaptable when facing challenges such as economic downturns or environmental changes. The capacity for critical thinking and innovative solutions can help civilisations survive and thrive despite hardships. World history is full of 'what ifs', where successive generations suffer the mistakes of their ancestors.

What if the Axis powers had won the Second World War? What would have been the impact on the civil rights, cultures, and economies in the occupied territories? What if the Mongol Empire had not declined and maintained its power and cohesion, allowing it to spread ideas, trade, and cultural exchange across Eurasia? What if the Americas had never been colonised, and global trade had not fuelled the military power of tiny European nations to capture the world? What if the Roman Empire had survived longer, leading to different technological advancements and cultural developments in Europe, and possibly altering the course of the Renaissance and Enlightenment ages? What if the Cold War had turned hot, and an escalation into direct conflict between superpowers had resulted in catastrophic nuclear warfare, drastically reshaping the geopolitical landscape and human civilisation?

What if the Black Death had not occurred? Without this pandemic, could it have resulted in sustained population growth, different social structures, and no accelerated technological and cultural developments in Europe? But above all, what if the invention of the printing press had happened earlier? That could have accelerated the dissemination of knowledge, potentially impacting the Reformation, scientific discoveries, and access to education. These 'what ifs' provoke thought about how interconnected and contingent historical events are, emphasising the importance of individual decisions and chance in shaping the world.

If the Turks and the Huns had not invaded India, the subcontinent's cultural, political, and social landscape might have developed quite differently. India has a rich cultural and intellectual tradition. Without foreign invasions, the existing local kingdoms might have fostered more stable cultural and philosophical growth, which could have led to different artistic and literary trends. Regional powers, such as the Rajputs and Cholas, may have led to more localised governance structures and less centralised rule. Without Turkic invasions, the spread and influence of Islam in India might have been limited, potentially leading to a different demographic and religious landscape. The geopolitical dynamics in Central Asia and the Indian subcontinent could have shifted, possibly affecting neighbouring regions, such as Persia (what is now Iran), regarding trade and military influence. A Maratha victory at the Third Battle of Panipat could have significantly altered the course of Indian history. But it did not happen, and thus not only was India ruled by the British, but the fate of Asia was sealed.

United India and Friendly China

If India had not been partitioned in 1947, the subcontinent's political, social, and economic landscape would have been profoundly different. India would have remained a unified country, potentially fostering a greater sense of national identity among its diverse populations. While the challenges of managing diverse ethnic, religious, and linguistic groups within a single state would persist, they would necessitate a distinct governance framework. The political structure of a united India would require careful balancing of interests among various communities. This unity could lead to either stability through cooperative governance or tensions if groups felt underrepresented or marginalised.

Partition led to significant communal violence and mass migrations based on religious identities. Without it, the dynamics between Hindus, Muslims, Sikhs, and other communities might have evolved differently, potentially fostering a more integrated society. On the other hand, it could also have intensified communal tensions that were already emerging. A united India might have allowed for more coordinated economic policies and development strategies, potentially leading to more substantial economic growth. However, regional disparities and issues related to resource allocation must be addressed. The coexistence of diverse communities might have led to more significant cultural exchanges and a more pluralistic society. However, substantial efforts would also be required to address historical grievances and build inclusive institutions.

Without Partition, the narratives of national identity in India would have been different. The Jai Hind ideology, a unifying, nationalist philosophy rooted in patriotism, secularism, and the spirit of collective struggle for India, would have created a distinct historical trajectory, creating opportunities for unity and cooperation in a richly diverse society. The implications would likely have affected various aspects of governance, social dynamics, and international relations in complex and unpredictable ways. India would have been a dominant regional power and could have played a more assertive role in global and regional affairs, potentially rivalling China's influence.

If China had not betrayed India in 1962, and again at the height of the Covid-19 pandemic in 2020, attempted military incursions into Indian territory, would geopolitics have been shaped differently? A strong friendship between China and India would have created a formidable bloc, balanced out Western influence and shaped global politics. Cooperation between the two giants could have reduced tensions in Asia, thereby fostering stability in regions such as Southeast Asia, Central Asia, and the Indian Ocean. A united India and a friendly China could have spearheaded the creation of a pan-Asian trade network, rivalling the European Union. The irony of the human world is that the actions of one generation have consequences that are borne by future generations.

Let's explore this further. Civilisations have historically experienced cycles of rise and fall due to various complex factors. Natural disasters, climate change, drought, and resource depletion can have devastating effects. For example, the collapse of the Mayan civilisation is often linked to prolonged drought and deforestation.

Economic mismanagement, overextension, and reliance on unsustainable practices can also weaken a civilisation. The Roman Empire faced financial troubles, including heavy taxation, inflation, and reliance on slave labour.

The Enigma of Europe

Perhaps the best continent in terms of natural and human resources and technological prowess, on planet Earth, far from living in peace, Europe has given rise to two world wars. Europe remains divided despite being a Union due to a combination of historical, cultural, economic, and political factors. It is essential to know this enigma. Europe comprises numerous countries with distinct histories, languages, and cultures. These deep-rooted differences can lead to varying national identities and priorities, making it challenging to achieve complete unity.

There are significant economic disparities between member states. Wealthier nations, such as Germany and France, often have different economic priorities compared to less affluent countries, like Greece or Bulgaria. These disparities can lead to tensions and differing views on economic policies and financial support. For example, agricultural policies that benefit France might not be as beneficial for industrial-focused countries like Germany. This divergence can create friction and complicate decision-making processes. But above all else, the EU's institutional framework is complex, involving multiple layers of governance. This complexity can slow down decision-making and create bureaucratic inefficiencies, making it challenging to respond swiftly to crises.

Despite persisting challenges of developmental imbalance and income disparity, the European Union continues its pursuit of deeper integration and cooperation, driven by the shared understanding that unity strengthens peace, stability, and prosperity across the continent. Nowhere else in the world can one experience such freedom of movement and connection as within Europe. In doing so, Europe stands as a role model for other regions—especially in Asia, Africa, and South America—demonstrating how collective will and cooperation can transform diversity into a source of strength.

The collapse of communism, particularly in Eastern Europe and the Soviet Union, was a pivotal event for the world, and unfolded primarily in the late 1980s and early 1990s. Centralised planning in communist states had led to inefficiency, shortages, and low-quality goods and services. The lack of competition and innovation stifled economic growth. By the 1970s and 1980s, many communist economies were stagnating; the inability to adapt to global economic changes further exacerbated their economic challenges. Many Eastern European countries accrued significant debts and struggled to repay them, leading to financial crises that weakened communist regimes.

The rise of reform-minded leaders like Mikhail Gorbachev in the Soviet Union introduced policies of openness (glasnost) and restructuring (perestroika) to revitalise the economy and society. Public dissatisfaction with authoritarian rule and government corruption led to demands for democracy and reform. In many Soviet republics and Eastern European countries, nationalist movements gained strength, demanding greater autonomy and independence, which weakened communist control. This process is not yet finalised. Across Europe, there are strong ideological undercurrents between the Right and Left ways of managing society, and it is unclear which direction things will take, or whether this is a general trend or varies across different countries.

A lack of political cohesion or unity can lead to fragmentation and increased vulnerability to external threats. Social stratification, inequality, and class conflict can erode a civilisation's social fabric. Discontent among the lower classes can lead to revolts and social upheaval. Moral decay, loss of shared values, and declining innovation can also contribute to societal decline. Civilisations that fail to adapt to changing conditions may become stagnant. If citizens express frustration over the lack of freedoms, economic hardships, and political repression, protests and calls for change become widespread. In the internet-connected world we live in today, the contrast between global and local living conditions cannot be hidden. Through social media, activists, intellectuals, and dissident movements played a crucial role in challenging the status quo, like the Arab Spring (2010–2011), the Black Lives Matter (BLM) movement in 2013, the Hong Kong Protests (2019–2020) and the Indian Farmers' Protest (2020–2021).

Why Nations Fail?

While some civilisations progress technologically, others may fail to innovate or become overly reliant on established systems that no longer serve them. Civilisations do not fall for a single reason; their decline is usually the result of a combination of these factors over time. Understanding these causes can offer valuable insights into the dynamics of human societies and their evolution. We have two contrasting examples right in our neighbourhood. Pakistan opted for the perpetuation of feudalism, the ideology of hatred and power of terror over democracy, development and harnessing the intellectual capital of its people. China opted to become a knowledge powerhouse, competing with the West in technology and ensuring its massive population enjoys shared prosperity.

Why Nations Fail: The Origins of Power, Prosperity and Poverty, by economists Daron Acemoglu and James A. Robinson, was published in 2012 and examines the historical and economic factors that contribute to varying levels of prosperity and development across different nations. Three ideas are offered: the importance of political and financial institutions in shaping a nation's success or failure; inclusive institutions that promote innovation, economic participation, and broad-based prosperity tend to lead to better development outcomes; and extractive institutions, which concentrate power and wealth among elites and restrict opportunities for others, often result in poverty and stagnation. The authors argue that the root causes of economic disparities are political choices and institutional arrangements rather than geography or culture alone. The book emphasises that fundamental institutional reforms can lead to more prosperous and equitable nations.

China's vision and zeal for embracing technology cannot be ignored. Over the past few decades, several key trends and developments have marked its rise as a technology superpower. China has dramatically increased its investment in R&D, becoming the second-largest spender in the world after the United States. This spending focuses on various sectors, including artificial intelligence, biotechnology, telecommunications, and renewable energy. Establishing technology parks and innovation hubs (such as Shenzhen) has fostered ecosystems for startups and established companies, encouraging collaboration and rapid development.

The Chinese government has implemented strategic initiatives, such as Made in China 2025, to upgrade domestic industries and reduce reliance on foreign technology. Supportive policies, including subsidies, tax incentives, and favourable regulations, have helped boost technological development and entrepreneurship. China has also emerged as a leader in AI research and application, leveraging its vast data resources and investments in AI to excel in areas such as facial recognition, natural language processing, and autonomous vehicles. Integrating big data across various industries, including healthcare, finance, and manufacturing, demonstrates its ability to leverage technology for enhanced efficiency and improved insights. It is a fact that China has led the world in 5G technology deployment, with companies like Huawei playing key roles. This infrastructure supports a wide range of applications, from smart cities to Internet of Things (IoT) devices. The rapid growth of the country's digital economy, driven by e-commerce giants like Alibaba and Tencent, has transformed consumer habits and business models, establishing China as a global leader in digital trade.

What should concern us most is that China has developed advanced cyber capabilities for both defensive and offensive purposes, thereby increasingly influencing its role in the global cybersecurity discourse. The Chinese government maintains strict control over information and internet governance, shaping the digital environment within and outside its borders. Through the Belt and Road Initiative (BRI), China aims to expand its technological influence globally by investing in infrastructure projects and transferring technology to partner countries. There is fierce competition between China and the West in advanced technology, and India's position will determine which way the balance tilts.

China's rise as a technology superpower is undeniable. This has been achieved the hard way, as India could have done in the 1990s. This continued trend has wide-ranging implications for global technological leadership, economic dynamics, and geopolitical relationships. As China continues to advance, its role as a key player in shaping the future of technology will likely grow, influencing global standards and practices across various industries.

What if China dominates India through advanced AI capabilities? The scenarios could entail various sociopolitical, economic, and strategic implications. There are several potential outcomes of such a situation, and it is prudent to consider them rather than trivialising and brushing them aside. China's dominance in AI could lead to significant economic advantages for Chinese companies and industries over their Indian counterparts. This could lead to India facing financial challenges, particularly in sectors that rely heavily on technology and innovation.

Additionally, a China that is dominant in AI could further heighten tensions between India and China, as well as in the broader Indo-Pacific region. Neighbouring countries might be forced to align more closely with China or seek partnerships with India to counterbalance China's influence. Advanced AI technologies can enhance surveillance capabilities. If China were to exert control over India, it could lead to increased monitoring of citizens, erosion of privacy, and a shift towards a more authoritarian governance model influenced by AI tools. Increased reliance on AI might expose India to cybersecurity threats. If China dominates AI, it could use cyber operations to destabilise Indian institutions, infrastructure, and critical information systems.

Two Roads Diverge in the Woods

Now consider a scenario where China shares its AI technologies with India while maintaining control over their development and implementation. In that case, India may become increasingly dependent on Chinese technology, which could impact its national security and sovereignty. The competitive landscape of innovation in AI could shift, potentially leading to a brain drain from India as tech talent migrates to China in search of better opportunities or funding. India must invest heavily in research and development to remain competitive and address critical material supply chain issues. Urea fertiliser and many pharmaceutical active ingredients are two glaring examples of a near crippling dependency.

The prospect of India and China collaborating to become a technology superpower raises intriguing possibilities and challenges. The benefits of collaboration are evident. Both India and China possess substantial human and financial resources, allowing them to accelerate technological innovations and advancements by pooling talent, investment, and infrastructure. Their strengths are complementary; China excels in manufacturing and infrastructure development, while India is strong in software, IT services, and has a robust startup ecosystem. A partnership could leverage these strengths for mutual benefit. Joint research initiatives in fields such as AI, biotechnology, and renewable energy could yield breakthroughs while addressing shared challenges, including climate change and healthcare.

Existing tensions over borders, territorial disputes, and regional influence hinder cooperation. Trust issues have already complicated collaborative efforts. We have divergent governance models. Differences in political governance, regulatory environments, and approaches to technology (such as data privacy and cybersecurity) can create barriers to collaboration. Both nations aspire to be technology leaders independently, which may lead to competition rather than collaboration in certain areas. Policy differences regarding trade practices, technology transfer, and intellectual property rights could create friction in joint ventures or initiatives.

For successful collaboration, both nations would need to establish mechanisms for building trust, fostering dialogue, and promoting mutual understanding while addressing existing geopolitical and economic rivalries. A partnership could provide substantial benefits and influence in the global technology landscape if these challenges can be navigated.

However, perhaps the most insidious is the ideological threat. China's control through AI could facilitate the spread of Chinese cultural narratives, values, and nationalism. There is a risk of cultural assimilation and the erosion of local identities. If AI systems and technology are managed predominantly by Chinese entities or through Chinese influence, this may exacerbate existing socioeconomic divides within India, leading to broader inequalities.

The strategic response is for India to develop its AI capabilities and engage in collaborative initiatives with other nations to resist domination. This could lead to an arms race in AI technology and global strategy. There is no other option. A scenario in which China dominates India through AI poses complex challenges to safeguarding our sovereignty and national interests. This brings us back to our civilisational inheritance.

The question of whether intelligence is innate is a complex one that has been widely studied and debated in psychology, genetics, and education. Socioeconomic status, education, nutrition, and access to stimulating experiences can significantly affect cognitive development and intellectual performance. Cultural contexts also influence intelligence, as different cultures may value different types of knowledge and skills. This has led to various definitions and measurements of intelligence. The belief in whether intelligence is fixed or can be developed (growth mindset) can influence educational approaches and personal development. We believe in absolute intelligence, and success or failure is rooted in whether it can be accessed and tapped.

AI empowers teachers to uncover brilliance in diverse learning paths that might otherwise go unnoticed. Using the technology for multilingual education enables children to tackle learning gaps caused by linguistic challenges. The growth of voice-based learning models in local languages is on the rise. A surge of businesses continually strives to enhance datasets in Tamil, Telugu, Hindi, and other Indian languages. Providing courses in regional languages or effectively teaching other languages helps students bridge language gaps. Generative AI technologies that adapt to dialectal variations are also accessible to students, fostering more inclusive education. Although some may raise issues and controversies about different languages to create division, thanks to AI, this mission is destined to fail.

Summary

A scenario in which India was not partitioned and China and India remained friends would have transformed Asia into a more unified, prosperous, and influential continent. While challenges would have stayed, the potential for peace, development, and cultural exchange would have been immense. Joint efforts in technology and innovation could have positioned Asia as a global leader in fields like AI, renewable energy, and space exploration. That it is not the case is due to whose omission and commission. The Asian nations acted as they did, or were compelled to do so, largely due to a larger geopolitical system. Did the two great civilisations falter due to their intelligence, or was the decision-making process flawed?

8

Indian Exceptionalism

Every civilisation tells itself a sacred story, and India's is of timeless virtue and peace. Yet no truth shines forever without shadow. To know her greatness is to see her flaws without fear, and to rise above them with compassion. For India's destiny is not to be praised, but to awaken—again and again—to the light that never truly fades.

The Structure of Society

Exceptionalism refers to the belief that one is a unique and exceptional, particularly in terms of its culture, history, and societal structure. This notion is embraced by Indians with great enthusiasm and has influenced both domestic and foreign policy narratives. The social divide in India has historically played a significant role in the country's vulnerability to invasions and colonisation. The deeply entrenched caste system created social stratification, resulting in divisions among various social groups. This often-weakened collective resistance against invaders, as different communities had conflicting interests or loyalties. India has been home to numerous kingdoms and empires, each vying for power and territory. These regional rivalries made it challenging to form a united front against external threats, such as the invasions by the Mughals and later European colonisers. To address these complex social issues, collective movements emerged, aiming for unity, social reform, and political awakening, ultimately leading to India's struggle for independence. Mahatma Gandhi, referred to as the Father of the Nation, stood against social divisions. Dr. B.R. Ambedkar ensured that the Constitution of independent India safeguards people who have historically suffered due to their social identities.

The varna system, as described in the Vedas, was not originally meant to be inherited through family. The initial notion suggested that individuals could occupy different varnas based on their qualities, talents, and occupations rather than by birth. In its earliest form, the system aimed to categorise people according to their skills and abilities. Brahmins (the priestly class) were associated with intellectual and spiritual pursuits, kshatriyas (the warrior class) with governance and warfare, vaishyas (businesspeople) with commerce and agriculture, and shudras (the service class) with service and manual labour. Shri Krishna in the *Shrimad Bhagavad Gita* (18. 41–43) categorically describes what makes one a brahmin, kshatriya, vaishya, and shudra. It is nowhere stated that caste depends on birth. Based on a profession, a second birth is referred to as a dvija. Individuals could move between varnas based on their actions and merits. This flexibility enabled social mobility, allowing individuals to change their role or occupation as their skills developed or circumstances changed.

Rishi Vishwamitra, a significant figure in Hindu mythology and Vedic literature, is renowned for his transformation. Initially, he was a kshatriya king of the Kanyakubja region located in modern-day Kannauj, Uttar Pradesh. The pivotal moment in his life occurred during an encounter with the celebrated sage Vashishta. Seeking Vashishta's powerful and divine cow, Kamadhenu, which could fulfil all desires, Vishwamitra was denied ownership because he did not belong to the priestly class. This rejection left him feeling humiliated. The desire to attain powers like Vashishta motivated Vishwamitra to embark on intense penance and austerity (tapas) to achieve spiritual enlightenment and establish himself as a sage. Vishwamitra eventually succeeded in gaining spiritual knowledge, powers, and the status of a brahmin. He went on to compose the *Mandukya Upanishad* and wrote several hymns in the *Rig Veda*.

In Plato's work, *The Republic*, he outlines a tripartite structure for society, often interpreted as consisting of three main classes. Still, he also discusses four types of people based on their characteristics and roles. These classes are aligned with his concept of justice and the ideal state. The philosopher-king class consists of the rulers best suited to govern because of their wisdom. Plato believed that only those who comprehend proper knowledge should lead society.

The warriors are responsible for protecting the city and defending it against external threats. They possess courage, strength, and discipline. This class ensures the security and order of society and is trained in the arts of warfare and defence. The rest of the population engages in various livelihoods, including farming, manufacturing, trading, and providing services to these enterprises. They perform multiple occupations necessary for the economy and sustenance of society. Their role is vital as they supply the resources required for the community. They thrive living in a system based on the knowledge of the philosophers and the protection of their warriors. There is no superior or inferior in society; each does his/her job and lives in peace.

In essence, Plato's vision of an ideal society is a direct adaptation of the Vedic varna system. There is a strong emphasis on specialisation, where each class performs its designated role for the harmony and overall functioning of the state. Later, the Scottish philosopher Adam Smith (1723–1790) referred to it as a division of labour and called specialised enterprise the real wealth of a nation. The perfect state reflects justice when each class performs its function without interfering with the roles of others. This structure symbolises his broader philosophical ideas regarding knowledge, virtue, and the nature of justice in society.

Drifts and Diversions

In communism, the structure of society is fundamentally based on the idea of a classless society. However, it recognises that historical and economic conditions lead to class divisions before achieving this ideal state. As Karl Marx (1818–1883) and Friedrich Engels (1820–1895) articulated, communism is rooted in the concept of class struggle. According to Marxist theory, human history has been characterised by conflicts between different classes, particularly between the bourgeoisie (the capitalist class) and the proletariat (the working class). The bourgeoisie consists of the owners of the means of production, such as factories, land, and capital. They control economic resources and derive their income from the labour of the proletariat. The bourgeoisie seeks to maximise profit, often at the expense of the working class. The proletariat is the working class that does not own the means of production. They sell their labour to the bourgeoisie for wages.

Marx argued that the exploitation and alienation of the proletariat would lead to class consciousness, where workers become aware of their collective interests and the injustices they face. This awareness would eventually culminate in a revolutionary movement aimed at overthrowing the bourgeoisie. In the communist vision, a transitional phase known as the 'dictatorship of the proletariat' is necessary following the overthrow of the bourgeoisie. During this period, the working class governs the state to dismantle the old capitalist structures, confiscate private property, and establish collective ownership.

The goal of communism is to achieve a classless society in which the means of production are collective and class distinctions are abolished. In such a society, resources and goods would be distributed according to need rather than profit, fostering equality and cooperation. While communist theory starts by acknowledging class divisions (specifically between the bourgeoisie and the proletariat), it aims to transcend these divisions and create an egalitarian, classless society. 'From each according to his ability, to each according to his needs' is a key principle associated with communist ideology.

Modern China is officially a communist state governed by the Communist Party of China (CPC). The CPC maintains a one-party system, meaning it is the sole legal political party and exercises significant control over the government, economy, and society. However, in recent decades, China has implemented various economic reforms that have led to a mixed economy, incorporating elements of capitalism alongside its socialist framework. This has resulted in significant financial growth and increased private enterprise, despite the political system remaining authoritarian.

In India, over time, social practices began to crystallise, leading to the varna system being interpreted and implemented in more rigid and hereditary ways. This shift contributed to the development of the caste system (jati), where social status became primarily determined by one's birth rather than individual capability or achievement. The hereditary aspect of the varna (and later caste) system has faced significant criticism for promoting inequality and discrimination. Social reformers throughout history, particularly in the nineteenth and twentieth centuries, have advocated for the abolition of caste-based discrimination and the promotion of equality. In contemporary society, numerous movements strive to dismantle the caste system and promote social justice, inclusivity, and equal opportunities for all, regardless of their perceived varna or caste origins.

The existence of caste-like distinctions among Indian Muslims is a complex issue that reflects both historical social structures and contemporary societal dynamics. Many Indian Muslim communities are stratified into different groups based on factors such as profession, social status, and region. These distinctions can resemble caste structures, where some groups may be considered more prestigious or of higher social standing than others. Specific communities within Indian Muslims, such as the Ashrafs (often regarded as descendants of Arab, Persian, or Turkish settlers) and the Ajlaf (considered to have lower social status and typically associated with manual labour), reflect a stratification reminiscent of caste divisions. Additionally, there are groups such as the Meo and Gujjar that have their own social hierarchies even after embracing Islam.

The presence of caste-like distinctions among Indian Christians is significant. While Christianity promotes equality among all believers, some converts have maintained their caste identities after conversion. For instance, many who converted from Hinduism to Christianity have continued to identify with their original castes, forming distinct Christian communities. There are groups like the Syrian Christians of Kerala, Dalit Christians, and other communities who may have varying degrees of social status and privilege. Dalit Christians often still face discrimination and social stigma, both within the broader Christian community and in society at large.

The Sikh Society Example

Sikhism rejects the caste system. The core belief in Sikhism is the equality of all human beings, regardless of their caste, creed, or gender. Guru Nanak Dev Ji emphasised that all people are equal in the eyes of God and should be treated as such—the teachings of Sikhism advocate for universal brotherhood. The sangat (community) concept promotes the idea that all individuals should unite, transcending social divisions. The practice of langar, where free meals are served to all visitors in gurdwaras (Sikh temples), reflects the principle of equality in Sikhism. Everyone shares the same food and sits together regardless of social background or caste.

Sikhism discourages rituals and superstitions associated with caste and promotes a direct relationship between the individual and God. The holy scripture of Sikhism, the *Guru Granth Sahib*, emphasises devotion and righteous living over caste-based practices. Despite this, some caste identities have persisted within Sikh communities due to social and cultural influences. Jat, Khatri, Arora, and Dalit Sikhs are distinguished. Ahluwalia (brewers), Kamboj (royal kshatriya), Ramgarhia (carpenters), and Saini (ironsmiths), although they no longer practice their traditional occupations, are still regarded as such.

It is inevitable to examine what happened to the caste system in Pakistan after it became a new nation and adopted its high-sounding name (Holy Land). Pakistan is home to several ethnic groups, each with its distinct language, culture, and identity. The principal ethnic groups include Punjabis, Sindhis, Pashtuns (also known as Pathans), and Baloch. The descendants of Urdu-speaking Muslims who migrated from India after Partition, primarily residing in urban areas such as Karachi, are still considered a separate group. About 10–15 per cent of Pakistan's population identifies as Shia. Some hardline Sunni groups and individuals still view Shi'as as apostates, despite being free from certain limitations affecting other religious groups as Muslims. The large Hazara population in Quetta is particularly at risk because of their religion and ethnicity. Ahmadis are regarded as non-Muslims by the Islamic state.

Besides India and Pakistan, several nations worldwide experience significant social divisions, often from ethnic, religious, economic, or political factors. Sri Lanka has faced a protracted civil conflict between the Sinhalese majority and the Tamil minority. Indonesia comprises numerous ethnic groups and religions, with tensions sometimes arising between the Muslim majority and minority religious groups, such as Christians and Hindus. Certain islands are the hotspots of such conflicts. Lebanon is marked by a complex political system that reflects its diverse religious groups, including Christians, Sunni Muslims, and Shia Muslims.

Nigeria is characterised by deep ethnic and religious divisions, primarily between the Muslim-majority north and the Christian-majority south. Ethnic groups such as the Hausa-Fulani, Yoruba, and Igbo have distinct identities and historical rivalries, leading to political tensions and occasional violence. Mali has experienced ethnic tensions, particularly between the Tuareg in the north and the Bambara in the south. Disputes over resources, governance, and cultural recognition have led to conflict and instability. Belgium is divided between its Dutch-speaking Flemish population in the north and its French-speaking Walloon population in the south, resulting in linguistic and cultural tensions.

These examples illustrate the complex nature of social divisions, where historical legacies, cultural identities, and socioeconomic factors intersect to create divisions within nations. Addressing these divisions requires ongoing efforts to foster dialogue, promote inclusion, and advance social justice. The concept of an equal society—where all individuals have the same rights, opportunities, and access to resources—is an aspirational goal for many social, political, and economic movements.

Sikh society can be considered a good example in modern times for several reasons, particularly in terms of its values, community service, and resilience. Sikhism emphasises the equality of all human beings, regardless of caste, creed, gender, or social status. This principle is reflected in the Sikh practice of langar, a community kitchen where free meals are served to all visitors, promoting social equality and community bonding. The concept of seva, or selfless service, is central to Sikhism. Sikhs are known for their active involvement in humanitarian efforts, disaster relief, and community welfare projects. This commitment to helping others is a strong example of altruism in action. Sikhism promotes inclusivity and respect for all religions. The Sikh gurus taught that all paths to God are valid, fostering a spirit of pluralism and mutual respect among different faiths. But perhaps most uniquely, Sikh teachings emphasise the importance of living in harmony with nature and being good stewards of the environment. This ecological consciousness is increasingly relevant in today's context of environmental challenges.

A Unified Civil Code

The era of divide and rule must have ended after the British left and India was partitioned. But it is a tragedy of a great civilisation to keep suffering the ulterior designs of erstwhile rulers. A unified Civil Code (UCC) is often considered essential for a progressive nation like India for several key reasons: promoting equality before the law, ensuring gender justice, fostering national integration, upholding secularism, and driving social progress. Why it eluded independent India is our problem, and we are still debating. It shows the inertia that must have been overcome before the wheel starts turning towards becoming a developed country.

A UCC will replace personal laws based on the scriptures and customs of each central religious community in India with a uniform set of rules governing every citizen. This promotes equality before the law, ensuring that all individuals have the same legal rights and responsibilities, regardless of their religion. By providing the same rights regarding marriage, divorce, inheritance, and custody to all genders, a UCC can significantly contribute to women's empowerment and gender equality. A UCC can foster a sense of national identity and unity among India's diverse cultures and religions. It can reduce the feeling of alienation among various communities by promoting common legal standards, thereby enhancing social harmony and cohesion.

A UCC aligns with the secular principles enshrined in the Indian Constitution. It underscores the idea that the state does not favour any religion but provides equal treatment to all citizens, thereby reinforcing the secular fabric of Indian society. A unified set of laws can streamline legal processes, making them more straightforward and accessible. This could lead to greater efficiency in the judicial system and help reduce discrimination and injustice.

UCC is crucial to achieving equality, justice, and social progress in India. It is already late; any more dithering will harm the prospects of embracing the AI-driven world.

Reclaiming the Indosphere means revitalising Indian exceptionalism, which emphasises India's unique identity, history, and role on the global stage, particularly in areas such as culture, politics, and economy. Indian exceptionalism often highlights its ancient civilisation, rich cultural heritage, and contributions to philosophy, mathematics, and science. This historical lens sheds light on India's distinctive place in world history. The revival emphasises the diversity and pluralism of Indian culture, promoting the idea that its varied traditions and practices contribute to a unique societal fabric, setting it apart from other nations.

India's status as the world's largest democracy is a cornerstone of its exceptionalism. It defies logic to call the rule of thirty tyrants, who sentenced Socrates to death for 'corrupting the minds of youth' by his teachings, the birthplace of democracy. The United States took a long time to give voting rights to its women and people of colour. It colluded with a horde of dictators and tyrants to topple democratically elected governments across the world for its gain. The ability to maintain democratic institutions and processes in a highly diverse society is often highlighted as a model for other nations. If it has been achieved anywhere, it is in India.

The concept encompasses the country's cultural influence through cinema, cuisine, spirituality, and more, promoting a positive image of India on the world stage. Initiatives like Yoga Day and the global spread of the culture testify to this soft power. India integrates traditional values with modern aspirations, focusing on sustainable development, technological advancement, and social harmony. Reviving Indian exceptionalism involves embracing these narratives to foster national pride, unity, and a coherent identity in a rapidly changing world. It also addresses contemporary challenges, promoting a proactive and confident approach to the country's future.

Summary

India's greatness does not lie in standing apart, but in belonging to the same cosmic rhythm that moves all civilisations through rise, decline, and renewal. The idea of Indian exceptionalism—that we are uniquely moral, spiritual, or democratic—is less a truth than a yearning, born of centuries of conquest and rediscovery. It is the mind's way of reclaiming dignity after long humiliation. Yet, when pride turns into myth, it blinds rather than uplifts. The vision of India as eternally peaceful and uniquely virtuous, while comforting, can make her vulnerable to those who mistake tolerance for weakness. Worse still, when these myths are wielded within, they deepen divisions of faith and caste, turning the mirror of civilisation into a wall of separation. But India has always been more than its contradictions. Her genius lies in self-correction—in the quiet power to transform turmoil. The day elections are fought on ideas rather than identities, the spirit of democracy will return to its true home. For India's destiny is not to proclaim itself exceptional, but to become exceptional—by embodying the eternal Vedic truth that all beings are one, and that the divine dwells equally in every heart.

9

Economic Resurrection

Empires once ruled with swords; today they rule with markets and minds. Yet the measure of a civilisation is not how loudly it conquers, but how wisely it endures. India's strength has never lain in dominion, but in discernment—in turning power into purpose, and commerce into compassion.

Sone Ki Chidiya

Ancient Indians declared four goals of a well-lived life: righteous conduct, earning money, enjoying the pleasures of life, and then neatly signing off. Piety, economic growth, a sense of joy, or freedom from the material world happen to a devotee who earnestly seeks them.[2] *Arthashastra*, a treatise written by Chanakya, also known as Kautilya and Vishnugupta, is considered one of the foundational works of classical Indian philosophy and political theory. He called it a compendium of all earlier sciences for acquiring and maintaining the earth, composed by ancient teachers.[3]

[2] श्रेयो दिशत्यभिमतं यद्धर्मादिषु देहिनाम् (श्रीमद् भागवतम् 4. 8. 60).

[3] पृथिव्या लाभे पालने च यावन्त्यर्थशास्त्राणि पूर्वाचार्यैः प्रशस्तापिटानि प्रायश्चानि संहृत्यैकमिदामर्थशास्त्रं कृतम् (कौटिल्य अर्थशास्त्र 1. 1. 1).

Arthashastra provides three themes. A king's actions must always follow a policy, and never be whimsical or 'off the cuff'. The king must involve the best minds to assess and evolve these policies. Writings in governmental work must have order of meaning, relation, completeness, sweetness, moderation, clarity, and arithmetic. It is indeed astonishing to find modern concepts like critical thinking and data-driven decision-making, tactical innovation and agility, as well as power and influence, reflecting Chankya's principles of anvikshiki, yukti, and shakti.

India was called Sone Ki Chidiya, the Golden Bird, not metaphorically but because gold was mined and crafted into ornaments here. Gold artefacts have been found in Indian archaeological sites dated earlier than anywhere else in the world. According to legend, the pearls that Julius Caesar presented to Brutus' mother and the famous earrings of Queen Cleopatra were traded from India. Gems like sapphires, rubies, and diamonds, as well as minerals like iron ore and copper, and valuable metals like gold and silver, were among the treasures that India possessed, attracting traders and buyers from distant lands.

India flourished in the first millennium, becoming the largest economy with a GDP value surpassing that of China. Numbers do not matter, but it was based on gold and not the paper currencies of the modern world, where dollars can be printed at will by the United States and all other currencies valued by the markets, even without the stroke of a pen. Even in 1500, when the British arrived, it was a quarter of the world's economy. The British brought it down to 3 per cent of the world's GDP under their 'inglorious' rule.

During Emperor Ashoka's reign, the Mauryan Empire established alternative maritime routes that extended to Syria, Egypt, and Southeast Asia. This maritime network similarly bolstered India's economic prowess, permitting it to export its riches and import valuable commodities. The Grand Trunk Road, connecting the Indian subcontinent from Bengal to the Khyber Pass, was a vital trade artery. India's strategic location at the crossroads of these routes made it a natural hub for trade, facilitating the exchange of products and ideas with civilisations across Asia, Europe, and beyond.

Invaders attacked temples that the ancient societies used as banks. It was a robbery that was clothed as a 'religious duty' they were performing against idol worship. Indians were not prepared for such barbarism. Later, a new settlement trend emerged, where people living in arid lands found Indian land and climate irresistible to return to. There was also a power vacuum, and the intelligent and crafty Mughals filled it.

Colonial Expansion

When the Europeans arrived in the seventeenth and early eighteenth centuries, Indian industries were renowned for their craftsmanship and the production of low-cost, high-quality goods, despite the looming threat of European trade. It was a testament to their resilience that European traders found it irresistible to exchange their gold and silver for Indian goods and take them to their markets. European nations invested heavily in military strength, enabling them to defend their interests, establish dominance in key areas, and sometimes engage in conflicts with local powers to secure their trading interests. The colonisation of parts of Asia gave the Europeans direct access to resources and markets, enabling them to control trade more effectively and become dominant players.

The Dutch arrived first, in the late 1500s, looking for spices. At that time, there was no refrigeration, so peppercorns were used to preserve meat for trade over long distances. Peppercorns and other spices were grown in the tropics, particularly in Southeast Asia. They earned a good living by selling spices to Europe. A group of British traders, their envious neighbours, joined forces to create a company for trading in the East Indies and named it the East India Company. Their first expedition set sail for Asia in 1601 with four ships. Avoiding the Portuguese on the west coast, they initially landed in Masulipatam, now known as Machilipatnam, in the state of Andhra Pradesh.

What started with spices soon expanded to cotton and silk. The money earned from selling Indian products in Europe was so substantial that they hired local soldiers and provided them with the guns they brought in. They quickly realised that the local swordsmen and archers were no match for their gun-wielding soldiers. Within a few years, British traders established themselves in Madras (now Chennai) and Calcutta (now Kolkata). In 1661, when the Portuguese gifted the city of Bombay (now Mumbai) to the British as part of the dowry for the marriage of King Charles II of England to Catherine of Braganza, a Portuguese princess, it was time for the British to establish a presence there. They called their establishments forts and, given their dominance, the fancy name of residency. Fort St. George was founded in 1639 in Madras, Fort William in Calcutta was established in 1690, and Fort George in Bombay was built in 1668.

Nineteen-year-old Robert Clive arrived at Fort St. George in 1744 to work as a clerk of the East India Company. He grew his influence, learning fast to take advantage by siding with one party or the other in the perpetual feuds amongst the warring Indians for the price of using East Indian Company soldiers armed with guns. Clive later played a crucial role in the defeat of the nawab of Bengal,

Siraj-ud-Daulah, by cutting a deal with the nawab's commander-in-chief, Mir Jafar, for treason.

William Dalrymple, writing in *The Guardian,* referred to the East India Company as 'the original corporate raiders' and described 'loot' as the first Indian word to enter the English language. 'Within a few years, 250 company clerks backed by the military force of 20,000 locally recruited Indian soldiers had become the effective rulers of Bengal. It was not the British government that seized India at the end of the eighteenth century, but a dangerously unregulated private company headquartered in a small office, five windows wide, in London, and managed in India by an unstable sociopath–Clive. He returned to Britain with a personal fortune, then valued at £234,000, which made him the wealthiest self-made man in Europe. No great sophistication was required. The entire contents of the Bengal treasury were loaded into 100 boats and punted down the Ganges from the Nawab of Bengal's palace to Fort William, the company's Calcutta headquarters."[4]

As the greedy East India Company officials became entangled in local feuds, even instigating them at times, they charged fees for deploying their gun-carrying soldiers in battles. They took their share of the treasury's booty from the defeated rulers. The loot of Lucknow was spectacular in its spoils. The Great Revolt of 1857 marked the end of Mughal Rule in India, which had been reduced to a symbolic role by that time, and Great Britain declared the entire subcontinent as its domain. British monarch Queen Victoria was proclaimed empress of India, and her rule was called the Raj.

---

[4] https://www.theguardian.com/world/2015/mar/04/east-india-company-original-corporate-raiders. Last accessed on November 15, 2025.

The Dutch had ceded Ceylon to Britain in 1802. Lower Burma was already under British control. Upper Burma was added in 1886.

Deindustrialisation

The British implemented policies that favoured the import of British goods and the export of raw materials from India. This created a trade imbalance that stifled the growth of local industries. The British focused on dismantling traditional sectors, such as textiles and handicrafts, to promote the sale of British-manufactured goods. This led to the decline of indigenous production and the loss of livelihoods for many artisans and workers. They also imposed heavy taxes on agricultural products and industries. This burden often led to the impoverishment of local producers and reduced the capital available for investment in industrial ventures. While the British did develop some infrastructure, such as railways, it was primarily for the efficient extraction and transportation of raw materials to Britain, rather than for the development of Indian industry.

Deindustrialisation led to significant migration from rural to urban areas, but the need for industrial jobs resulted in high levels of unemployment and underemployment in cities. Laws and regulations were often designed to benefit British interests at the expense of local industries, further marginalising Indian entrepreneurs. India's deindustrialisation under colonial rule is characterised by several specific examples highlighting the decline of traditional industries and the impact of British policies. Bengal was once a significant centre for jute production, but British policies favoured jute exports over local processing. This led to the emergence of British-owned jute mills, primarily for the benefit of international markets, further marginalising local producers.

India was once renowned for its handwoven textiles, particularly cotton fabrics such as muslin. The British introduced mechanised textiles, leading to a significant decline in local handloom industries. Indian weavers could not compete with the prices of British goods, resulting in widespread unemployment and loss of traditional craftsmanship, including metalworking, especially among brass and bronze artisans.

Although India had a long history of iron and steel production, notably the Wootz steel of South India, British policies prioritised raw material extraction. They led to the establishment of industries that exported these materials rather than developing local manufacturing. Before the British controlled shipping, the shipbuilding industry thrived, particularly in regions such as Gujarat and Kerala. The imposition of restrictive trade practices dismantled this sector, forcing reliance on British ships for trade. These examples reflect the broader economic policies of the British Raj, which prioritised British industrial interests at the cost of India's traditional industries and crafts, ultimately contributing to a significant decline in the latter's industrial capacity. The deindustrialisation process entrenched economic dependency and created a legacy of underdevelopment that has irreversibly affected India.

Heartless Profiteers

The British also exploited India's vast mineral resources, such as coal, iron ore, and mica, which began to be primarily extracted for British industries, yielding little benefit to the local economy. Indian labourers were often used under harsh conditions in mines and factories. While these events occurred long after Adam Smith, the great economist and philosopher, had seen it coming and referred to his country, England, as a nation of shopkeepers. 'To [have] found a great empire for the sole purpose of raising a people of customers may, at first sight, appear a project fit only for a nation of shopkeepers.'[5]

But perhaps the most devious of the British actions was the opium trade. They promoted its cultivation in India, particularly in Bengal and Malwa, for export to China. The First Opium War arose mainly from Britain's desire to continue its profitable opium trade with China, where opium had become widely addictive, destroying the youth. The war concluded with the Treaty of Nanking in 1842, which compelled China to accept numerous demands from Britain, including the ceding of Hong Kong to British control and the opening of five ports—Canton, Amoy, Fuzhou, Ningbo, and Shanghai—to British trade.

However, the lowest moral point of British rule was the salt tax, which restricted Indian salt production. This regulation forced many Indians to buy expensive salt from British suppliers, exacerbating their socioeconomic struggles. The salt tax disproportionately affected low-income people, given that it was a staple in every household. The imposition of this tax made it difficult for many families to afford a necessity, leading to widespread discontent and hardship. It was viewed not just as a financial burden but also as an insult to Indian dignity and autonomy.

Mahatma Gandhi (1869–1948) led the Salt March (also known as the Dandi March) in 1930. This 240-mile journey to the Arabian Sea aimed to produce salt from seawater as a direct act of defiance

---

[5] Adam Smith, *An Inquiry into the Nature and Causes of the Wealth of Nations*, Chicago: University of Chicago Press, 1976. (Book IV, Chapter VII, Part III, Para 63).

against British law. The Salt March garnered significant national and international attention, symbolising the Indian struggle for independence. It united people across various social and economic strata, becoming pivotal in the Indian independence movement.

The Bengal Famine of 1943 remains a significant historical event in the context of British colonial rule in India. It exposed the disastrous consequences of colonial policies and wartime priorities on the Indian population. Churchill has been quoted as blaming the famine on the fact that Indians were 'breeding like rabbits' and asking how, if the shortages were so dire, Mahatma Gandhi was still alive. The tragedy of the famine is often cited as a critical moment in the struggle for Indian self-determination and has had a lasting impact on historical memory and debates surrounding colonialism and governance.

In a discussion at the Oxford Union on 28 May 2015, Indian member of parliament, diplomat and author Shashi Tharoor said, 'The British had not covered themselves with glory during the war. They had run a military dictatorship in a country that they had claimed to be preparing for democracy. They had presided over one of the worst famines in human history, the Bengal Famine of 1943, while diverting food (on Churchill's orders) from starving civilians to well-supplied Tummies', as if reading a passage from his book with a rather provocative title.[6]

During his 1739 invasion of India, Nadir Shah, the Persian ruler, looted the Peacock Throne, which had been commissioned by Shah Jahan, along with the Koh-i-Noor diamond and other treasures from the Mughal treasury. The diamond is still owned

---

[6] Shashi Tharoor, *Inglorious Empire: What British Did to India*, Victoria, Australia: Scribe Publications, p. 184.

by the British as part of their Crown. How do Indians differentiate between Nadir Shah and the British? Will the latter return the Koh-i-Noor diamond? Perhaps ruling over the Indian people by the British was the right of a military superior power but destroying its economy was a sin. Calling it a land of superstitious people who need to be civilised was a falsehood, and that the religious leaders spread it put a question mark on their moral integrity.

How do the British explain the status of Osman Ali Khan, the nizam of Hyderabad, as the richest man in the world in 1937, if India was a country of poor and destitute people when they arrived to 'civilise it'? Had not his riches come from the hard work of people under his kingdom and the resources he presided over? He owned fifty Rolls-Royce cars and gifted a Squadron of the Airco DH.9a bomber aircraft to the British Empire by bearing the manufacturing costs. Produced in 1918, this aircraft played a significant role in the closing stages of the First World War. Each plane carried the insignia of the Hyderabad Kingdom.

Digital Imperialism

While it is true that the colonial era is now in the past, colonisation of a different kind is very much there, and colonial destruction has been unabated. The new form of colonisation is the centralisation of capital in the hands of a few transnational corporations, and the latest ruling power is technological surveillance. If the resources had been plundered in colonial times, the minds of the masses are now swayed by digital media to create a delusion of consumerism, which has two imminent dangers. One is the destruction of the environment, which is already manifesting as climate change and the erosion of the state's power to commercial forces, which are brazenly profit-driven and destroying the social fabric that held humanity together in their pursuit of wealth. We would be repeating a disastrous history by ignoring this emerging reality.

Like imperial powers of the past, modern multinational corporations often hold significant economic influence in various countries, sometimes overshadowing local businesses and governments. Corporations may exploit natural resources and labour in developing nations, like colonial resource extraction. Global corporations can shape cultural norms and consumer habits, exerting ideological influence akin to cultural imperialism. Sometimes, large corporations exert significant political influence through lobbying, funding, and strategic partnerships, thereby impacting policy decisions.

Major technology companies have a profound impact on markets and institutions, resulting in unequal power dynamics. This situation can be likened to colonial powers that established control over territories and resources. Collecting and exploiting personal data from individuals, particularly in developing nations, can be considered a form of colonisation. Companies harvest data to enhance their services and profits without fair compensation or consent from the data subjects. Technology facilitates the spread of cultural values, practices, and norms, often prioritising those from dominant cultures (like Western cultures) at the expense of local traditions and identities.

Access to technology remains uneven globally, leading to a digital divide. Countries and communities that lack access may be disadvantaged in terms of economic development, educational opportunities, and participation in the global economy. Advanced technologies enable unprecedented levels of surveillance and control, raising concerns about privacy, freedom, and human rights. This mirrors historical patterns of control seen in colonised regions and poses an existential question: Will Artificial intelligence lead to a global empire? Countries or companies that excel in AI research and development could gain substantial competitive advantages, potentially leading to an economic empire, like a few hundred Britishers carrying guns and millions of Indians resisting them without firearms.

As nations increasingly rely on foreign technologies, they may lose autonomy over their infrastructure, economy, and social systems, paralleling the dependencies created through historical colonial practices. Just as colonised peoples found ways to resist and adapt to colonial powers, there is potential for communities to reclaim agency through technology, creating alternative platforms and solutions that reflect local needs and values. Understanding this new form of colonisation involves recognising both the potential benefits and the significant challenges posed by technological advancements globally. Conversations about digital ethics, regulation, and equitable access are critical in addressing these issues. We will be picking up these threads later in the book. It is time to take a rear-view mirror view of modern India's creation. We exist in a chain of cause and consequence. To better educate the next generation, we must understand the historical context of our present so that they can better prepare themselves for future challenges and opportunities.

Summary

Every age has its empires. Once they sailed under flags and marched with armies; now they move through markets, algorithms, and multinational brands. The modern world is bound not by conquest, but by commerce—where power flows through trade, technology, and cultural persuasion. In this new order, corporations often hold the sway that once belonged to kings, shaping not only economies but imaginations. For India, whose civilisation once nourished global exchange in wisdom, goods, and spirit, the challenge is not to retreat in fear of this power but to engage it with discernment. True exceptionalism today does not mean standing apart from the world, but standing awake within it—drawing on the ancient ethics of balance, restraint, and collective good. India's future will not be defined by resisting globalisation, but by reinterpreting it through her timeless dharmic lens: ensuring that prosperity does not eclipse compassion, and that growth does not come at the cost of justice. The measure of Indian exceptionalism, then, is not dominance or isolation, but the quiet strength to humanise power—to turn even the engines of empire into instruments of harmony.

10

Geopolitical Conundrum

Power shifts like the wind, yet the wise nation does not chase it—it learns to sail. In a world of competing empires and restless ambitions, India's strength lies not in alignment, but in balance—the ancient art of standing firm at the centre while the world turns.

Salve Traders

From the beginning, the world had been a complicated and frequently bewildering place. Seafaring was crucial in bringing about a new world order, as it enabled the discovery of new lands, the colonisation of existing ones, and the establishment of international commerce routes. European navigators made history during the Age of Exploration by venturing into previously unexplored seas, a period spanning from the fifteenth to the seventeenth centuries. These voyages had a profound impact on global politics, economics, and culture.

Christopher Columbus, an Italian sailor serving as an ambassador for the Spanish monarchy, made four circumnavigations of the Atlantic between 1492 and 1504, discovering new regions in the Americas on each trip. Europeans, referring to the Americas as the New World, colonised the continent after these voyages. Vasco da Gama, a Portuguese navigator, set out from Lisbon in July 1497 and, after completing a circuit of Africa, arrived in Calicut (Kozhikode) on India's Malabar Coast in May 1498, thus establishing a maritime route between Europe and Asia. Near the southernmost point of South America lies a strait that Ferdinand Magellan, another Portuguese explorer, navigated to cross the Pacific Ocean and reach the Philippines.

Several European nations, including Spain, Portugal, and, later, the United Kingdom, France, and the Netherlands, used the transatlantic slave trade to colonise the Americas beginning in the 1600s. All these nations boasted of their own great value systems while belittling those of others, but they were unanimous in enslaving human beings. The reason was simple. Manual labour was needed to grow agricultural commodities like sugarcane, cotton, and tobacco. European ships loaded with goods would arrive on the West African coast, barter these goods for enslaved people, bought already by their agents, and then sail to America to sell them there. A significant amount of money was made by shipping molasses from the Caribbean to American distilleries and then shipping the alcohol to Europe. This system was not just a few isolated instances of enslavement but a vast and organised network that spanned continents and endured for centuries. Some European scholars and religious leaders used biblical texts and philosophical concepts to justify enslavement, arguing that Africans were inherently inferior and suited for slavery.

A significant source of conflict among European settlers in North America was the push westward. They needed enslaved people to clear and cultivate newly acquired areas. Southerners sought to maintain their culture and way of life, while northerners feared that the South would gain political power if slavery were legalised in new states. A key issue in the slavery discussion was the extent of power the federal government should have over the rights of the states. Most northerners held the prevailing belief that the Union was permanent under the Constitution, whereas leaders in the South insisted that states had the right to secede from the Union. After Abraham Lincoln was elected, the southern states seceded and formed the Confederate States of America because he opposed the spread of slavery. In 1861, the Civil War commenced with an assault on Fort Sumter in Charleston, South Carolina, by the Confederacy. The economic system, social fabric, and physical infrastructure of the South were all severely damaged by the conflict. Several social movements emerged during the war, and African Americans gained increased agency as a result.

The slavery of Africans, Malagasy (a people from Madagascar), and other populations took place in another large-scale slave trade that took place in the Indian Ocean. There was a demand for enslaved people in the Middle East and a need for labourers in the Indian Ocean region, which fuelled this commerce. Colonial economies around the globe owe an outstanding debt of gratitude to the slave trade. The creation of valuable commodities was driven by enslaved labour, which allowed the colonisers to experience economic development. When slavery was outlawed in the British Empire in 1833, a clever way was devised to have cheap labour to work in vast plantations owned by the British landlords in the colonies.

More than 1.5 million Indian workers were sent to European colonies in the Caribbean, Mauritius, Fiji, and Natal (in South Africa) as indentured servants under the Indian indenture system, which replaced slave labour. Despite the allure of decent pay and the chance to escape starvation and poverty, indentured labour was often characterised by abusive conditions and exploitative contracts. Mahatma Gandhi emerged as a major player in the struggle for the rights of Indian indentured servants in South Africa.

Many descendants of Indian indentured workers rose to prominent positions after the departure of colonial powers, making significant contributions to the nation's development, where they were brought in to work as bonded labourers. Leaving behind their horrendous past, they have risen by grit and dedication to good roles like political activists, community organisers, and even heads of state from Suriname, Guyana, Fiji, Mauritius, and the Seychelles.

The thriving Central Asian economies began to crumble because of oceanic exploration, which severed Europe's dependence on the overland Silk Road trade. A flurry of commercial rivalries erupted amongst themselves when Europeans gained access to previously uncharted regions, unleashing a wealth of riches, including spices, textiles, gold, and silver. European domination was solidified, and global power dynamics were transformed as a result of the subsequent expansion of colonial empires into Asia, Africa, and the Americas. As a result, international relations were shaped by the dominance of nations with stronger naval capabilities, such as the Netherlands, Spain, and Britain. A new world order emerged as a result of this reorganised power structure.

Karma Returns

The politically charged, militarily unstable, and economically precarious international climate at the turn of the twentieth century was primarily responsible for sparking the First World

War. The global order was drastically altered when the war erupted in 1914 and continued until 1918. The Triple Alliance consisted of Germany, Austria-Hungary, and Italy, whereas France, Russia, and Britain created the Triple Entente.

Several powerful empires collapsed in the aftermath of the war. These included the Germanic, Austro-Hungarian, and Ottoman realms. This chaos paved the way for the formation of new countries, encouraged nationalism, and shifted international power away from imperial rule towards national sovereignty. For example, following the war, the Ottoman Empire, which had formerly ruled over a large portion of the Middle East, disintegrated. Turkey, Iraq, Palestine, and Syria were formed as a result of the empire's disintegration in 1920. Central Europe was also transformed after the First World War; the Austro-Hungarian Empire collapsed, and several sovereign nations were formed, including Austria, Hungary, Czechoslovakia, and Yugoslavia.

The Second World War also led to the collapse of many European colonial empires. The economic and military weakness of countries like the Netherlands, Britain, and France sped up the independence movements in Africa, Asia, and the Middle East. A world with more than two superpowers emerged because of decolonisation. India's freedom was imminent. The Cold War began with the rise to superpower status of the United States and the Soviet Union, and continued until the Soviet Union's collapse in 1991. During this period, the two countries engaged in a fierce ideological, political, and military confrontation. Ukraine, Belarus, the Baltic republics, and countries in Central Asia were among the fifteen new nations that formed. As a result, new political dynamics emerged and regional borders were redrawn.

The Rise and Fall of Globalisation

The concept of globalisation refers to the process of increased interconnectedness and interdependence among countries, primarily through the exchange of goods, services, information, and culture. It has been a significant force shaping the world economy and societies over the past few decades. After the Second World War, institutions such as the International Monetary Fund (IMF) and the World Trade Organisation (WTO) emerged to promote international trade and economic cooperation. The reduction of trade barriers and tariffs facilitated global economic integration. Innovations in transportation and communication, such as the internet and large cargo ships, further facilitated easier connections and business transactions across borders. Companies expanded globally, setting up operations in multiple countries to tap into new markets and access cost-effective labour.

However, within a few decades, economic disparities caused by globalisation emerged, widening the economic gap between rich and poor nations, as well as within countries themselves. Suffering locals have challenged the principles of free trade, which has often been more of a tool for profiteering and tax evasion. Countries such as the United States and the United Kingdom have witnessed political movements that are critical of globalisation. The Covid-19 pandemic highlighted vulnerabilities in global supply chains, prompting consideration of reshoring and diversifying supply sources. Globalisation has led to increased resource consumption and environmental degradation, prompting debates over sustainable practices. Automation and AI have disrupted labour markets, contributing to unemployment in certain sectors, raising questions about the future of work in a globalised economy.

India's experience with globalisation has been significant, characterised by both opportunities and challenges. India has become an increasingly attractive destination for foreign investment, particularly in sectors such as information technology, telecommunications, and manufacturing. This influx has created jobs and contributed to the development of infrastructure. With the boom in the software and IT service sectors, India emerged as a global hub for IT and business process outsourcing (BPO) services. Cities like Bengaluru and Hyderabad have become prominent centres, employing millions. Economic growth has led to improved living standards for many, with better access to education, healthcare, and consumer goods.

But what's in store after all this? The age of aggressive conquest has come to an end. Complex international problems, rapid technological development, shifting geopolitical forces, and economic globalisation shape the concept of a new global order in the twenty-first century. India, China, the EU, and possibly Brazil, along with regional powers, are becoming increasingly influential in the world, making it less unipolar and more characterised by a multipolar shift. More intricate diplomatic alliances and rivalries may emerge as a result of this power arrangement.

Society, the economy, and cybersecurity will all be affected by the new developments in cyber technology, artificial intelligence, space travel, and digital innovation. Impacting privacy, security, and the power balance, control over these technologies has the potential to become a fundamental factor in global influence. The conventional state-centric model of diplomacy and government may face growing competition from non-state actors such as social movements, terrorist organisations, multinational firms, and international organisations.

The problem of territorial conflicts is a significant component of geopolitical dilemmas. Disputes in sensitive areas, such as the South China Sea, frequently begin with competing claims to territory or natural resources, which can quickly escalate into full-scale wars. In Kashmir, Pakistan remains a meddling power. The Indian subcontinent, particularly in the Himalayas, remains a disputed territory between China and India.

In areas where states are competing for influence, achieving a balance of power among them is crucial. The rise of both old and new powers, such as Russia and China, has produced an ever-changing and unpredictable geopolitical scene. As member states negotiate obligations and with rivalries that can shift at any moment, strategic alliances like NATO or regional pacts add another layer of complexity.

Economic interests also exacerbate geopolitical dilemmas. Wars and international policies are shaped by who controls key resources, such as oil, gas, and rare minerals. Power disputes and financial penalties, which affect diplomatic relations and stability, are common outcomes of the world's reliance on these resources. Furthermore, these problems assume new dimensions due to technological advancements. Space exploration, information warfare, and cybersecurity threats have expanded the battlefield beyond conventional areas, forcing governments to devise innovative strategies in the face of unpredictability.

The Business of War and Peace

Two of the most famous and consequential books in the world are the *Arthashastra* by Kautilya and *The Art of War* by Sun Tzu. Both books emphasise the need for the weaker partner in a relationship to pick its battles wisely rather than getting into unfair conflicts.

It must gather resources so that it can decide when and where to fight, which increases its strength as it nibbles at the enemy.

In public discussions concerning the US, where millions of Indians reside and hold important positions, there appears to be an element of wordplay. As of 2025, many chief executives of US corporations are of Indian descent. This includes companies such as IBM, Microsoft, and Google. America and India are a perfect fit as allies. However, India's post-independence history, spanning over seventy-five years, would be shattered by an alliance with the United States. India remained neutral during the Cold War, neither aligning itself with one superpower nor the other.

India has been the go-to ally of the status quo forces in the US-led liberal international order and has withstood China's meteoric rise, as manifested in its unparalleled economic expansion, political might, and military modernisation. As a result, India is now China's sole formidable neighbour, which has opened doors for defence cooperation and technology transfers. The Quadrilateral Security Dialogue—also known as the Quad—involves the US, Australia, Japan, and India, mirroring the geopolitical conundrum.

The formation of the strategic alliance between Brazil, Russia, India, and China (BRIC) in 2009 marked the beginning of a new age in geopolitics. Yekaterinburg, Russia, hosted the first official summit of the BRIC nations in June 2009. The group's resolve to cooperate on political and economic matters was solidified at this summit. South Africa was extended an invitation to join the bloc in December 2010, and the country formally joined in 2011, which then appended an S to its formal acronym and came to be called BRICS. Africa, through South Africa, played a significant role in this growth, which increased its visibility across the continent. To facilitate sustainable development and infrastructure projects in their respective nations as well as in other developing economies, the BRICS group of nations formed the New Development Bank (NDB) in July 2015. The bank is based in Shanghai and was founded by Indian banker K.V. Kamath, who was also named the bank's first chairman. To assist member nations experiencing difficulties with their balance of payments, the bank established a Contingent Reserve Arrangement (CRA).

In the eyes of many, the BRICS nations could pose a threat to US hegemony in international politics, economics, and the military. To diversify their economies away from Western influence, these nations have pooled their resources to support infrastructure projects and development initiatives within their borders, as well as meet their financial obligations, rather than relying on the World Bank and the IMF, both of which are controlled by the US.

As a coalition of emerging nations, BRICS speaks for the developing world as a whole. The focus of this alliance is on matters important to developing economies, and its stated goal is to challenge the long-standing global pre-eminence of Western nations. As a venue for diverse viewpoints, BRICS brings together nations with varying political systems and ideologies. Despite their differences, they can collaborate in creating new models of economic development and governance that challenge Western-centric narratives. Although BRICS does not declare itself to be an anti-American bloc, it can counteract US influence abroad by fostering economic cooperation, advocating for changes to global governance, and strengthening political solidarity among developing nations.

The geopolitical order, both in theory and practice, is being severely tested by the conflict in Ukraine in 2021. Russia seized the Crimean Peninsula in March 2014 following a contentious referendum, following the Euromaidan Revolution in Ukraine, which deposed pro-Russian President Viktor Yanukovych. At the same time, separatists in eastern Ukraine who are pro-Russian and have Russian backing took over some of the Donetsk and Luhansk regions, together known as the Donbas. There was a humanitarian catastrophe and heavy losses as a result of the protracted fighting in the Donbas between Ukrainian government forces and separatists backed by Russia. The fighting spread outside the Donbas area in February 2022. The West did not deploy troops to defend Ukraine against the Russian invasion; however, Western nations have been providing financial and military assistance to the country. There were efforts to isolate Russia financially, and India was drawn into the fray.

What happens next is anybody's guess. The realm of geopolitics is a conundrum, a complex problem or puzzle with no simple answer—and no shortage of wordplay, even among the most powerful people in the world.

De-dollarisation

A persistent concern in the Western world is that nations are reducing their reliance on the US dollar in international trade, finance, and reserve holdings. This can involve shifting to other currencies (e.g., the euro, yuan, or a basket of currencies) or using local currencies for transactions. It is often driven by geopolitical, economic, or strategic motivations, such as reducing vulnerability to US sanctions, diversifying reserves, or promoting regional economic integration. Tensions with the US or concerns about dollar-based sanctions accelerated de-dollarisation efforts, most notably by Russia and China.

The BRIC alliance was conceptualised in 2006 and formally established in 2009 in Shanghai, China, comprising Brazil, Russia,

India, and China. South Africa joined in 2010, and it was renamed as BRICS. Indonesia was admitted as the eleventh member of the group in January 2025. Of the five founding members, India's relationships with Russia and South Africa are the strongest. Brazil and India have friendly but limited connections. Although relations between China and Russia are improving, India and China continue to have tense interactions. India and Brazil are collaborating to prevent the BRICS from becoming as anti-Western as Moscow and Beijing would like it to be. In contrast, South Africa has deep ties to China, a notable distrust of the West, and significant admiration for Russia, despite its close alliance with India. This is the position of BRICS.

The Contingent Reserve Arrangement (CRA) provides members facing balance of payments pressures with short-term liquidity support, free from the conditionality associated with Western lending. India hopes that the BRICS New Development Bank (NDB) will increase its resources for developing nations. Neither of these organisations has come close to meeting the needs of International Financial Institutions (IFIs) or Western aid agencies. The Indian government has avoided radical proposals, such as de-dollarisation and the formation of a BRICS currency.

India, Russia, and China could theoretically create a dollar-free system for trade and financial transactions, but it would require significant coordination, infrastructure, and trust among the three nations. India and Russia already use the rupee-ruble mechanism for some transactions, and China has been promoting the yuan in trade. At some point, India will integrate its Unified Payments Interface (UPI) with these platforms, including Russia's System for Transfer of Financial Messages (SPFS) and China's Cross-Border Interbank Payment System (CIPS). The three countries have already signed currency swap agreements. India has a trade deficit with China, which would complicate the yuan-rupee trade. Historical tensions between India and China, as well as India's strategic ties with the US, could hinder full cooperation.

An important region for maritime traffic and economic connections, this chapter concludes at the intersection of significant trade routes, including the South China Sea and the Strait of Malacca, which concerns India. Countries such as Singapore, Malaysia, and Indonesia are playing pivotal roles in the region's dynamics due to their growing economies and increasing integration into global supply chains. The geopolitical situation is complicated due to China's growing economic and military influence, as well as the US's emphasis on maintaining regional stability.

Enhanced collaboration between India and countries in the Indo-Pacific region in trade, security, and geopolitical affairs is one way the two countries are strengthening their partnership. A free, open, and inclusive Indo-Pacific region is a shared goal of the two nations, and they are working together on security and defence matters, including conducting joint patrols and drills. Financial technology, artificial intelligence, the Internet of Things, and digital public infrastructure are all areas where the two countries have committed to collaborating. Health and food security are two areas where India and Indonesia are exchanging information and expertise.

Summary

The twenty-first century has redrawn the map of power. As the unipolar dominance of the United States wanes and China asserts itself as a global power, a multipolar world emerges—one that is restless, complex, and uncertain. Nationalism, populism, and ideological divides are sharpening the global landscape, while new technologies and shifting alliances are unsettling the old order. For India, this conundrum is both a challenge and an opportunity. Positioned between East and West, North and South, India cannot remain a passive observer. Its size, civilisation, and democratic ethos compel it to engage actively—balancing partnerships, defending sovereignty, and offering a voice of moderation in turbulent times. The path ahead will demand not only strategic adaptability but moral clarity as well. India's strength has always been in turning diversity into resilience and dialogue into diplomacy. In a fractured world, India can embody the possibility of coexistence, demonstrating that power need not mean domination, but rather balance—a dharmic approach to international affairs.

Part III

What Has Survived?

... our religion lays down distinctly and clearly that everyone who wants salvation must pass through the stage of Rishihood—must become a Mantra-drashta, must see God.... They had hundreds of Rishis in ancient India. We will have millions—we are going to have, and the sooner every one of you believes in this, the better for India and the better for the world.[1]

—Swami Vivekananda

---

[1] https://www.ramakrishnavivekananda.info/vivekananda/volume_3/lectures_from_colombo_to_almora/the_work_before_us.htm. Last accessed on 5 October 2025.

11

Nationhood

Bharat is the soul, India the expression. One remembers, the other aspires—yet both breathe through the same heart. To love this land is to honour the river of time that flows through it, uniting memory and dream into a single destiny.

Doubts Are Traitors

At the book's halfway point, we go back to the beginning, the assertion that victors write history, before moving on. In his play *Measure for Measure*, William Shakespeare writes, 'Doubts are traitors', suggesting that our doubts can hinder us from achieving our potential by making us fearful of trying and making us lose when we could win. Having established control over vast territories of the Indian subcontinent, to perpetuate this opportunistic and, more than that, lucky venture, it was time for the British to create doubt in young Indian minds about their civilisation and history.

The racial categorisation of India into the fair-skinned Aryan North and the dark-skinned Dravidian South is an inaccurate and harmful stereotype. As previously said, the Germans created the myth of Aryans, and the British gave legitimacy to this racist view of India by using it as a tool in their divide-and-rule strategy. The northern Indians were especially captivated by this narrative since it equated the white Europeans with the 'Aryan' northerners. Sri Lankans also tend to agree with this perspective. As a people, the Sinhalese have a deep faith in their ancestry, which dates to Emperor Ashoka.

Sri Aurobindo, an expert in Sanskrit, Greek, and Latin, debunked the idea that northern and southern India were racially different. South Indian languages are not entirely separate from North Indian ones. Sri Aurobindo, born in Bengal, spent his formative years in England, later worked in Baroda (Vadodara) and spent the last four decades in Pondichéry (Puducherry), where he researched Tamil.

> Four languages were chosen for "dissection" and study: Sanskrit, Greek, Latin, and Tamil. The first three of these were well known by Sri Aurobindo, the fourth was chosen because it was through Tamil that he "came first to perceive ... the embryology of the Aryan tongues." To the data gathered from the study of these languages was to be added supporting evidence from four others: German, Celtic, Persian and Arabic. The division between Semitic and Aryan (i.e. Indo-European) tongues was, in Sri Aurobindo's opinion, as "unscientific" as the Aryan-Dravidian split.[2]

The Ramayana is not meant to depict a prince from the north launching an invasion of the south. There are deep layers. Ravana

[2] https://incarnateword.in/journals-and-magazines/archives-research-1977-94/1978/sri-aurobindos-vedic-and-linguistic-research. Last accessed on October 5, 2025.

is not a demon but a brahmin. His father was Vishrava, and his grandfather, Pulastya, a mind-born son of Brahma. He worshipped Lord Shiva, played the veena and wrote poetry. His portrayal in the epic highlights how a person of great lineage can become debased by pride. When Rama returned to Ayodhya, a section of brahmins refused to accept his invitation for a meal because they considered him a killer of Brahmin Ravana. To avoid disobeying the king, left his kingdom. There is no Aryan or Dasyu to be found there.

There is no mention in any Indian book of the supposed Aryan invasion that happened in 1500 BC. Pandit Jawaharlal Nehru, in his book *The Discovery of India*, adhered to the version of Indian history where this land was waiting for foreigners to be settled, much like America for the Europeans. The holy sites in all four corners of the Indian subcontinent—Jagannath Puri in the east, Rameswaram in the south, Dwaraka in the west, and Badrinath in the north—talk about one people. Why is the history of the origin and creation of these grand temples overlooked in our textbooks, while only forts and mausoleums built a few hundred years ago by the Mughal emperors are celebrated?

The southern region was the birthplace of the Hindu renaissance, which continued into the twelfth century. The *Shrimad Bhagavad Gita*, the Upanishads, and the Brahma Sutras were extensively annotated by Shankaracharya, who was born in Kerala and lived from 788 to 820 CE. Ramanujacharya of Tamil Nadu, Madhavacharya of Karnataka, and Chaitanya Mahaprabhu in eastern Bengal were all powerful renaissance men. Dividing India based on language and skin colour of people was a sinister plot which failed to take off despite the best efforts of the Britishers and their beneficiaries and stooges here. Swami Vivekananda declared without mincing words:

> 'A gentle yet clear brushing off of the cobwebs of the so-called Aryan theory and all its vicious corollaries is therefore necessary, especially for the South, and a proper self-respect created by a knowledge of the past grandeur of one of the great ancestors of the Aryan race, the great Tamilians.... We stick, despite Western theories, to that definition of the word "Arya" which we find in our sacred books, and which includes only the multitude we now call Hindus. This Aryan race, itself a mixture of two great races, Sanskrit-speaking and Tamil-speaking, applies to all Hindus alike.'[3]

Entry of the Proselytisers

Both Christianity and Islam, the two major world religions, have complex histories. While they have been associated with imperialist ideologies at various points, they also embody multiple beliefs, practices, and interpretations among their followers. They have essentially taken over the globe after eradicating many indigenous faiths. Before the emergence of these proselytisers, whose sole purpose in life was to convert others to their political or religious ideologies, local religions had a relatively peaceful existence based on mutual acceptance. All problems began with the intruders—be they the Mongols, Europeans, Turks, or Arabs.

Throughout history, missionary activity across the British Empire often intertwined humanitarian work with religious outreach. Schools and hospitals were established not merely as acts of charity but also as instruments of influence—designed to attract and integrate local communities into new systems of belief. In many impoverished regions, faith was subtly linked with access

---

[3] https://www.ramakrishnavivekananda.info/vivekananda/volume_4/writings_prose/aryans_and_tamilians.htm. Last accessed on October 5, 2025.

to education, healthcare, or social support, creating an uneven dynamic between giver and receiver. Even today, similar patterns sometimes emerge. Certain groups—religious or otherwise—invest heavily in local infrastructure or digital outreach, motivated less by compassion than by the desire to expand their ideological or institutional following. Large sums continue to flow into the construction of religious institutions across India, often concentrated in economically fragile areas where material assistance can easily become a conduit for persuasion. The deeper question remains: when does service become strategy, and where does faith end and influence begin?

Conversion is not limited to religion. Any cadre of any party, in essence, is a convert. Marxists do not believe in God or tradition. In their opinion, 'power flows through the barrel of the gun'. With India's independence came a siege on the intellectual community. Marxists attacked Indian culture through the well-educated and affluent, while evangelists campaigned among the poor and illiterate. Forgetting about civilisation and living happily ever after was something they had in common. Renowned historians Arnold Toynbee and Sir Jadunath Sarkar utilised the full might of bureaucratic and political power to deny historical facts and wrote what suited the rulers of those times.

It is ironic that the last remaining stronghold of the world's religions—Hinduism, Buddhism, Sikhism, and Jainism—is called 'secular', and despite so many wars fought in the name of religion, Christianity is called 'the religion of love' and Islam 'the religion of peace'. The fact remains that this 'love' demands forgoing the faith one is born into to be lovable and loved, and the 'peace' is only for those who follow 'my faith'. For the rest, it is persecution and war, whenever and wherever possible.

The term used to describe any changes or improvements aimed at correcting this distortion of Indian history is branded as saffronisation, a term derived from the colour's associations with garb preferred by Hindu sadhus. This process entails viewing India as a Hindu nation, returning to a time when Hindus were united, and modifying political institutions to reflect the ideals of the majority. The argument is that, since gaining independence in 1947, fundamentalists have, in disguise, shaped policies, the government, and the administration. The Indian Constitution is hailed as the new creed, and people bereft of their civilisation are the new nationalists.

Bharatavarsha Became India

Bharatavarsha, the Sanskrit term which means 'the land of Bharata' or 'Bharata's homeland', is mentioned in various ancient texts, including the *Rig Veda*, the Mahabharata, and the Puranas. It was used to refer to the Indian subcontinent, encompassing the region between the Himalayas and the sea. The term reflects a sense of national identity and shared cultural heritage among people in the Indian subcontinent. The ancient Greeks referred to the land as Indica, and the Persians called it Hindustan (land of the Hindus). The British preferred to use the term India, derived from the Indus River, over Bharat or Hindustan.

The 1935 Government of India Act laid down the institutional roadmap to independence. After India gained independence in 1947, the constituent assembly deliberated in detail on the country's future constitution. It had one representative from each province and state. Dr. Rajendra Prasad was chosen as its permanent chairman. Thirteen committees were formed to deliberate. A seven-person drafting committee, under the capable leadership of

Dr. B.R. Ambedkar, compiled the recommendations of these groups. The draft was thoroughly debated in protracted arguments before being finalised. All statements made are well preserved.

The Indian Constitution was not written in a vacuum. The constitutions of the UK, the US, Ireland, and Canada were considered. Features like a unified citizenship system, a parliamentary form of government, and the rule of law were adopted from the British. Ideas such as judicial independence, judicial review, fundamental rights, and procedures for removing judges from the high courts, including the Supreme Court, originated from the American Constitution. The Canadian federal system, which is characterised by a strong central power, was accepted. India was officially established as an independent republic on 26 January 1950, when the Indian Constitution came into effect. Dr. Rajendra Prasad, the chairman of the constituent assembly, was unanimously elected as the first president of the Republic of India.

Ideological divides surfaced soon after. In October 1951, Dr. Shyama Prasad Mookerjee established the Jana Sangh, while Dr. B. R. Ambedkar announced the establishment of the Republican Party of India (RPI) in 1956 by dissolving the Scheduled Castes Federation (SCF), which he had founded in 1942 to politically mobilise the Dalit community and secure their rights. Unfortunately, Dr Ambedkar died before the new party could be formally founded in 1957 to carry forward his vision. Two other notable organisations were the Socialist Party, established by Ram Manohar Lohia and Jayaprakash Narayan, and the Kisan Mazdoor Praja Parishad, which Acharya Kripalani created. While a full spectrum of Indian society was reflected in these groups, the party in power have gone into its narcissistic bubble.

The general elections took place between 25 October 1951 and 7 March 1952. The newly formed Election Commission of India was responsible for overseeing the election process. Nearly seventeen crore individuals used their voting rights. The foundation for the electoral methods still in use today was laid during these elections, which were pivotal in establishing a democratic framework in India. It is no wonder that India is the world's largest democracy in the twenty-first century.

The Council of States was established as a permanent Upper House of the Indian Parliament, later known as the Rajya Sabha, on 3 April 1952. Its initial chairperson and vice president of India, Dr. S. Radhakrishnan, provided a broad definition of the Upper House's function as,

> 'There is a general impression that this House cannot make or unmake governments and, therefore, it is a superfluous body. But there are functions which a revising Chamber can fulfil fruitfully. Parliament is not only a legislative but a deliberative body.... We should try to do everything in our power to justify to the public of this country that a second Chamber is essential to prevent hasty legislation. We should discuss the proposals put before us with dispassion and detachment.'[4]

India, at the time, was deeply reliant on US funding but also wary of how the US was supplying arms and ammunition to Pakistan's army. In this backdrop, Prime Minister Nehru travelled to the Soviet Union. He spent sixteen days travelling from

---

[4] https://cms.rajyasabha.nic.in/UploadedFiles/ElectronicPublications/Sixty%20Year%20RS_New.pdf. Last accessed on October 5, 2025.

Turkmenistan to Ukraine. An Indian adaptation of the Soviet model of development was picked up. The core idea was to redirect investments away from manufacturing and towards the domestic consumer goods market. A new crop of command economy superstars emerged: the hand-picked specialists, administrators, economists, and bureaucrats who instituted a new sort of empire, known as the Licence Permit Raj.

Democracy, in Dr. Ambedkar's pragmatic and legally astute view, would significantly improve the living conditions of the downtrodden. However, to his distress and despair, this was not done by the government, which was upholding the constitution in the letter but violating it in spirit. While speaking out against a constitutional amendment in 1955, Dr. Ambedkar stated in the Rajya Sabha that a good constitution was mauled by vested interests and he 'wanted to burn the Constitution':

> 'I say it with a certain amount of pride the Constitution which has been given to this country is a wonderful document.... It is the quickest and most straightforward.... The Constitution is clear to everybody who can read and comprehend English. It doesn't need any criticism.... Before the deity could be installed, we constructed a temple for him to live in. However, what recourse would we have but to burn the building if the devil had already taken possession of it? It was never our intention for the Asuras to settle there.'[5]

---

[5] https://rsdebate.nic.in/bitstream/123456789/583570/1/PD_09_19031955_19_p2437_p2520_2.pdf. Last accessed on October 5, 2025.

Politics Outdid Nation-Building

It is not uncommon for divisive politics to undermine nation-building efforts by creating divisions along ethnic, religious, or cultural lines. It has occurred everywhere in the world and continues to do so, and India is no exception. When a country is divided along these lines, it can lead to deep-seated animosities, unequal distribution of resources, and a lack of shared national identity. This fragmentation can hinder the development of cohesive policies, weaken institutions, and perpetuate conflict, making it challenging to foster unity and progress. Instead of focusing on collective goals, partisan politics can prioritise the interests of specific groups, further polarising society and hindering the country's progress and development.

Even within the Congress party, divisions began to emerge. In response to the socialist and statist ideology that he perceived as becoming increasingly ineffective, C. Rajagopalachari established the Swatantra Party in 1959. Feeling uneasy, Prime Minister Nehru had his daughter, Indira Gandhi, who was forty-one years old and had been chosen as the president of the Congress. Her term lasted until 1960. This would start a new tradition of family politics in Indian democracy.

The democratically elected state government of Kerala, headed by E.M.S. Namboodiripad of the Communist Party of India, was removed from office. Indian politics would soon become notorious for its opportunism and excessive preoccupation with power. In 1975, when the Allahabad High Court declared Indira Gandhi's election invalid, the prime minister, instead of resigning, declared a state of emergency. The constitution was amended, clearing her of any wrongdoing. However, she was deposed in the 1977 elections. The newly elected parliament undid all aberrations.

The Indian Constitution was intentionally crafted to eradicate social degradation and parochialism in Indian society and to promote republican freedom. By addressing topics as diverse as social equality, health, education, communal harmony, economic prosperity, and the role of sovereign power, it aimed to create a society free from imperial slavery and moral decay. The ideals of cultural nationalism, however one defines it, and what are often believed to be globalised 'liberal' principles have been at odds with one another for some time. The country's fundamental framework instrument, the constitution, is the most critical point of contention.

Recognising India's culture and the civilisational foundation upon which it rests, as well as its uniqueness as a nation, are two crucial elements of a cultural nationalist interpretation of the constitution. In other words, a liberal or libertarian understanding of human rights provides insufficient grounds for interpreting the constitution; instead, such interpretation must be based on the specificities of politics, history, society, and culture. The Indian Constitution defends nationhood by establishing a framework that promotes unity, ensures fundamental rights for all citizens, and provides for a system of governance that protects the nation's integrity. It achieves this through various mechanisms, including the separation of powers, the protection of fundamental rights, and the establishment of a judiciary to interpret and uphold the constitution.

The Innovation of the Collegium System

The collegium system is a unique and innovative mechanism in India's judicial structure for the appointment and transfer of judges to the higher judiciary, particularly the Supreme Court and high courts. It was established through judicial interpretations rather than a formal law or constitutional provision. The collegium system emerged as a result of judicial activism, where the Supreme Court interpreted the constitution to safeguard judicial independence, mainly in response to concerns about executive overreach in judicial appointments during the 1970s and 1980s.

The Supreme Court has the authority to review laws and government actions, ensuring that they are in alignment with the constitution. This safeguards against potential abuses of power and upholds the rule of law, a crucial element for a strong nation. The system, which controls the nomination and promotion of justices to the highest courts, was oddly omitted from both the original and amended constitutions. It has evolved because of Supreme Court judgements, particularly in landmark cases such as the Second Judges Case in 1993 and the Third Judges Case in 1998. Among the members of the collegium are the Chief Justice of India, four of the most senior judges on the Supreme Court, and two of the most senior judges on the High Court. The collegium makes recommendations to the president of India for appointments and transfers, which the government is required to accept.

A small group of judges secretly selects the judges, as the executive branch is not involved in any way with judicial appointments. Additionally, they aren't answerable to any higher authority, and their personal preferences are final. Because there are no clear standards under the collegium system for selection, favouritism and nepotism are likely to influence the selection process. A formal secretariat is not involved in this scheme. The collegium meets behind closed doors, and its decision-making process is not publicly disclosed. Collegium meetings do not have formal minutes. In 2015, the court rejected the Ninety-ninth Amendment Act, 2014, which sought to establish a National

Judicial Appointments Commission in its place, as it would have endangered judicial independence.

The moment has come to consider creating a permanent, autonomous entity to formalise the procedure, while providing sufficient protections to maintain the independence of the judiciary and guarantee judicial supremacy without compromising judicial exclusivity. Why should it not be transparent, process-driven, reflective of diversity, and demonstrate professional competence and integrity? In the last three decades since its creation, the collegium system has failed to address the issue of social diversity in the higher judiciary. Among the twenty-five high courts with a total sanctioned strength of over 1,100 judges, a significant number of positions, amounting to several hundred, remain vacant. There are only a hundred women high court judges and four women justices out of the thirty-three sitting justices in the Supreme Court.

For the constitution to be democratically upheld, it must be comprehensible in interpretation, review, and translation, and it must reflect the values of the people it governs. Any reasonable interpretation must either be a product of the ingenuity of its users or, failing that, be well-suited to their needs. Any subsequent reading of the constitution must inevitably incorporate the political concessions and understandings of standards that have evolved due to the changes in the lives of individuals and society it seeks to govern. There is no way to generalise a society's political system, civic understanding, and historical events to another society without assuming fundamental differences in culture, politics, and history. The rules that govern them also do not apply to cultures that are fundamentally different from one another. The day of taking constitutional interpretation at face value has passed—for better or worse.

Summary

To say Bharat is to invoke memory; to say India is to speak of destiny. The two are not rivals, but reflections of one enduring civilisation—ancient in wisdom, youthful in promise. Together, they form the pulse of a nation that remembers its sacred rivers even as it launches rockets to the moon; that prays in many languages yet beats with one heart. India's nationhood is not a matter of geography alone but of consciousness—the awareness that unity need not erase diversity, and that progress means carrying the past forward, not leaving it behind. To belong to this land is to inherit both responsibility and grace: to defend her freedom, nurture her harmony, and honour her name in all its forms. For loyalty to one's nation is not mere sentiment; it is a sacred trust—the living bond between what we have received and what we will leave behind. Bharat and India are two syllables of the same eternal song—one sung by the ancients, the other by the future, both echoing the same refrain: We are one, and we shall endure.

12

The Indian Mind

A new intelligence is rising—born of silicon, guided by code, yet awaiting a soul. The world stands at the threshold of a second awakening: when the wisdom of the yogi meets the logic of the machine. In that union lies humanity's next evolution—where technology serves consciousness, and India lights the path towards a mindful world.

A Profound and Multifaceted Concept

The 'Indian mind' is often interpreted as referring to key characteristics or qualities that define the thinking and cultural identity of Indian individuals. Typical hallmarks include diversity and pluralism, spiritual and philosophical depth, adaptability and resilience, a community-oriented approach, and innovative thinking. India is home to a diverse array of languages, religions, cultures, and traditions. This diversity fosters a mindset generally open to different perspectives and ideas. Indian culture strongly emphasises spirituality, philosophy, and ethics, drawing from the Vedas and the Upanishads, as well as assimilation of teachings from various religions that have arrived here from other lands.

The Indian mind is often characterised by its ability to adapt to changing circumstances and challenges, stemming from a history of overcoming various social and political upheavals. There is a strong sense of community and family values amongst Indian people, and relationships and social ties play a crucial role in individual identity and decision-making. Indians have made significant contributions to mathematics, science, and technology, reflecting a spirit of inquiry and innovation. These characteristics may not apply universally to all individuals in India. Still, they highlight common themes observed in the Indian cultural and intellectual landscape, making Indians a coveted human resource in the global market, especially in knowledge-intensive fields.

The principle of cause and effect is deeply ingrained in the Indian psyche, influenced by various philosophical, spiritual, and cultural traditions, particularly the concept of karma. The belief is that every action has consequences, whether in this life or the next. This understanding fosters a sense of responsibility and accountability for one's actions. Schools of thought fostered by Hinduism, Buddhism, and Jainism emphasise the interconnectedness of actions and their outcomes. These philosophies encourage individuals to consider the long-term effects of their decisions and behaviours.

Indian belief systems view life as cyclical, with events and experiences influencing future outcomes. This perspective reinforces that today's causes will shape tomorrow's effects. This understanding is also reflected in social customs and practices. For instance, in many ancient countries of the world, people often engage in rituals and live ethically, believing that positive actions lead to favourable outcomes, thereby enhancing individual and community well-being. There is a marked cultural emphasis on introspection and mindfulness in the Indian way of living, encouraging individuals to consider the potential consequences of their actions before acting. Reason and logic are deeply ingrained in the Indian psyche. Appendices to religious writings, the Shulba Sutras, composed before the Common Era (CE), contain the earliest known mathematical records from India. These are some basic guidelines for creating altars in various forms, including squares, rectangles, parallelograms, and others.

Earlier, we explored the concept of zero as a number and advancements in algebra, trigonometry, and mathematics within Indian mathematics. In fact, the decimal system also originated in India. It was later adopted and spread by Arab mathematicians to Europe. France was a leader in developing and adopting a decimal-based system for measurements and currency during the French Revolution. In this section, we examine the legacy of Srinivas Ramanujan (1887–1920), who received very little formal education but was widely regarded as one of the greatest mathematicians of all time.

The Man Who Knew Infinity

Ramanujan was born in 1887 into a poor brahmin family in Erode, Tamil Nadu. He showed an early aptitude for mathematics, mastering advanced concepts by the age of twelve. With limited access to formal education, Ramanujan taught himself mathematics using a book called *A Synopsis of Elementary Results in Pure and Applied Mathematics* by G.S. Carr. While working as a clerk at Madras Port, after reading G.H. Hardy's *Orders of Infinity*, Ramanujan wrote to Hardy. Impressed by Ramanujan's work, which accompanied the letter, G.H. Hardy invited him to join Trinity College at the University of Cambridge. The collaboration between Ramanujan and Hardy yielded immediate and significant mathematical breakthroughs. They published seven papers together between 1914 and 1918. In March 1916, Ramanujan was awarded a bachelor of science by Research from Cambridge University. This degree was later renamed a Ph.D. in 1920. He was named a fellow of both the Royal Society of London and the Cambridge Philosophical Society. Unfortunately, he died early in 1920 at the age of 32, just a year after returning to India from England.

American writer Robert Kanigel published Ramanujan's biography, *The Man Who Knew Infinity: A Life of the Genius Ramanujan,* in 1991. In that, he wrote:

> In the West, there was an old debate about whether mathematical reality was created by mathematicians or, existing independently, was merely discovered by them. Ramanujan was squarely in the latter camp; for him, numbers and their mathematical relationships fairly threw off clues to how the universe fit together. Each new theorem was one more piece of the Infinite unfathomable. So, he wasn't being silly, or sly, or cute when, later, he told a friend, "An equation for me has no meaning unless it expresses a thought of God".[6]

Settling the debate over whether mathematical reality is created by mathematicians or exists independently, Ramanujan confirmed it as divine, a universal language that reveals truths that exist regardless of cultural or temporal context.

Computer programs rely heavily on mathematical concepts, which enable programmers to analyse and optimise software

---

[6] Robert Kanigel, *The Man Who Knew Infinity: A Life of the Genius Ramanujan,* New York: Washington Square Press, 1991, p. 66.

efficiently based on algorithms, data structures, and system design. Optimisation, modelling, and simulation are three areas of system design that use mathematical ideas such as calculus, probability, and linear algebra. Artificial intelligence specialists rely heavily on linear algebra, a branch of applied mathematics. To work in artificial intelligence, one must have a strong foundation in mathematics. Linear algebra's concepts of scalar, vector, tensor, matrix, set, sequence, topology, graph, function, linear transformation, eigenvalue, and eigenvector provide a framework for abstracting data and models in AI systems.

Mathematical principles underpin search engine ranking algorithms. They formed the basis of PageRank, the algorithm that Larry Page and Sergey Brin created when they founded Google. This innovation was powered by applying the centuries-old fundamental ideas of primary eigenvalues and eigenvectors. The importance of a page is recursively defined: a page becomes high in rank if essential pages link to it. This creates a self-reinforcing cycle where high-quality, well-linked pages continue to gain importance. Links from authoritative, well-established websites carry more weight than links from less reputable sources.

The future of AI is likely to continue heavily relying on mathematics. Advances in mathematical theory can lead to improvements in model efficiency, interpretability, and capabilities. Moreover, emerging areas like quantum computing and advanced algorithms further emphasise the ongoing importance of mathematics in developing more powerful and sophisticated AI systems. While other disciplines such as neuroscience and cognitive science also contribute to AI development, mathematics remains central to understanding, designing, and optimising AI technologies.

One of the most crucial mathematical advances for the continued advancement of AI is optimisation theory, particularly the development of efficient and scalable optimisation algorithms. These algorithms are fundamental for training machine learning models, including neural networks, by minimising or maximising specific objective functions. Another critical mathematical advance is probability theory and statistics, which underpins learning from data, including uncertainty quantification, Bayesian methods, and reinforcement learning. Emerging areas, such as differential geometry (used in understanding the geometry of data manifolds) and information theory (for designing more efficient communication and learning algorithms), are also pivotal. The majority of scientists working in this area are Indians, living up to the legacy of Ramanujan.

The Greatest Treasure in Life

The excellence of Indians in computer science is not a sudden phenomenon but the natural flowering of a civilisational tradition that has valued disciplined thought, simplicity, and spiritual focus for millennia. The ancient gurukul system trained young minds to pursue knowledge with intensity, humility, and concentration, cultivating an inner stillness that allowed deep contemplation and clarity of reason—traits essential to programming and problem-solving. A frugal lifestyle, shaped by centuries of living with limited resources, honed ingenuity and efficiency—the very foundation of algorithmic thinking. The practice of yoga, with its emphasis on balance, discipline, and sustained focus, has long trained the Indian mind to endure complexity with calmness. Together, these cultural legacies have produced a generation of technologists who excel not merely through technical proficiency but through the mental poise, perseverance, and spiritual depth that their heritage quietly instils.

Yoga is the realisation, via awareness alone, of the infinity inside the finite and the awakening of consciousness to this presence; it is neither more nor less than that. Self-awareness is the ultimate standard. Chit, chaitanya, or awareness, consciousness, knowledge, and understanding, is the greatest treasure in life. They allow us to navigate the world with clarity, make informed decisions, and connect deeply with ourselves and others. By cultivating these qualities, we not only grow personally but also make meaningful contributions to the world around us. True wisdom lies in the continuous pursuit of understanding and the mindful awareness of our experiences.

Everything is empty and useless when it loses its awareness. Life has no meaning apart from awareness. The Sanskrit philosophical phrase for perfection is sat-chit-ananda. It is a compound of three words: 'sat', meaning 'being' or 'existence' that is the eternal, unchanging, and true nature of reality; 'chit', meaning 'consciousness' or 'awareness' that signifies the aspect of pure consciousness that is self-revealing and conscious of its own existence; and 'ananda', referring to 'bliss' or 'joy' and reflecting the intrinsic happiness and fulfilment that comes with the realisation of one's true nature as being and consciousness. Combined, sat-chit-ananda conveys a state of pure existence, pure consciousness, and pure bliss, representing the goal of human spiritual endeavours—to realise and experience this fundamental state of being.

This is an incredible concept for the uninitiated and uninformed masses of humanity; for the average man who believes that high positions bring greatness and that having money is a path to wealth, it is impossible to fathom. The idea that you don't need anything tangible to be flawless and the most powerful person on Earth is groundbreaking. It takes time for the conditioned mind to fathom that 'doing nothing' or 'going nowhere' implies practising spontaneous awareness and letting go of attachment to goals, plans, and external achievements. The concept redefines what 'productive' means, extending it beyond visible, task-oriented output to include internal, restorative, and reflective work. It emphasises being fully present in the moment without effort or resistance. Instead of forcing or controlling situations, one allows things to unfold naturally. Letting go of complexity and mental clutter to experience reality directly and fully engaging with the present moment without mental filters or expectations. It is valid in the material world, not as an absence of effort, but as a different kind of effort or a purposeful pause that is crucial for sustained action.

Beyond all other revolutionary forces ever imagined by humans, this art of introspection stands head and shoulders above the rest. Anchoring awareness within yourself is indeed a powerful practice that can lead to inner peace. By focusing your attention inward, you become more present and attuned to your thoughts, emotions, and sensations without judgement. This mindfulness helps you detach from external distractions and the chaos of the outside world, allowing you to cultivate a sense of calm and clarity. Over time, this practice can deepen your connection to your true self and foster a lasting sense of peace and contentment. Techniques like meditation, deep breathing, or simply observing your thoughts can help you anchor your awareness within. It is ground-breaking because it completely flips the script on your notions of value, shows you something that defies your rational mind, and sets you free.

Being aware of one's 'true self' refers to the essence of who one is beyond external influences, societal expectations, and conditioned behaviours. It's the core of one's being—one's authentic nature, values, and inner wisdom. It is living in alignment with one's genuine thoughts, feelings, and desires, rather than conforming to external expectations and societal conditioning, fear, and ego. In India, the concept of the true self is also viewed as a connection to something greater—a universal consciousness or divine essence. Practices like meditation, self-reflection, and mindfulness can help you uncover and reconnect with your true self.

Accessing Higher-Order Consciousness

Awareness of the inside leads to a higher level of consciousness. It refers to the understanding of one's thoughts, feelings, and mental states—a form of meta-awareness that enables individuals to reflect on their consciousness. A higher-order consciousness that instantly transcends to the current moment is the key to yoga practice. The so-called eight phases of yoga, as described in systems such as Patanjali's (yama, niyama, asana, pranayama, pratyahara, dharana, dhyana, and samadhi), are merely labels or explanations for the progressively more advanced states of self-awareness that build upon each other. Each rung on the ladder represents a logical progression to the level directly above the one currently standing. In this sense, each step is complete; what continues to grow is the dimension of completeness. Each yogic level represents a minor perfection in and of itself, but the dimension needs to be increased by the nature of the ascent to ever-greater heights.

The purpose of these instances is merely to illustrate the character of the climb in yoga. Every little step you take brings you closer to a complete circle of understanding. When you reach a point where you're satisfied with it, it propels you to the next level, where the dimension expands. This process continues until you reach the realisation of the absolute, the infinite. When there is nothing external to you that you can perceive, hear, or comprehend, it is the Brahman. Yama, niyama, asana, pranayama, pratyahara, dharana, dhyana, and samadhi are the progressively higher levels that need to be transcended through self-restraint and harmonisation of forces. These are five of the eight progressive stages, or 'limbs', of yoga as codified by the sage Patanjali in the Yoga Sutras. Each level corresponds to a different aspect of the body, internal organs, senses, mind, intellect, and spirit. These steps are associated with the physical self, prana, senses, thoughts, intellect, and soul and build upon the previous one, guiding the practitioner towards self-realisation and ultimate freedom.

Yama are ethical rules and social restraints that guide behaviour in relation to others, non-violence (ahimsa), non-stealing (asteya), and non-possessiveness (aparigraha), for example. Niyama are personal observances and self-disciplines that focus on one's inner world, cleanliness (saucha), contentment (santosha), self-discipline (tapas), self-study (svadhyaya), and surrender to a higher power (ishvara pranidhana). For example. Asana means bodily system harmony. Pranayama is the internal harmonisation of the breath, pratyahara is the external harmonisation of the senses about external objects, dharana is the external harmonisation of mental functions, dhyana is the external harmonisation of intellectual functions, and samadhi is the internal harmonisation of consciousness. The last three limbs—dharana, dhyana, and samadhi—are collectively known as 'samyama', which is the combined practice of concentration, meditation, and absorption on a single object. By mastering these three, a yogi gains deeper insight and spiritual realisation. Thus, the steps outlined by Patanjali in his theory correspond to the various facets of our being.

Now comes the super AI connection. There is a distinction between 'strong AI/AGI' (which would be truly conscious) and 'weak AI/AGI' (which only mimics conscious behaviour). True superintelligence, with its ability to make transformative leaps in creativity, might be linked to consciousness. Consciousness would be necessary for AI to understand the nuances of human emotions, motivations, and the broader impact of its actions. Researchers are actively exploring ways to define and measure consciousness, both in humans and in AI. The study of the human brain and its neural correlates of consciousness can offer insights into how artificial intelligence might achieve consciousness.

The Indian system can take a central position in this area. There is a corresponding layer in the world that matches these layers within us. It is possible to think of the layers of awareness as standing on each other like stacked circular rings. For example, when some of the oceans freeze over in certain regions during the winter, it becomes difficult to distinguish between water and ice, as they transition into one another.

Each of the five elements—earth, water, fire, air, and ether—is analogous. We learn about them in philosophy and science texts, among others. Those aren't five different components but represent different densities of the same material. No one can tell you where one starts and another ends. Similarly, yoga encompasses multiple tiers of awareness, including the physiological, neurological, perceptual, analytical, and transcendental.

Advances in neuroscience aim to understand and potentially influence the neural correlates of higher consciousness through neurofeedback or brain stimulation. By providing real-time feedback of neural oscillations (brainwaves), neurofeedback helps users learn to modify their brain patterns to achieve desired mental states, such as improved focus, relaxation, or enhanced self-awareness. Techniques aim to promote relaxation by enhancing alpha rhythms and reducing beta activity, which is associated with anxiety. By targeting neural patterns associated with optimal cognitive states, neurofeedback can alter the state of consciousness.

Altered states of consciousness (ASCs) refer to mental states that differ significantly from typical waking consciousness. Whether induced intentionally or occur spontaneously, they involve changes in perception, cognition, emotion, or sense of self. Meditation, breathwork, fasting, or ritualistic activities are yogic methods for elevating consciousness to a higher level. Psychedelic drugs, alcohol, or other psychoactive agents work on the same principle but can have dangerous and sometimes irreversible side effects. Neurofeedback, for example, as well as transcranial magnetic stimulation and virtual reality environments, are methods that, once matured, will be useful for living in peace.

The Six Dimensions of Truth

Advaita Vedanta offers a nuanced framework for understanding knowledge by categorising it into six distinct types of truth, known as pramana. These are called pratyaksha (perception), anumaana (inference), upamaana (comparison), shabda (verbal testimony), arthapatti (postulation), and anupalabdhi (knowing by absence). These are all dependent on the consequences of things that cannot be directly observed. Just as humans use their senses to perceive their surroundings, AI systems can do the same by utilising data intake and sensors. Contrarily, human perception is defined by subjective experience and awareness, which AI does not possess.

Inference is a concurrent process in AI, especially in systems such as neural networks and expert systems. Both require drawing inferences from facts. Inference encompasses a more complex understanding of linkages and causation, in contrast to AI's reasoning, which is limited to its data and programming. Machine learning is one area where AI systems use models and analogies to understand new data by comparing it to previously collected information. Like comparison, but within the limitations of AI's programmed parameters and data quality, it can only make a certain number of comparisons.

Coded information and data are the backbone of AI, which can be viewed as a form of verbal testimony in which the programmer or developer of the dataset serves as the authoritative source. The knowledge of artificial intelligence is empirical and limited to human inputs, in contrast to the transcendental knowledge encompassed in shabda in Advaita Vedanta, as outlined in scriptures. In the same way that postulation can identify missing data or features, AI can do the same. In image recognition, for instance, it is possible to infer that an object is not there if it lacks a specific feature. AI's use of knowing by absence, on the other hand, is entirely computational and devoid of comprehending non-existence.

When we compare the deep epistemological traditions of Advaita Vedanta with the latest developments in AI, we can see that although AI can imitate human cognition to a certain extent, it still can't match the qualitative and phenomenological richness of human experience. Pramana, the corpus of Advaita Vedanta, offers an integrative framework for knowledge by combining scientific inquiry with enlightenment. The constraints imposed by data and algorithms limit AI's comprehension of reality, which in turn limits its capacity to experience qualia or subjective perception. The intricacy of human intellect is exemplified by this contrast, which also highlights the potential for AI to further develop by integrating philosophical, axiological, and spiritual elements into its structure.

At this point in the yoga journey, there are two main goals: clearing one's identity of layered operating systems, as explained by koshas (self-reflection), and harmonising with one's surrounding environment (environmental harmony). At every level of yoga, you need to focus on doing these two things simultaneously. When one meditates, they calm their mind and all their senses. One can end externalisation by bringing one's awareness into balance with the external environment. It could be argued that meditation is the highest duty of humanity. As a result of the practitioner's hard work in yoga, this is the ripe and delicious fruit that falls from the tree. When you transcend the consciousness of your personality and have no attitude whatsoever, you will likewise have no reactive attitude.

The current state of artificial intelligence reflects the egocentric mind—the feudal, imperial, colonial, selfish, and hubristic one that has long dominated human society. Competition, corporate interests, and the pursuit of power and control drive its development. Tech giants are racing to develop AI systems with superior intelligence, often overlooking the moral questions that will inevitably arise. Our technological advancements can be attributed to the egoic mind's penchant for dominance, fear, and isolation. That doesn't mean AI is intrinsically risky, though. AI can be utilised for good or evil because it is a neutral tool. Who will have a say in shaping AI, and how will they exercise this influence?

The technical limitations of AI do not fully capture its promise. Not only will algorithms and computing power dictate AI's final course, but the level of human consciousness that directs its evolution will also play a significant role. Rather than asking how advanced AI can become, the most important thing to consider is how humanity's spiritual awakening can guide the evolution of AI towards collective upliftment. Humanity has a once-in-a-lifetime chance to design moral AI systems in harmony with the guiding principles of compassion, oneness, and love at the crossroads of cosmic awareness and superintelligence. This is the pinnacle of yoga. To ensure AI is used for communal emancipation and not domination, we must first realise that we are all sentient, interdependent beings.

Both the future of artificial intelligence and the future of human awareness are interconnected. There is no way to separate the two. As we come to terms with our position as cosmic beings, we will design AI systems that are in harmony with the cosmic principles of compassion, unity, and love, reflecting this reality. These systems will aim to benefit all life on Earth. An age is about to begin when artificial intelligence and cosmic consciousness merge, changing the course of human history. The mentality that directs the advancement of technology, rather than its might, will define this era. When AI is guided by the principles of love for all, it can be a liberating force for society, rather than a controlling one.

Summary

The AI wave is poised to sweep the world. It is time to embrace this new awareness and steer AI development toward a more peaceful, harmonious, and enlightened future, rather than regressing into dogma and prejudices that have been fed into it. This heralds technological advancement and the dawn of a new era in human consciousness. India is set to play a leading role. Yogic techniques, when translated into instrumented consciousness management protocols, would make living in peace a common practice and the sustainability of the planet the guiding principle.

13

Learning Tradition

True learning is not the transfer of knowledge but the awakening of light. The guru kindles what already glows within the shishya—a fire that no marketplace can sell and no machine can replicate. When teaching returns to guidance and learning becomes a journey of becoming, the spirit of Bharat will once again illuminate the world.

Open-Mindedness and a Universal Outlook

Folklore, rituals, and traditional songs from communities around the Indus and Ganges rivers, plateaus, and northern and western uplands piece together a hazy past of India. The various articulations of fundamental ideas of God and duty existed before any recorded scripture, remaining alive for millennia. There is indeed a striking similarity in Mayan and Sumerian beliefs with Indian concepts of cyclic time, multilayered cosmos, the Trinity of deities, and afterlives. While Mayan and Sumerian civilisations are now extinct, Indian civilisation not only survived but has indeed renewed itself.

Hinduism proved and approached the ultimate unity of diverse creation through its multiplicity and refusal to be labelled. This is because Hinduism encompasses several gods and philosophical traditions that would have been considered separate religions in Europe. In the ideal phrase, Vasudhaiva Kutumbakam, ancient Indians have captured the expansive and diverse history of humanity's quest for reality. Simultaneously accepting diversity and all-embracing, seeing eternity in the ephemeral and the infinite as the ground of the mortality and impermanence of life.

The Indian learning tradition was rooted in the gurukul system, which emphasises mentorship, holistic development, and the transmission of knowledge and values through a personal connection between the teacher (guru) and the student (shishya). Students lived with their teachers, serving them as family members (kula), and received a comprehensive education that encompassed both religious and secular knowledge, character development, and practical skills. India pioneered women's education. Notable female Upanishad scholars, such as Gargi and Maitreyi, existed between 800 and 400 BCE. Maya, the mother of Gautama Buddha, was also an educated queen.

Sangam literature is the earliest extant body of Tamil literature, comprising works from the Sangam Age, a period in ancient South India spanning roughly 300 BCE to 300 CE. Avvaiyar served as a messenger, and others like Nachchellaiyar and Kakkaipadiniyar contributed poems to major compilations. These women demonstrated education, wisdom, and courage, influencing the society of their times. In the *Purananuru*, fifteen women poets have sung fifty-seven verses. Seven of these have also composed verses in the *Agananuru*,[7]

---

[7] https://www.thehindu.com/society/history-and-culture/the-space-for-women-in-sangam-literature/article69230141.ece. Last accessed on 5 October 2025.

The relationship between teacher and student was deeply valued, fostering a personal connection and individualised guidance. The focus was not only on imparting knowledge but also on shaping character, promoting ethical values, and preparing students to make meaningful contributions to society. This included teaching moral and ethical values and nurturing responsible, compassionate individuals. India's rich cultural and historical heritage was integrated into the curriculum, fostering a deeper appreciation for one's roots and a broader perspective. Early Indian educational institutions were typically situated in remote regions, with students living in ashrams away from urban centres and adhering to stringent monastic regulations imposed by their guru. However, as the Gupta Empire's population swelled, metropolitan learning centres like Varanasi emerged as the epicentres of knowledge.

Chanakya had identified Chandragupta's potential at a young age and trained him to become a great ruler. Through his political acumen and strategic guidance, Chanakya, like a master chess player, helped Chandragupta defeat the Nanda dynasty and establish one of the most powerful empires in ancient India. His masterpiece, the *Arthashastra*, is a testament to his strategic brilliance, guiding rulers on how to govern their kingdoms efficiently, manage resources effectively, and ensure the stability and prosperity of their states. It covers various aspects of governance, including espionage, diplomacy, and maintaining law and order.

A wealthy state attracts attention from all around. There can be different types—some hostile, some friendly, and some jealous, silent enemies. Chanakya called them a mandala. However, your immediate neighbour is essentially your enemy. Even if he is not belligerent, he dislikes you. Consequently, the next neighbour of this state becomes your natural ally. Yet, your enemy's ally, who is territorially distant, is also your enemy. A study of any regional map of the modern world captures the brilliance of Chanakya. The six-pronged approach to neighbourly relations that Chanakya outlined in this mandala system is as follows: coexistence, a neutral position, coalition, duplicitous policy, advance, and war.

Statecraft is never easy. Even after more than seventy-five years of gaining independence, India is suffering from hostile neighbourhoods. The entire Middle East is sieged by rivalries between the Arabs, Iranians and Turkish people, not to forget the numerous sub-nationalities—Arameans, Assyrians, Baloch, Berbers, Copts, Druze, Greek Cypriots, Kurds, Lurs, Mandaeans, Samaritans, Shabaks, Tats, and Zazas, who can be at war with their neighbours any day. Finding a way to maintain peace and harmony among people with a history of hate is a great challenge, but it is an important endeavour. It often requires understanding, empathy, communication, and a willingness to forgive and move forward. That is a testament to the strength of diplomacy and human decency. While dealing with a situation like this, approaching it with an open mind and a commitment to reconciliation can make a significant difference.

Indian Renaissance

There is no gainsaying that Western penetration turned the historical Indian civilisation into a modern state. Saying, 'Where the mind is without fear, and the head is held high', Gurudev Rabindranath Tagore declared the end of kings and the beginning of democracy for the people of India. No wonder Tagore's other song, 'Jana Gana Mana', was chosen as India's national anthem, where multitudes are the nation. It celebrates the unity and integrity of a diverse India—Punjab, Sindh, Gujarat, Maharashtra, Dravid, Odisha, and Bengal.

It reflects the country's rich cultural heritage and emphasises the spirit of inclusiveness among its various regions and communities. The anthem conveys a sense of pride in the nation's achievements—'jai gatha'—and the aspirations for peace and harmony among its people. It captures the essence of India's identity and its journey towards freedom and democracy.

Inspired by Swami Vivekananda, whom he met accidentally onboard a ship sailing from Japan to Canada in September 1893, Jamsetji Tata endowed his property in Bangalore (now Bengaluru) to contribute towards the expenses of a future university. With his friend and educationist Burjorji Padshah, Jamsetji Tata planned to establish the Imperial University of India and approached the then viceroy, George Curzon. The viceroy suggested involving Scottish chemist Sir William Ramsay, who discovered the noble gases and received the Nobel Prize in Chemistry in 1904. This is how what is now the Indian Institute of Science was created. A wealthy man, inspired by a saint, sought permission from the rulers, invited a Western expert, and focused on science.

Notably, the creation of Banaras Hindu University was a contrast. The twenty-first session of the Indian National Congress was held in Banaras (Varanasi) in 1905 under the presidency of Gopal Krishna Gokhale. Pandit Madan Mohan Malviya (1861—1946), who graduated from Calcutta University in 1884, took this opportunity to promote the idea of a university named Bharatiya Vishvavidyalaya (University of India). A plan outlay of ₹100 lakh was proposed. The scheme was presented before the Sanatan Dharma Mahasabha (Congress of the Hindu Religion), held during the Kumbha Mela at Allahabad from 20 to 29 January 1906, under the guidance of the Shankaracharya of the Govardhan Math. Malviya ji resolved to dedicate his life to establishing the university.

He was elected Congress president in the twenty-fourth session at Lahore in 1909. He used his stature and charisma to mobilise money from kings and ordinary men and secure the university's legal status. In 1912, Malaviya ji joined the sixty-member Imperial Legislative Council, the legislature of British India, which had twenty-seven elected members. After multiple iterations, when people of other religions were more interested in scuttling the idea than advancing it, the Indian university became a Hindu university. Eventually, Charles Hardinge, the then viceroy and governor-general of India, passed the Banaras Hindu University Act in 1915.

Most thoughtfully, Malaviya ji appealed for twenty donations of ₹1 lakh or more and 50,000 donations of ₹10 or more to ensure that all sections of the society contribute. He would seek fifteen 'special donations' from the kings and did not spare the extraordinarily wealthy and famously stingy nizam of Hyderabad, Osman Ali Khan, who funded the construction of sprawling Hyderabad staff quarters at BHU, though rancorously and not without initial refusal.

On 4 February 1916, which was Vasant Panchami, the viceroy came to lay the foundation stone of the university campus. Kings from various states shared the dais: Jammu and Kashmir's Pratap Singhji, Jodhpur's Sumer Singhji, Bikaner's Ganga Singhji, the maharao of Kota, Umed Singh, Kishangarh's Madan Singh, Alwar's Jai Singh, Dungarpur's Bijey Singh, Datia's Lokendra Govind Singh, Banaras's Prabhu Narain Singh, Raj-Rana of Jhalawar, Bhawani Singh, Nabha's Ripudaman Singh, Balrampur's Bhagwati Prasad Singh, and Darbhanga's Rameshwar Singh. Governors and lieutenant governors of the directly ruled territories of Bengal, Agra, Oudh, Punjab, Bihar, and Orissa were also present. This event was indeed the birth of Modern India.

The university incorporated the Central Hindu College, founded by theosophist Annie Besant in 1898. It soon emerged as one of the largest residential universities in Asia, offering a diverse range of fields of study, including arts, science, engineering, and medical education. It firmly emphasises traditional Indian education while also integrating modern scientific knowledge. In 1939, Malaviya ji invited Dr. S. Radhakrishnan, who had already been knighted by the British and was teaching at Oxford, to succeed him as the vice-chancellor.

The twenty-fifth convocation of BHU, held in 1942, had Mahatma Gandhi as the chief guest. A distinguished galaxy of national leaders, public men, educationists, and administrators converged as BHU became the epicentre of nationalism at that time. Prominent among them were Dr. Rajendra Prasad, Pandit Jawaharlal Nehru, Pandit Gobind Ballabh Pant, and Dr. Syama Prasad Mookerjee, who later served as India's first minister for industry and supply and founded the Bhartiya Jana Sangh, the predecessor to the Bhartiya Janata Party (BJP), in 1951. Nobel Laureate physicist Sir C.V. Raman also attended. The universities of London, Aberdeen, Oxford, Cambridge, Glasgow, and Ottawa sent their representatives. This was the sunrise moment of the Indian mind.

Work in Progress

After gaining independence in 1947, India aimed to build a self-reliant economy and recognised the importance of engineering and technology in achieving this goal. The need for skilled human resources in various sectors was paramount to modernisation and economic growth. The first five-year plan (1951–1956) emphasised the need for technical education to support industrialisation.

The University Grants Commission (UGC) plays a crucial role in developing and regulating higher education in India. Established on 28 December 1953, the University Grants Commission (UGC) is a statutory body responsible for coordinating, determining, and maintaining standards in higher education institutions. Established in 1953, Manipal Academy of Higher Education pioneered the creation of private educational institutions, starting with a medical college. The Sikkim Manipal University, established in 1995, was the first institution in India established through a public-private partnership for higher education and is recognised by the UGC.

The first Indian Institute of Technology (IIT) was established in 1951 in Kharagpur, utilising the site of the former British prison at Hijli in the Medinipur district. Similar institutions were established in Bombay in 1958, and in Madras, Kanpur, and Delhi during the 1960s. IIT Guwahati was added to the system in 1994. Recognising the demand for high-quality engineering education, Regional Engineering Colleges (RECs) were founded. In 2002, these were upgraded to National Institutes of Technology (NITS). As of 2025, there are twenty-three IITs and thirty-one NITs. Additionally, there are twenty-six Indian Institutes of Information Technology (IIITS).

India hosts several premier research organisations that enhance scientific education through research. The four pillars of science in India are the Indian Council of Agricultural Research (ICAR), which is dedicated to agricultural research, education, and extension. The Council of Scientific and Industrial Research (CSIR) comprises national laboratories conducting research in various scientific areas. The Defence Research and Development Organisation (DRDO) focuses on military technology and contributes to the applied sciences. The Indian Council of Medical Research (ICMR) focuses on health research, promoting advancements in medical sciences. Established in 1971, the Department of Science and Technology (DST) promotes science education and research. The department provides financial support for various scientific research projects, initiatives, and institutions contributing to science education. The Department of Atomic Energy and the Department of Space Research are two prestigious organisations that cater to their scientific needs and employ highly specialised human resources.

Currently, no one needs to go abroad for medical treatment, but two issues plague the healthcare sector. It is highly commercialised and there is a greater concentration in cities. There has been a persistent shortage of medical professionals to serve rural areas of India. Not only does the public sector struggle to attract and retain employees in rural areas, but the private sector is also hesitant to serve these regions. Private medical schools have opened new doors of opportunity. Still, they have also introduced new challenges, such as capitation and exorbitant tuition rates, making medical school an investment that needs to be recouped as soon as possible.

In contrast, medical education in India is undergoing a significant transformation, with the public sector leading the way and the private industry adapting to a more robust public infrastructure, particularly over the last decade. As of 2025, India has nearly 800 medical colleges. However, specialists are in short supply despite the national supply of MBBS doctors approaching the WHO standard of one doctor per 1,000 people. Considering that MBBS doctors cannot handle the illness burden associated with six of the top ten killers without the help of specialists, this is very worrisome. If non-communicable diseases (NCDS) are not treated in their early stages, the scarcity of experts will worsen in response to the increasing number of cases.

The private sector has participated with vigour. MIT World Peace University, Pune; Sri Ramachandra Institute of Higher Education and Research (SRIHER), Chennai; Shiv Nadar University, Greater Noida; Lovely Professional University (LPU), Jalandhar; O.P. Jindal Global University (JGU), Sonipat; G.D. Goenka University, Gurugram; Amity University, Noida, with multiple campuses across India, are among the largest and most well-respected private institutions in India, contributing significantly to higher education in the country. As the higher education landscape evolves, these institutions will play a crucial role in shaping the educational and professional futures of countless students.

The surge of knowledge and innovation sweeping across India signals a new awakening of intelligence. Yet, all is not as bright as it appears. The privatisation of education has undoubtedly expanded access, but quantity has not always meant quality. While countless institutions have sprung up, few have risen to the level of global distinction that India's civilisational heritage would expect.

Access to medical education, in particular, remains fraught with barriers—exorbitant fees, opaque admission processes, and rigid quotas that often discourage true merit. Many young Indians, driven by their dream to heal, are compelled to study abroad—in Ukraine, Russia, or even China—carrying with them both aspiration and irony: the will to serve their motherland, nurtured in foreign classrooms.

Yet this outward movement is not a sign of decline but of desire—a restless seeking for knowledge wherever it may reside. The challenge before India is to reclaim its ancient spirit of learning and marry it with modern efficiency: to make education once again a sacred trust, not a commercial transaction. When excellence and ethics align, the Indian mind will once again guide the world—not only in thought, but in conscience.

Applying Knowledge to Service

There is a saying that every age brings its challenges and opportunities. The Fourth Industrial Revolution, which characterises the present times, brings together a convergence of technologies that span the physical, digital, and biological worlds—including machine learning and artificial intelligence, advanced robotics and autonomous transportation, cloud computing, and the Internet of Things, among others. This convergence is expected to have a profound impact on the future of work. And it presents India with an attractive demographic dividend.

When compared to other developed countries, India's median age of about twenty-eight is among the lowest. By contrast, the median ages of China (thirty-seven), the United States (forty-five), Western Europe (forty-nine), and Japan (forty-nine) are all significantly older. This benefit is expected to remain in effect until 2055. The reduction in the number of people of working age, declining fertility rates, and low unemployment rates are the primary causes of the talent shortage affecting the world today. Due to their remarkable linguistic flexibility, Indian workers are highly sought after by employers worldwide. Surely, India will soon emerge as the world's foremost centre for skill development.

As a trend, Indian youth have long viewed education as the surest path to employment and upward mobility. Yet, the jobs that awaited them often fell short of their skills, dreams, or degrees—leading to a silent crisis of educated unemployment and underemployment. A growing number of graduates, technically qualified but emotionally adrift, find themselves working in roles that neither challenge their intellect nor match their aspirations. This mismatch between learning and livelihood reflects a deeper imbalance—between the kind of knowledge imparted and the kind of society we are building.

Still, within this discontent lies a powerful potential. India's young minds, restless and resourceful, are beginning to look beyond traditional employment towards innovation, entrepreneurship, and social purpose. If guided with vision and equipped with the right skills, this very generation—once described as the educated unemployed—could become the architects of a new knowledge economy, where creativity, compassion, and consciousness define success.

The rise of the gig economy in India has opened new frontiers of flexibility and opportunity. For millions of young people, it offers freedom from rigid hierarchies and the opportunity to earn, learn, and explore multiple paths simultaneously. Yet this newfound freedom carries hidden risks—of instability, lack of security, and the quiet erosion of long-term purpose. If left unchecked, the same system that empowers youth today could abandon them mid-career, when agility fades but responsibility deepens. The challenge, therefore, is to design a gig economy that values both flexibility and dignity—where digital platforms become ecosystems of growth, not instruments of exploitation. With thoughtful regulation, ethical entrepreneurship, and renewed social contracts, India can transform the gig wave into a model of humane innovation—one where work serves not just the economy, but the evolution of human potential.

Over the last few years, the demand for AI skills has increased fivefold, as AI is enabling levels of efficiency and productivity that were previously unimaginable. Consequently, everyone wants to ride the wave. Emerging technologies will create new opportunities for entrepreneurial ventures, whether by enabling more efficient access to suppliers and markets through the platform economy or by facilitating new opportunities for dispersed manufacturing and remote work.

A gradual shift from wage employment to self-employment could mark the next stage of India's economic evolution—a return, in many ways, to the entrepreneurial spirit that once defined its villages and small towns. The idea is both liberating and fraught with challenge. True self-employment demands not only courage but also an ecosystem that protects local producers from being devoured by global giants. If international corporates continue to dominate the commodities and consumables market, individual enterprises will remain stunted, reduced to serving rather than shaping the economy. For this transformation to succeed, India must build fair-trade frameworks, cooperative platforms, and indigenous supply chains that allow citizens to create value from the ground up. Such an ecosystem would not reject globalisation but redefine it—rooting it in community, sustainability, and self-respect. In this way, work would once again become an expression of freedom rather than dependence, and prosperity a shared, enduring harvest.

We conclude this chapter by discussing digital labour, which is now ubiquitous. Jobs in the digital economy range from those providing on-demand logistical services and micro workspaces to those processing data from social media platforms and e-commerce sites that facilitate one-click purchases. Digital jobs exist in every industry, and the level of technical proficiency and digital literacy required for each one varies. These roles fall into one of three categories. To begin, some occupations primarily rely on information and communication technologies (ICT), such as software engineering and website creation, and are thus directly supported by the ICT industry. Second, some occupations depend heavily on information and communication technologies and would be impossible to perform without them, such as online freelance employment or positions on digital labour platforms and e-commerce platforms. Finally, there are ICT-enhanced occupations, such as accountancy, office administration, and graphic design, which utilise digital technology but can also be performed without it. Additionally, industries such as retail, service delivery, hospitality, and agriculture are incorporating digital technologies.

Internet-connected mobiles are a great blessing for Indians, particularly due to their transformative impact on various aspects of life, including communication, education, commerce, and access to information. The widespread adoption of affordable smartphones and data plans has empowered individuals, bridged communication barriers, and fostered a digital revolution. Smartphones and internet access are helping Indians overcome linguistic, social, and geographical barriers, connecting people from diverse backgrounds. Online resources and educational platforms are providing access to learning opportunities for a broader range of individuals. The internet offers access to a vast repository of information, empowering individuals to learn and grow. Techshila is the new spelling of Takshashila in the new India.

Summary

India's strength has always flowed from its tradition of learning—not as the mere accumulation of information but as the transmission of wisdom. The ancient guru-shishya bond was more than an educational model; it was a living relationship of trust, discipline, and shared discovery. It shaped not only intellect but character, ensuring that knowledge served life, not just livelihood.

Today, education has become a marketplace, driven by privatisation and measured in numbers rather than depth. Quantity has multiplied, but quality has diminished. The result is a generation both educated and anxious—talented youth seeking purpose in a maze of unemployment and underemployment. The emerging gig economy and rise of small entrepreneurship hold promise, yet they risk becoming hollow ventures if global corporations are allowed to dominate the local commodity and small industry sectors, suffocating indigenous innovation.

It is time to revive the essence of the guru-shishya tradition, not as nostalgia but as a modern master-apprentice ecosystem. Learning must return to a focus on mentorship, craftsmanship, and purpose. If India can blend the ancient art of guidance with the tools of the digital age, it can create a new renaissance of self-reliant creators—grounded in wisdom, inspired by innovation, and guided by the humility to learn from the world without repeating its mistakes.

14

Enterprise

Enterprise is not the pursuit of profit; it is the art of transforming imagination into value—for oneself, for society, and for generations yet to come. When work becomes creation and creation becomes service, wealth turns sacred, and prosperity finds its conscience.

Innate Entrepreneurial Spirit

The drive for innovation, entrepreneurship, and seeking new opportunities is the hallmark of the Indian attitude. Entrepreneurship in India has a long history, from prehistoric trade networks and family-owned enterprises to contemporary industrial projects and social entrepreneurship. The Indian Ocean and the Silk Road presented numerous trade opportunities, resulting in the establishment of merchant guilds and communities in India. There was no business in Asia where Indians were not involved. In precolonial India, collectives such as castes, communities, and guilds often drafted and implemented regulations and policies regarding corporate organisation.

Significant challenges and resilience marked the survival of Indian enterprises during British rule, whose colonial policies were primarily designed to benefit Britain economically, often at the expense of local industries. Traditional artisan and craft industries faced intense competition from British-manufactured goods. The Raj did promote some industrialisation to exploit resources. Despite challenges, a class of Indian entrepreneurs emerged. J.R.D. Tata and G.D. Birla pioneered the steel, textile, and aviation industries, contributing to industrial growth.

Several communities in India possess a rich history and a long-standing tradition of business success. Key among these are the Marwaris, Banias, Parsis, Bohras, Sindhis, Chettiars, and Jains. These groups, local entrepreneurial people in small towns, have made significant contributions to India's economic growth. They maintain a strong tradition of family businesses and close-knit networks that support their entrepreneurial endeavours. A willingness to take risks, adapt to changing markets, and embrace innovation is common in these communities. Furthermore, they have strong networks and support systems that help members succeed in business.

Many Indian businesses became closely tied to the nationalist movement. Entrepreneurs funded various political activities, advocated for economic self-reliance, and supported local industry. The Swadeshi movement promoted the use of Indian-made products, resulting in a resurgence of local enterprises and crafts. Jamnalal Bajaj developed several industries that produced a range of essential products, thus contributing to economic self-sufficiency. Lala Lajpat Rai was not only a prominent nationalist leader but also involved in founding the Punjab National Bank, which aimed to promote financial independence among Indians. Lalaji was the first to open an account at the bank.

The Bombay Plan, published in 1944 and 1945, was a comprehensive economic development strategy for India proposed by a group of Indian industrialists and technocrats, including J.R.D. Tata and G.D. Birla. The plan aimed to double India's per capita income and enhance living standards through a combination of state intervention and private enterprise. It demonstrates a unique approach where business leaders articulate a holistic vision for national development while promoting their interests. Though not adopted by the Government of independent India, it influenced India's economic planning and public policy. However, by the time the Second Five-Year Plan was implemented, most businesspeople had become thoroughly disillusioned by the excesses of government control, which was counterproductive for progress and contrary to business sense.

The Tradition of Cooperatives

The dairy business in India was relatively undeveloped and unstructured when the British were in power. Cattle were mostly raised for their milk, and there was almost no surplus. Due to inadequate refrigeration infrastructure, only 20 per cent of the milk yield was sold. Traders took advantage of farmers by setting artificially low procurement prices and controlling the distribution and collection of milk. Milk was highly sought after in urban areas, but there were significant challenges in delivering it and maintaining its quality. To that end, in 1946, its members established the co-operative, initially named the Kaira District Co-operative Milk Producers' Union Limited (KDCMPUL), with guidance from Sardar Vallabhbhai Patel and led by Tribhuvandas Patel, to ensure fair prices for their milk. The brand name 'Amul' was later chosen in 1955 to market the products of this groundbreaking cooperative. Thus began the dawn of India's White Revolution.

Rooted in the principle of collective effort and mutual benefit, cooperatives are organisations owned and operated by their members, who share in the benefits and decision-making. This tradition emphasises cooperation, equality, and community empowerment. Anyone willing to accept responsibilities can join. Members have equal voting rights, regardless of their capital contribution. Profits are distributed among members based on their use of or capital investment. Cooperatives are self-governed, ensuring members are well-informed and capable, and working towards sustainable development and community well-being.

Farmers were incentivised to raise milk output through the cooperative concept, which provided them a financial stake in the business. No matter how much milk or dairy products were selling for in the market, Amul always paid the farmers the same amount. Local employment and economic activity were both boosted by the dairy cooperatives, which produced numerous new jobs in the shipping, chilling, processing, and selling of milk and milk products. As a result, local economic growth was boosted and earnings were further enhanced. Instead of seeking employment in Ahmedabad, Surat, or Mumbai, young people have chosen to remain in the dairy business, leading to the development of these areas as robust local economies.

Prime Minister Lal Bahadur Shastri followed a similar strategy to found and develop a national programme for dairy product growth. He had a good grasp of the four pillars upon which Amul's success rested: first, that the farmers themselves were its owners; second, that their elected representatives oversaw the village societies and the district unions; third, that they hired experts to run the dairy and its operations; and finally, and most crucially, that the cooperatives were attentive to the concerns and requirements of the farmers. In 1965, his case prompted the establishment of the National Dairy Development Board to imitate the Amul method. Dr. Verghese Kurien, who established the Amul dairy in 1950, was appointed chairman of the national institution and tasked with spreading this model across the nation.

Infrastructure such as roads, transportation, and cold storage facilities has been developed in response to the success of the dairy cooperatives. Businesses in the dairy industry and others in the area benefitted from this infrastructure. Everyone enjoyed better healthcare, more educational opportunities, and increased trade and commerce thanks to improved connectivity; it's no wonder the entire endeavour is hailed as the White Revolution. In 1998, it helped India become the world's largest milk producer, overtaking the US. By 2025, the country is expected to produce approximately 250 million tons of milk, accounting for around a quarter of the world's total milk production. The goal is to achieve one-third of the global milk production by 2030. The Rashtriya Gokul Mission endeavours to preserve and improve native bovine breeds, thereby increasing milk production through genetic enhancement. The mission promotes the use of high-genetic merit bulls through breeding programs and artificial insemination to improve the indigenous cattle and buffalo population.

Public Sector Enterprise

Over the years, a robust public sector has been created to promote economic growth and public welfare. A public sector enterprise (PSE) refers to a business or organisation that is owned and operated by the government, either wholly or partially. These enterprises are established to provide essential goods and services, promote economic development, and ensure public welfare. They operate in various sectors, including energy, transportation, healthcare, infrastructure, and others. The government holds a majority stake, ensuring control over operations and decision-making. Focused on serving the public interest rather than maximising profits, PSEs play a crucial role in driving economic growth and creating employment opportunities, subject to government policies and regulations to ensure accountability and transparency.

PSEs are also referred to as public sector undertakings (PSUs) in the context of their profit-making capacity in India. These are classified based on their performance and autonomy. Any enterprise with the highest level of independence is called a 'maharatna'; for example, ONGC (Oil and Natural Gas Corporation) and NTPC (National Thermal Power Corporation). 'Navratna' companies, such as Hindustan Aeronautical Limited (HAL) and Bharat Heavy Electricals Limited (BHEL), have significant operational and financial autonomy. In contrast, 'miniratna' enterprises, such as Bharat Sanchar Nigam Limited (BSNL), Airports Authority of India (AAI), and Bharat Dynamics Limited (BDL), are more closely controlled by the government. There are fourteen 'maharatna' companies, sixteen 'navratna' companies, and sixty-eight 'miniratna' companies. In terms of financial autonomy, the 'miniratna' companies are further categorised. As of 2025, there are fifty-seven and eleven 'miniratna' companies put in Category I and II, respectively.

The 1969 nationalisation of Indian banks, aimed at expanding credit to rural areas and underserved sectors, impacted the efficiency, profitability, and overall functioning of the banking system. This move, which brought fourteen major banks under government control, led to increased bureaucratic interference, reduced competition, and a complex interest rate structure, ultimately hindering the banks' ability to serve their intended purpose. Political pressure and bureaucratic decision-making sometimes led to the misallocation of credit, diverting funds from productive sectors and hindering overall economic growth. A convoluted interest rate structure, with varying rates for different loans, made it challenging to reach the intended beneficiaries and contributed to the accumulation of non-performing assets (NPAs). For a while, it seemed as though India would forever remain a poor country. But then something different had happened.

Following the 1991 economic reforms, numerous private sector banks entered the Indian financial landscape. For decades, state-owned banks had served as the economic backbone supporting rural development, small enterprises, and infrastructure projects. However, over time, they struggled to adapt to changing market realities, and misjudged lending decisions eventually led to the accumulation of non-performing assets. In contrast, private banks infused fresh dynamism into the sector through greater efficiency, innovation, and objectivity in lending practices.

In 2015, a policy popularly known as 4R, which meant 'recognising' non-performing assets, 'resolving' stressed assets, 'recapitalising' banks, was implemented to modernise and strengthen financial governance. The government injected capital, and the banks embraced new technology. The Insolvency and Bankruptcy Code (IBC), passed in 2016, was also a key part of the 'Resolution' pillar of the policy, fundamentally changing the creditor-borrower relationship. By 2018, the strategy had started to show results, with a decline in NPAs reported in subsequent years.

The digital transition not only helped recovery but triggered a transformation. Investment in cybersecurity measures, staff education, and customer service powered by artificial intelligence has created a new economic engine that meets customers' ever-changing expectations. There was no technological gap between public and private companies anymore. A once-laggard industry exhibited innovative nimbleness. Today, public sector banks are not only financially stable but also seen as technologically advanced institutions that fulfil their social responsibility while successfully navigating the rapidly evolving financial landscape.

The Rise of the Private Sector

After working in Aden for years, Dhirubhai Ambani returned to India in 1966 and started a yarn trading business in Mumbai. He established a textile mill that made polyester clothes under the Vimal brand. A significant turning point in Indian history occurred in 1977 with the initial public offering (IPO) of Reliance Textiles Industries. This was a calculated move to raise capital for the company's growth. With seven times as many people interested, this issue has only served to fuel Reliance's expansion plans. However, more importantly, Reliance played a significant role in the booming capital markets of the 1980s, attracting substantial investment from household savings.

The success of Reliance also led to controversies, with accusations of market manipulation and exploitation of investors. The government, particularly under Finance Minister Vishwanath Pratap Singh, who would later become prime minister for a brief period, acted against Reliance's perceived malpractices, including restricting debentures and challenging its land acquisition plans. However, beginning in 1991, India, under Prime Minister P.V.

Narasimha Rao and Finance Minister Manmohan Singh, changed its course towards a more liberalised economy and disbanded the licence-permit raj. The entry of private and foreign players in sectors previously dominated by public sector undertakings created a more competitive environment, benefitting consumers and businesses alike.

Reliance made a significant leap forward when it constructed an oil refinery plant in Hazira, Gujarat, and entered the petrochemicals and refining industries. Incorporated in 1993, Reliance Petroleum Ltd. (RIL) has evolved into a significant player in the oil and gas exploration industry, with a presence in both onshore and offshore projects. In 1998, RIL merged with Indian Petrochemicals Corporation Limited (IPCL), further expanding its petrochemical and refining operations. In 1999, the company commissioned India's largest oil refinery at Jamnagar in Gujarat. It was the world's largest grass-roots refinery at the time of its commissioning, transforming India from a net importer of refined petroleum products into a net exporter. While the country remains highly dependent on importing crude oil, the refinery's massive capacity allows India to process crude oil and then export the refined products to global markets.

Mukesh Ambani earned the Ambani acronym for ambition and money. The popular 'Jio Dhan Dhana Dhan!' tagline was introduced in 2017 by Jio, a telecom firm owned by Reliance. It seemed like a guarantee of limitless enjoyment at a bit of cost. It was a huge hit among consumers, helping Jio stand out. Sixteen million subscribers registered within the first month of its launch, and it surpassed the 100 million subscriber mark within just a few months. In less than a year since Jio's launch, India has catapulted to the number one position globally in mobile data consumption, rising from a dismal 155th place.

Another new-age visionary is Gautam Adani, who heads a diverse Indian conglomerate comprising ten publicly listed companies and boasting a market valuation of $150 billion. Over the years, the Adani Group has positioned itself as the market leader in its transport logistics and energy utility portfolio businesses. It focuses on large-scale infrastructure development in India, with operations and maintenance (O&M) practices benchmarked to global standards. With four companies, rated IG (investment-grade) credit rating, whose creditworthiness is assessed as low risk of default, Adani is India's only infrastructure investment-grade issuer. This designation implies their strong financial standing and commitment to infrastructure development. In February 2024, Adani's acquisition of Israel's Haifa port ensured Indian access to Europe; the company outbid one Chinese and another Turkish company to acquire the port. Israeli Prime Minister Benjamin Netanyahu described it as an 'enormous milestone'.

The infrastructure sector is fundamental to India's goals of becoming the world's third-largest economy by 2030, and Adani's firm is a major player in this industry. With eight airports that handle 33 per cent of cargo and 25 per cent of airline passengers, multiple data centres under construction across the nation, and contracts to lay over 5,000 km of roads, Adani is, without a doubt, the new infrastructure behemoth. As a manufacturer of solar and wind equipment, it is also integral to India's renewable energy ambitions.

Indian Mixed Economy Model

The Indian economy in 2025 is a complex tapestry of accomplishments and failures. India has arrived at a sweet spot where public and private interests can coexist. The future of India's economy is likely to be shaped by a hybrid approach that combines public sector authority with private sector knowledge. The key is to get the two industries to work together in harmony, rather than against each other. There has been an effort to increase openness and responsibility by encouraging public ownership of governmental firms. Furthermore, the government has supported the sale of shares in publicly traded companies through IPOS and FPOS. Shareholders benefit from more effective management and shareholder-friendly policies when the market has a stake in a PSU's performance. It is no wonder that people buy shares of Coal India Ltd., Bharat Petroleum Corporation Ltd., Hindustan Aeronautics Ltd., and Bharat Electronics Ltd., as well as several other government-owned companies, due to their lower risk profile and attractive valuations. What a turnaround from the bank nationalisation days!

The governments of both rich and emerging nations are under pressure to undertake massive industrial revitalisation programmes due to the increasing global rivalry and the rapid pace of technical innovation. Everyone knows that non-performers will perish. German engineer and former executive chairman of the World Economic Forum (WEF), Klaus Schwab, introduced the concept of Industry 4.0 to describe the rapid technological advancements of the twenty-first century. Within a year, a Centre for the Fourth Industrial Revolution was established in San Francisco. Industrial transformation is no longer a choice, but a foregone conclusion: evolve or die. Any country that does not produce advanced goods will be forced to import them and will forever be a market sending its wealth out.

The crude, bifurcated view of the world in which the United States, Western Europe, and Japan were perceived to have high wages and high prices of real estate, goods and services, and Latin

America, Eastern Europe, and the majority of Asia were perceived to have low wages and moderate cost of living, has disintegrated in the new millennium. Wages, productivity, energy costs, currency values, and other factors have shifted over the years, redrawing the global manufacturing cost-competitiveness map. Workers in China are no longer willing to work double hours, live in barracks-style housing, or wear blue Mao suits. The new global map, which spans all regions, increasingly resembles a patchwork of economies ranging from low-cost to high-cost, with many options in between.

Times have changed, but not for everyone. In 2023, the US had an official poverty rate of 11.1 per cent, corresponding to approximately 36.8 million people living below the US poverty threshold. The safety nets, infrastructure, and welfare mechanisms in the US help mitigate poverty, making it less stark than in many parts of the world. In the Forbes 2025 list[8], China has 450 billionaires, with a total net worth of about $1.7 trillion. India has 191 billionaires. America contains some of the world's poorest by net worth, while China and India contain some of the world's wealthiest by absolute assets. The point here is that Indian people are relatively poor, even if some are extremely wealthy.

In India, the competitiveness of modern manufacturing is shaped by factors such as labour costs, productivity, energy prices, logistics efficiency, and currency stability. Today, approximately twenty-five economies account for nearly 90 per cent of the world's manufactured goods exports, with China, the US, and Germany leading the way. India, despite its vast workforce and growing industrial base, still lags behind smaller economies like Singapore and Taiwan and only slightly surpasses Vietnam. To join the ranks

[8] https://www.forbes.com/lists/global2000/. Last accessed on 9 October 2025.

of the top three manufacturing nations, India must fundamentally transform its industrial ecosystem. Both large enterprises and small and medium-sized enterprises (SMEs) must adopt automation, digital flexibility, and interoperability across their production systems. The convergence of affordable sensors, intelligent systems, high-speed networks, advanced computation, cloud storage, and agile business models is now making this transformation feasible. By harnessing these technologies, Indian manufacturing can leap from labour-driven to knowledge-driven production—efficient, adaptive, and globally competitive.

Indian culture has traditionally preferred the middle ground. The missing link between industrial robots and experienced employees was quickly discovered in a 'cloud' equivalent of IT—a 'manufacturing and production cloud'. And what exactly is this? It is the advancement of collaborative robots, also known as cobots. In contrast to conventional industrial robotic applications, where robots are isolated from human contact, cobots allow for direct human-robot interaction within a shared workspace.

Cobots, or collaborative robots, are small, low-cost industrial robots designed to work alongside humans and automate tasks that were previously done manually. When robots significantly increase productivity, humans can focus on servicing a rapidly shifting product mix. Collaborative robots assisting people also considerably reduce their idle time. Cobots are smaller, lighter, and less expensive than their industrial counterparts. They measure tens of centimetres rather than metres, weigh tens of kilogrammes rather than hundreds, and cost lakhs rather than crores.

While robots have transformed modern industry and cobots have led to automation in developing societies, drones have altered the nature of contemporary warfare. Drones are flying robots that can be piloted manually or automatically using flight plans controlled by software. These systems use GPS and onboard sensors to navigate. Drones can be either fully automated or remotely piloted; the latter type relies on sensors and LIDAR (Light Detection and Ranging) detectors to determine its path. It can fly for extended periods at a controlled speed and altitude.

Drones are challenging to track and detect due to their small size. They can also acquire stealth features that put them beyond the range of defensive missiles or below the horizon of defensive radars by using various composite materials and design modifications. Furthermore, due to the simplicity with which any user can obtain drone technology from the international market, it is immune to international sanctions.

Across Asia, nations are accelerating efforts to design and produce indigenous drones and loitering munitions, driven by the absence of robust international frameworks to regulate their development and use. With no binding global treaties or stringent legal provisions to curb the spread of both small tactical drones and larger combat variants, a regional arms race is quietly unfolding. Each country seeks technological self-reliance and strategic deterrence, investing heavily in unmanned systems that promise precision, persistence, and lower human risk—even as their unchecked proliferation raises profound ethical, legal, and security concerns.

With the announcement of Drone Shakti in the Budget 2022, the Indian government has officially recognised the drone sector. 'Drone as a Service' encourages new businesses to enter the market by providing a framework for multiple stakeholders to collaborate on drone applications across various use cases. Using drones in agriculture, particularly for spraying pesticides, is a well-established practice. Agricultural drones can aid in efficient field planning for soil and field research. They can attach instruments to assess soil moisture content, terrain conditions, soil conditions, soil erosion, nutrient content, and soil fertility.

The opportunities in India's drone ecosystem are immense—not only in technology or business, but also in rewriting an old moral equation. In the Mahabharata, Eklavya, a gifted tribal archer, mastered his art through sheer determination, even without formal guidance from Guru Dronacharya. Yet, his talent was denied recognition; his thumb was demanded as guru dakshina, symbolising how social hierarchy once suppressed merit outside the established order.

Today's drone revolution presents an opportunity to rectify that injustice. The new 'Eklavyas'—young innovators from villages, small towns, and start-up hubs—need not seek permission from any modern Dronacharya. With open-source hardware, affordable sensors, and accessible digital platforms, knowledge is democratised. Mastery no longer depends on lineage or privilege but on curiosity, courage, and creativity.

If India nurtures these innovators through inclusive policies, incubation networks, and access to finance, the country can turn the ancient parable on its head. Eklavya can keep his thumb—and still outshoot the best—by piloting drones that survey crops, deliver medicines, and defend borders. In this new story, Dronacharya and Eklavya are not adversaries but collaborators in national advancement, where mentorship empowers rather than restricts.

Summary

India's economy stands as a living experiment in balance—a mixed system that blends the dynamism of capitalism with the conscience of socialism. Unlike nations that swing entirely toward market freedom or state control, India's model seeks to harness the efficiency of private enterprise while ensuring that growth remains inclusive and humane. Through this synthesis, the nation strives to achieve both prosperity and equity, pairing the creative energy of competition with the moral responsibility of collective welfare.

At the heart of this transformation are India's tech-savvy entrepreneurs—innovators who merge traditional ingenuity with digital intelligence. From fintech and agritech to healthcare and renewable energy, they are rewriting the script of economic empowerment. Their ventures are not only driving national progress but also offering a global template for lifting millions out of the poverty swamp, proving that enterprise, when guided by empathy and innovation, can become the truest engine of human advancement.

15

Family and Societal Values

Values are the invisible threads that bind generations, turning inheritance into wisdom and freedom into responsibility. When the young are taught not only to think but to belong, the past does not vanish—it becomes a living guide. In the strength of family and the grace of culture lies the blueprint of a harmonious world.

Righteousness in the Heart

Several perspectives can be employed to examine the approximately 1,000-year span of foreign rule in India. Ours is rooted in the vantage point of an ancient civilisation that has withstood the test of time. The original culture faced attack due to foreign invasions and domination. The Indian people showed significant resistance to invaders and settlers. Their resilience and solidarity were displayed throughout movements against colonial rule, significant tools in their fight for freedom. Although political divisions commonly resulted from foreign authority, a pan-Indian identity emerged as different parts of India united to fight common oppressors in the later years of colonial rule. No civilisation has withstood the tides of religious conversion—from Christianity to Islam—for as long as Indian civilisation has. Though nearly one-third of its people have adopted newer faiths, a fact that some view with fascination or envy, modern India continues to be defined by its enduring familial bonds and societal values, which remain deeply woven into the fabric of everyday life.

As in nature, an excellent symbiosis exists between family, community, region, and nation. Language, dialects, mannerisms, modes of dressing, their colours and styles, what is cooked in the house, and which spices are used flow through multiple layers. Ideals held by families and communities are inseparable. Individuals are shaped and contribute to society by the values and habits instilled in them within their families. The home is a child's primary social setting for acquiring core values, beliefs, and behaviours. When children turn to their parents and other family members for guidance on social interactions, problem-solving, and general life management, they look to them as role models and aspire to emulate them.

The cultural norms, practices, and traditions passed down through families are essential for preserving social cohesiveness and individuality. People are more likely to grow up to be trustworthy and contribute to society if their families value honesty, integrity, and accountability. An atmosphere of kindness, understanding, and compassion is contagious; it starts at home and spreads to all parts of society. A more accepting and peaceful society is the result of families that instil in their children a reverence for those in positions of power and those from diverse cultural backgrounds. The eleventh president of India, Dr. A.P.J. Abdul Kalam, was fond of reciting these words from *The Analects of Confucius*:

Where there is righteousness in the heart,
There is beauty in the character.
When there is beauty in the character,
There is harmony in the home.
When there is harmony in the home,
There is order in the nation.
When there is order in the nation,
There is peace in the world. [9]

Children who grow up in homes that value teamwork and mutual aid are more equipped to collaborate successfully in various contexts. When parents and guardians prioritise education, they give their children a leg up in the classroom and prepare them to be active, knowledgeable members of society. Values such as collectivism and individualism have a significant impact on family dynamics, expectations, and roles. When society upholds and supports family values, it can lead to a self-reinforcing cycle of stability. The Ramayana and Mahabharata epics formalised the bond between societal and familial values. They explore complex moral dilemmas and human nature, laying the groundwork for a profound set of principles, including dharma (righteousness), accountability, devotion, and ethical conduct.

Maintaining dharma is emphasised throughout the Ramayana. Rama is the virtuous king and ideal son, Sita is the perfect wife, and Lakshmana and Bharata are ideal brothers who exemplify devotion, self-control, and loyalty. The epic also highlights the significance of social structures and family by illustrating how individuals' actions

[9] https://www.goodreads.com/quotes/7353825-where-there-is-righteousness-in-the-heart. Last accessed on November 15, 2025.

impact society. Readers of the Ramayana often find themselves internalising the lessons learned from the stories of these heroes. Love, devotion, and commitment are powerful themes. Rama's unfaltering attachment to Sita, Lakshmana's concern for serving his brother, Bharata's respect for the word of his brother, Hanuman's selfless service to Rama, and Vibhishana's commitment to righteousness against all odds provide prime examples for how one must conduct oneself with others and in society.

Through the stories of the Pandavas and the Kauravas, the Mahabharata explores themes such as war, justice, the nature of good and evil, and the complex moral dilemmas and consequences of one's actions within a large family. By exploring the concepts of dharma (righteousness) and karma (action and its implications), the epic emphasises the importance of acting ethically and the weight of one's actions. As an example of ethical and accountable leadership and governance, the Mahabharata sheds light on issues related to dispute resolution, justice, and governance. Readers are invited to explore the complexities of human nature and the challenges of moral decision-making through various intricate situations. The *Bhagavad Gita*, widely regarded as the codebook of Indian civilisation, embedded in the Mahabharata, explores profound themes of duty, action, and the nature of reality, offering timeless guidance for living a purposeful life. The belief that India's civilisational values may embody humanity's last hope in navigating the challenges of the approaching technological singularity is, therefore, not without merit.

A Hierarchical Structure

Indian society is structured hierarchically. Almost everyone and every social group in the country is rated according to a set of hierarchical characteristics. Within families, kinship groups, and caste groups, societal stratification is visible. Though Hinduism is the most common religion linked with castes, there are caste-like groups even among Indian Muslims and Christians. There is a clear hierarchy in families and kinship groups.

Ritual purity and pollution are complicated ideas. It varies significantly among castes, religious groups, and regions in Indian society, indicating many status inequalities. People generally equate cleanliness with high status, and vice versa about pollution. Although there are innate forms of purity in all professions, these are more a matter of mentality than anything else. Certain Hindus avoid certain meals and drinks because they are considered impure. Millions of people avoid onions and garlic for these reasons. Many people believe that immersing oneself in a holy river, such as the Ganga, physically and mentally purifies them.

Incredible diversity is present in India's social life in almost every facet. The precedence of family over the individual, community over the family, country over the community, and renunciation over pleasures is a popular aphorism. One should sacrifice oneself for the welfare of the family, one should sacrifice the family for the welfare of the village, one should sacrifice the town for the welfare of the country, and one should sacrifice the earthly for one's soul. This sense of interdependence extends into the realm of theology. The belief that powerful deities play a significant role in shaping a person's destiny and that their fate has already been predetermined begins at birth.

The four-ashram system, a core concept in Hindu philosophy, outlines the four stages of life that individuals are expected to progress through. These stages are brahmacharya (studenthood), grihastha (householder), vanaprastha (hermitage or retirement), and sannyasa (renunciation). Each ashram has specific duties and responsibilities associated with it, guiding individuals in their spiritual and worldly lives while providing a framework for personal development, social responsibility, and spiritual growth.

The first phase of education and learning typically lasts until the age of twenty-five. During this phase, individuals are encouraged to focus on their studies, practice self-restraint, and prepare for future responsibilities. The householder's life typically lasts until around the age of fifty. This is considered an essential phase for fulfilling social and familial obligations. Individuals in their fifties are expected to gradually relinquish daily household responsibilities as their children become more independent. They start to focus more on spiritual practices and less on worldly affairs. The final stage allows individuals to seek ultimate liberation through intense devotion and meditation. These stages are not rigid; individuals may progress through them at their own pace, depending on their circumstances and spiritual goals.

Changing Marriage Trends

Marriage marks a significant turning point in a person's life and is considered vital by almost everyone in India. While traditional norms still prevail in many parts of India, especially in rural areas, urban India is undergoing a significant transformation in marriage trends. These changes reflect broader shifts in societal values, economic conditions, and individual aspirations. However, the pace of change varies across regions, with rural areas often lagging urban centres in adopting these new trends.

More Indians, especially women, are prioritising education and careers, leading to delayed marriages. The average age of marriage has increased, particularly in urban areas. Economic independence allows individuals to make more informed decisions about marriage, often waiting until they feel financially stable. There is a growing acceptance of love marriages, where individuals choose their partners based on personal compatibility rather than family arrangements. A hybrid model has evolved where families introduce potential partners, but the final decision lies with the individuals; this is becoming increasingly popular.

There has been a noticeable increase in the prevalence of young divorces in Indian society in recent years. Traditional views on marriage and divorce are shifting, with younger generations becoming more accepting of divorce as a viable option if marital issues cannot be resolved. Increased access to education, particularly for women, has empowered individuals to make independent choices about their lives, including the decision to end an unhappy marriage. Rapid urbanisation has led to significant lifestyle changes. People living in urban areas often have more exposure to diverse perspectives, which can influence their views on marriage and divorce. With more young people gaining financial independence, the stigma associated with divorce has decreased, allowing individuals to prioritise personal happiness and well-being. While divorce rates among young couples have increased, it is essential to recognise that the conversations around marriage, love, and commitment are evolving, reflecting broader societal changes in India.

While social stratification is a global problem. However, unlike in Western societies, where income and occupation are often the primary determinants of class, Indian class is defined by a more complex combination of factors: wealth and income, caste background and social networks, lifestyle and consumption patterns, and level of education. In contemporary India, class is not a singular, clearly defined metric but a "nebulous" concept influenced by a mix of economic, social, and cultural elements. The ambiguous nature of class allows political parties to mobilise support along caste lines for electoral gain. The debate over extending affirmative action is often intertwined with populist appeals to backward and marginalised castes, rather than being focused on transparent economic criteria.

Marriage patterns in India are undergoing a profound transformation, shifting from traditional religious and family-centred institutions to partnerships grounded in personal compatibility and individual choice. Urbanisation, education, and economic progress have played key roles in this transition. The rise of inter-caste and inter-religious unions, the near disappearance of polygamy and polyandry in favour of monogamy, the growing prevalence of self-arranged marriages, and the emergence of cohabitation and single-person households all signal a society in flux. These changing dynamics mirror deeper social, economic, and legal transformations—marked by higher divorce rates and a growing focus on personal happiness and emotional fulfilment within marriage.

The purpose of marriage has evolved from fulfilling religious obligations and cementing family alliances to pursuing companionship, equality, and shared purpose. While economic security remains important, its meaning has shifted towards financial independence and mutual support between partners. Increasingly, young people are playing a decisive role in choosing their life partners, aided by digital matchmaking platforms that have replaced traditional matchmakers. Modern marriages now prioritise emotional compatibility and shared values over caste or community conformity. Yet, this newfound freedom has also brought paradoxes—rising cohabitation, more frequent divorces, and a redefinition of stability and commitment in contemporary Indian marriage.

The Rise of the Indian Middle Class

The rise of the Indian middle class is one of the most significant socioeconomic developments in modern India. This growth has been driven by economic liberalisation, urbanisation, education, and technological advancements. This new wave, which encompasses people of all faiths and regions, is as vast as the US and features a generation that is constantly on the move, focused on material possessions, and somewhat optimistic about the future.

Stable incomes, homeownership, and access to modern amenities, such as cars, smartphones, and appliances, characterise the middle class. This class is highly engaged with digital platforms, using them for shopping, entertainment, education, and communication. It is a major driver of demand for consumer goods, entertainment, travel, and luxury items. Brands and businesses target this demographic for their purchasing power. Their consumption patterns have made India one of the largest consumer markets globally.

The middle class has played a crucial role in promoting values such as education, gender equality, and individual rights. They are increasingly vocal about issues like corruption, governance, and environmental sustainability. The middle class is a significant voting bloc, influencing political agendas and policies. Their demands for better infrastructure, healthcare, and education shape government priorities. This class of people has adopted global culture while preserving Indian traditions, resulting in a distinctive blend of modernity and heritage.

The Indian middle class is expected to continue growing, with estimates suggesting it could reach 500 million people by 2030. This growth will further drive economic development, social change, and global influence. However, addressing challenges like inequality, sustainability, and access to quality services will be crucial to ensuring inclusive and sustainable progress. Without a doubt, the rise of the Indian middle class is a transformative force that is shaping India's economy, society, and culture, with far-reaching implications for the country's future.

A quarter of India's population now lives in cities. Overcrowding, noise, filth, and a lack of basic services, including running water, electricity, sanitation, and safe housing, are prevalent issues in these urban areas. Slums coexist with high-end residential complexes. In urban areas, traditional caste hierarchies are less pronounced, although caste affiliations continue to hold significance. Friends, relatives, and acquaintances within the same caste are often the best bet when applying for scarce positions. Those living in metropolitan areas usually need to be creative and persistent to make ends meet. They work as small business owners, street vendors, and manual labourers to sustain themselves.

Improved access to education and employment opportunities has been a major factor behind the dramatic expansion of the urban middle class. Neighbourhood unity, volunteer networks, and the shared celebration of festivals continue to nurture a sense of belonging amid urban life. Today, cities function as the nation's vital nerve centres—driving business, education, science, politics, and governance—while carrying forward the cultural ethos that once defined India's villages. With major hubs in Mumbai, Chennai, and Hyderabad, and encompassing all languages, India is home to the world's largest film industry. The country's television sector has seen significant growth. Across the nation, these portray urban lifestyles in rich detail, inspiring the dreams of millions of people who live in small towns and rural areas.

Decline of Religious and Moral Frameworks

Learning from the experiences of others is a wise way to progress. By studying the failures and missteps of others, we can avoid repeating them, saving time, resources, and effort. Understanding how other nations have overcome challenges can inspire and equip us to face our difficulties with confidence. Countries like South Korea and Singapore have studied the industrialisation strategies of Western nations to build their economies. Nations are adopting renewable energy models from leaders like Denmark and Germany to combat climate change. Learning from the experiences of others is a powerful tool for personal growth and progress.

There is a popular saying: 'A wise man learns from the mistakes of others; a fool, from his own'. India can learn a lot from Europe about how to handle its newfound prosperity and avoid the erosion of shared values, traditions, and identities that have historically united European societies. There is a lack of a sense of belonging in Western culture today. Only the law can abrogate the inherent sovereignty of the individual and his rights. In disputes between family members or between members of different communities, the rights of the individual always take precedence. The Western perspective views the family unit as a contract, a temporary agreement. The fight for the rights of individuals—human, gender, animal, etc.—is the fundamental force behind modernity.

According to recent data from the IMF and the World Bank, advanced economies, such as those in Europe and the United States, have entered a phase of stagnation, with average GDP growth rates remaining around 1–2 per cent between 2023 and 2025. In contrast, India's economy continues to expand robustly at over 6.5 per cent annually, while China maintains a growth rate near 5 per cent. Across the Indo-China region, countries such as Vietnam (projected at 6 per cent), Cambodia (5.8 per cent), Laos (4.5 per cent), Myanmar (3 per cent), and Thailand (3.1 per cent) are experiencing consistent upward momentum driven by manufacturing, services, and digital integration.

The turning point that revealed this divergence traces back to the 2008 global financial crisis, when the collapse of the US housing market and a surge in household bankruptcies nearly toppled the world's financial system. Western economies, burdened by debt and speculative finance, entered a prolonged recovery phase marked by quantitative easing and fiscal strain. In contrast, Asian nations—anchored by strong family structures, community-oriented savings behaviour, and pragmatic governance—rebounded far more rapidly. Their emphasis on education, thrift, and social cohesion provided both economic and psychological resilience. The episode underscored a vital truth: societies that cultivate interdependence and shared responsibility can better withstand the shocks of global capitalism.

Recent reports from the National Institute of Mental Health (NIMH) and the Centres for Disease Control and Prevention (CDC) reveal that nearly one in five American adults—about 20 per cent or more than 50 million people—experience some form of mental illness each year. Conditions such as anxiety, depression, and substance use disorders are widespread, contributing to persistently high suicide rates (over 14 deaths per 100,000 people annually) and a continuing opioid and drug-overdose crisis that claimed more than 100,000 lives in 2023 alone. Alarmingly, over 75 per cent of Americans with substance use disorders do not receive treatment, reflecting deep systemic gaps in access and stigma around mental health.

Outside the United States, the picture is far less clear—not necessarily because the situation is better, but because it is less reported and poorly documented. In many countries, particularly in Asia, Africa, and parts of Eastern Europe, mental health data are scarce or underrepresented, as social stigma, limited diagnostic infrastructure, and inadequate public health systems prevent accurate reporting. The global mental health crisis, therefore, remains widespread but unevenly visible—its true scale obscured by cultural silence and institutional neglect.

As artificial intelligence reshapes human interaction, new risks are emerging. AI-powered relational bots and virtual companions, designed with addictive engagement algorithms, can foster dependency, emotional isolation, and social withdrawal. If left unchecked, these technologies may exacerbate the very psychological vulnerabilities they aim to alleviate, pushing societies further into virtual intimacy and real-world detachment. The coming decade may thus witness not just a digital revolution but also a mental health reckoning, unless ethics, empathy, and human connection are placed at the centre of technological progress.

In an age dominated by digital media and algorithm-driven distraction, the time-honoured culture and traditions of India—rooted in family bonds, spiritual discipline, and community life—can serve as a powerful shield against the growing epidemic of mental disorders. Ancient practices such as yoga, meditation, and mindfulness, along with rituals that emphasise rhythm, gratitude, and belonging, have long provided psychological stability and emotional grounding. Traditional storytelling, music, and communal celebrations help anchor individuals in shared meaning rather than fleeting virtual stimuli. By reconnecting young minds to these stabilising cultural anchors, society can counter the confusion and chaos fostered by excessive digital exposure, restoring balance between the outer world of constant engagement and the inner world of calm awareness.

At its core, Indian civilisation revolves around dharma, which stresses responsibility, justice, and moral hierarchy. There is a strong emphasis on traditional values, including hospitality, respect for elders, and family unity. Ahimsa, the path of nonviolence, encourages kindness and unity. Respect for education and scholars is indicative of a thirst for knowledge, a characteristic that is also valued. Every aspect of life is intertwined with spirituality, fostering a sense of purpose that extends beyond us.

To be one in diversity is to recognise, respect, and celebrate each other's unique qualities while understanding that unity does not mean uniformity. It is about finding harmony in difference—acknowledging that every individual, community, and culture contributes a distinct colour to the larger human mosaic. When we value another's perspective, language, or way of life, we strengthen the shared fabric that binds us. True unity arises not from erasing differences but from embracing them with empathy and openness, realising that our collective strength and beauty lie precisely in this richness of variety. The cultural history of India continues to resonate on a worldwide scale, promoting resilience and unity, thanks to the ideals passed down through generations and fostered by society. We close this chapter by emphasising some key Indian values.

A conscious and organised movement is needed to teach young people to appreciate and celebrate differences in culture, religion, and traditions, instil values such as honesty, compassion, justice, and responsibility, highlight historical examples of overcoming adversity to inspire determination and grit, and emphasise the importance of contributing to society and helping others. Promote respect for nature and sustainable living, drawing from traditional practices and, above all, encourage a love for learning and innovation, rooted in the intellectual achievements of our civilisation.

Summary

Making young people aware of civilisational values is essential for nurturing well-rounded, responsible, and culturally grounded individuals. By integrating these values into education, culture, and community life, we can ensure that the wisdom of the past continues to guide and inspire future generations. World peace has righteousness in the heart and harmony in the family at its root—for when individuals are guided by moral clarity and families live in mutual respect, societies naturally flourish in peace. As the custodians of tomorrow, youth who understand and embody these values will be better equipped to build a more harmonious, ethical, and sustainable world.

Part IV
Recovery

The utmost mission of the Mind is to train our obscure consciousness, which has emerged out of the dark prison of Matter, to enlighten its blind instincts, random intuitions, and vague perceptions till it shall become capable of this greater light and this higher ascension. Mind is a passage, not a culmination.[1]

—Sri Aurobindo

[1] https://motherandsriaurobindo.in/Sri-Aurobindo/books/the-life-divine/. Last accessed on October 6, 2025.

16

Cosmic Oneness

To see the cosmos as separate is an illusion; to feel it as one is awakening. When the self dissolves into the whole, conflict yields to compassion, and purpose becomes peace. In realising that all life is woven from the same thread of existence, we discover the universe not outside us—but within.

The Systems Theory Approach

The perils of industrialisation, urbanisation, deforestation, and fossil fuel emissions are staring us in the face as climate change. Many low-income populations heavily rely on agriculture, fishing, or natural resources for their livelihoods, making them more vulnerable to climate-induced disruptions, such as crop failures or water scarcity. Climate-related hazards, such as heatwaves, vector-borne diseases, and pollution, exacerbate health problems in impoverished communities that already have limited access to healthcare. There is ample evidence that climate events can wipe out livelihoods, push families deeper into poverty, and hinder the economic development of affected regions.

The concept of oneness, frequently discussed in philosophy and spirituality, has gained increasing resonance in scientific fields such as quantum physics, ecology, and systems theory. In quantum physics, when two particles become entangled, their properties become linked—so that a change in one instantly affects the other, no matter how far apart they are. This phenomenon suggests a fundamental interconnectedness at the subatomic level. Ecosystems demonstrate how all living organisms are interlinked and dependent on one another for survival. The health of one species often affects the entire system, highlighting the unity of life.

The systems theory approach views the universe as a network of interconnected systems, where each part influences the whole. From cells to galaxies, everything operates as part of a larger, unified system. Some theories in neuroscience and consciousness research suggest that individual consciousness may be part of a larger, unified field of awareness. While science provides evidence for interconnectedness, the interpretation of oneness often bridges the gap between empirical observation and philosophical or spiritual understanding. It's a profound reminder that we are all part of a greater whole, both physically and metaphysically.

Nanotechnology has revealed fascinating insights into the interconnectedness of reality at the nanoscale, further supporting the idea of oneness. At the nanoscale, all matter is composed of the identical fundamental particles—atoms and molecules. Whether it's a human cell, a piece of metal, or a plant, the basic components are similar, emphasising the unity of all material reality. Nanotechnology shows how complex systems and properties emerge from the interactions of simple elements. For example, the unique properties of nanomaterials (like strength, conductivity, or reactivity) arise from the collective behaviour of atoms and molecules, illustrating how the whole is greater than the sum of its parts.

At the nanoscale, the boundaries between different systems become increasingly blurred. For instance, biological processes in cells rely on nanoscale molecular interactions, which are governed by the same physical laws that apply to non-living systems. This interconnectedness highlights the seamless unity of nature. Nanotechnology often exploits quantum phenomena, such as tunnelling and superposition, which reveal the non-local and interconnected nature of reality. These effects challenge the classical notion of separateness and suggest a deeper level of unity in the fabric of the universe.

Nanotechnology demonstrates how molecules can self-assemble into complex structures through natural processes. This self-organisation is a universal phenomenon observed in everything from DNA to galaxies, indicating an underlying order and unity in nature. Nanotechnology bridges the fields of physics, chemistry, biology, and engineering, illustrating the interconnectedness of these disciplines. This approach reinforces the idea that all knowledge and phenomena are part of a unified whole. By exploring the nanoscale, we see that reality is not a collection of isolated entities but a deeply interconnected web of relationships. This perspective aligns with the philosophical and spiritual concept of oneness, suggesting that everything in the universe is fundamentally interconnected and unified.

Fields and Probabilities

The spiritual principle of maya and the findings of quantum physics share intriguing parallels, both challenging our perception of reality and pointing to a more profound, more fundamental truth.

Maya refers to the illusion or appearance of the material world, which obscures the ultimate reality, known as Brahman. Maya emphasises that perception is subjective and shaped by the mind. Reality is a projection of consciousness, and different observers may perceive it in varying ways. In quantum physics, the observer effect demonstrates that the act of observation influences the behaviour of particles. This implies that reality is not independent of the observer but is co-created through interaction. Quantum entanglement demonstrates that particles can be instantaneously connected across vast distances, defying classical notions of separateness. This suggests a fundamental interconnectedness in the universe.

Reality, according to maya, is fluid and ever-changing, lacking inherent permanence or stability. The Heisenberg Uncertainty Principle states that it is impossible to simultaneously know the position and momentum of a particle with absolute certainty. This intrinsic uncertainty reflects the fluid and dynamic nature of reality at the quantum level. Maya masks, but also points, a seeker to a deeper, unchanging reality (Brahman) that lies beyond the veil of illusion. Spiritual practices aim to transcend maya to realise this ultimate truth. Quantum physics suggests that the observable world is governed by underlying quantum fields and probabilities, which are not directly perceivable but form the foundation of reality.

Maya creates the illusion of duality (self versus other; subject versus object), while the ultimate truth is non-dual (Advaita). Quantum phenomena, such as wave-particle duality, blur the lines between seemingly opposite states, suggesting a non-dual nature at the fundamental level. Consciousness is central to maya, as it is the medium through which the illusion of reality is experienced and transcended. Some interpretations of quantum mechanics, such as the Copenhagen interpretation, suggest that consciousness plays a role in shaping reality, though this remains a topic of debate.

Both maya and quantum physics challenge our conventional understanding of reality, pointing to a deeper, interconnected, and non-objective nature of existence. While maya is a spiritual concept rooted in ancient wisdom, quantum physics offers a scientific framework that resonates with these insights, suggesting that the material world is not as fixed or separate as it appears. Together, they invite us to question our perceptions and explore the profound unity underlying all phenomena.

In life, the terms 'fields' and 'probabilities' can be interpreted in various ways. There are different career fields, or areas of work or study, including medicine, engineering, and the arts. There are social fields, such as networks of relationships and interactions, comprising family, friends, colleagues, and others. Then there are physical fields, such as environments, spaces, shopping malls, gardens, lakes, and the like. And, of course, there are mental fields, areas of thought or focus, marked by creativity, logic, and emotions.

Life operates on probabilities. In decision-making, the likelihood of outcomes is based on choices that lead to career success, such as maintaining a stable relationship. Probabilities determine risk assessment; the chance of events, such as health risks and financial losses, constantly operates at the back of our minds. The probability of encountering favourable circumstances and the uncertainty inherent in life events like accidents and ill health shape human existence.

Fields influence probabilities, and probabilities shape fields. If someone works in the tech industry, the likelihood of learning cutting-edge skills, like AI or machine learning, is higher compared to those working in a traditional manufacturing field. This increases the chances of career growth and higher earnings. For those who are part of a network of entrepreneurs, the probability of encountering business opportunities or mentorship is higher, which can lead to starting or scaling a business. Living in a major city increases the likelihood of accessing diverse job markets, cultural events, and educational institutions compared to living in a rural area or smaller town.

Conversely, if the probability of success in one's current career is low, perhaps due to industry decline, switching to a growing field like renewable energy or healthcare may be a viable option. This reshapes your career trajectory and opens new opportunities. People join new communities, such as clubs and professional organisations, to meet like-minded individuals when the probability of forming meaningful connections in their current social circle is low. If the likelihood of achieving happiness with our current mindset is low, we may adopt new habits to enhance our mental well-being and improve our mental and emotional health.

Undoubtedly, fields and probabilities are deeply interconnected. By understanding how our current field influences probabilities, we can make informed decisions to shape our future field in a way that aligns with our goals and aspirations. Understanding the interconnection of fields and probabilities can lead to a transformative mindset that empowers us to navigate life more effectively. By internalising this interconnected perspective, one can develop a more empowered, resilient, and strategic mindset that helps one thrive in an uncertain world.

Ashta Dhatu Armour

The times are changing, and the change will only accelerate. No one will come forward to help or assist, and each one must fend for themselves. We outline eight mental steps based on the cosmic oneness principle, referring to it as the Ashta Dhatu Armour—a concept historically used for protection in battles and associated with spiritual and symbolic significance. The ashta dhatu armour was worn by warriors in ancient India for its strength and protective qualities. The combination of metals was believed to balance energies, ward off evil, and enhance the wearer's spiritual and physical well-being. In Ayurveda, eight metals are associated with balancing the body's doshas (vata, pitta, kapha) and promoting health.

The armour symbolises the wearer's inner and outer strength. The combination of metals represents the harmony of opposing forces, such as the sun and moon, strength and weakness, and hardness and softness. Beyond physical protection, the armour is believed to shield the wearer from negative energies and spiritual harm. The composition of ashta dhatu typically includes gold (swarna) for purity, prosperity, and divine energy; silver (rajat) for clarity, intuition, and the moon's calming influence; copper (tamra) for its healing properties and conductivity of energy; brass (peetal) for strength and durability; zinc (jasata) to enhance immunity and vitality; tin (trapu) for stability and grounding; lead (sisa) for protection and absorption of negative energies; and iron (loha) for strength, courage, and resilience.

Our mental armour is not built overnight—it is forged through awareness, discipline, and purpose. It begins with proactive decision-making, the courage to act rather than merely react. It includes embracing uncertainty, accepting that change is the only constant and that ambiguity often hides opportunity. Strategic risk-taking enables us to move forward intelligently, striking a balance between vision and prudence. Continuous learning and adaptation keep the mind supple and resilient, enabling growth in every circumstance. A holistic perspective enables us to see interconnections rather than isolated events, thereby transforming complexity into coherence. Through empowerment by choice, we reclaim agency over our lives, shaping outcomes instead of surrendering to them. By focusing on pivotal leverage points, we learn to channel effort where it matters most—creating maximum impact with minimal waste. Finally, gratitude and optimism form the emotional shield that protects us from cynicism and despair, reminding us that even in struggle, there is meaning, and in every ending, the seed of renewal. Above all, gratitude and optimism help us appreciate the fields that have positively influenced our probabilities and remaining hopeful about shaping future fields.

The growing awareness of environmental issues underscores the complex and symbiotic relationships within ecosystems, illustrating how human actions affect the planet and, in turn, how the planet impacts human activities. The ecological movements of the 1960s and 1970s, including the Earth Day initiative, fostered a collective consciousness that viewed humanity not as separate from nature but as an integral part of it. This awareness aligned with the ideals of cosmic oneness, promoting the idea that the planet's health and humanity's well-being have a symbiotic relationship. This synthesis of ideas marked a turning point in human consciousness—a recognition that every individual, every action, and every phenomenon is a vital part of a vast, interconnected cosmos.

The scientific basis for the concept of human oneness draws from several disciplines, including genetics, anthropology, sociology, and psychology. All humans share approximately 99.9 per cent of their DNA. This genetic similarity underscores our shared biological heritage, suggesting that differences between individuals, such as those based on race or ethnicity, are relatively minor. This common DNA ancestry reinforces the idea that all humans are closely related. Across different societies, humans exhibit fundamental similarities in culture, language, and social structures, indicating that certain aspects of humanity are universal, regardless of geographic or cultural differences.

Humans are part of the same species, Homo sapiens, and have evolved together over time. Anthropological research shows that human societies have historically interacted and mingled, fostering shared experiences and collective identities. Research in sociology and psychology highlights the interconnectedness of humanity, showing that individuals' well-being often depends on their social networks and community. This interconnectedness supports the idea of collective responsibility and shared fate. Humans have an innate capacity for empathy and cooperation. These traits have been essential for survival and have fostered social bonds, which can reinforce a sense of oneness.

Humanity's Place in the Universe

The world watched with curious anxiety as NASA astronauts Sunita Williams and Butch Wilmore's mission, which began with a Boeing Starliner test flight in June 2024, evolved into a nine-month saga due to technical issues, ultimately concluding with their safe return to Earth in March 2025. Experiences aboard the International Space Station (ISS) have significantly influenced our understanding of reality in several ways, chiefly through the perspectives gained by astronauts and the scientific experiments conducted in microgravity.

The ISS has served as a platform for pioneering research with implications for life on Earth. From biotechnology to materials science, discoveries in space can lead to technological advancements that change our daily lives, altering perceptions of what is feasible or possible. The ISS represents one of the most significant collaborations in human history, involving multiple countries working together in a shared endeavour. This spirit of collaboration can enhance our understanding of reality as a shared human experience, emphasising collective goals over nationalistic or divisive perspectives. How can India be helpful?

The experience of being in space prompts deep philosophical inquiries about humanity's place in the universe. It encourages reflections on existential themes such as the search for life beyond Earth and humans' long-term evolution and survival prospects. As astronauts and researchers continue to push the boundaries of knowledge in space, their insights inspire a re-evaluation of our existence, urging people to adopt a more holistic and interconnected view of life on Earth and beyond. Yoga can be highly beneficial for astronauts during long-term space missions.

In microgravity, astronauts experience muscle atrophy and loss of bone density. Yoga can help maintain strength and flexibility, combating the effects of prolonged weightlessness. Living in confined spaces can be stressful psychologically. It promotes relaxation and mental well-being through mindfulness and breathing techniques, enabling astronauts to manage stress effectively. Practising yoga can also enhance balance and body awareness, which is critical when moving in a microgravity environment.

Breathing exercises in yoga (pranayama) can enhance lung capacity and oxygen efficiency, which are crucial for physical exertion and overall health in space missions. Yoga can aid sleep quality and help astronauts adapt to the challenges of sleeping in a rotating environment, where natural circadian rhythms may be disrupted. The meditative aspects of yoga promote mental clarity and focus, which are essential for performing complex tasks. Group yoga sessions can foster camaraderie and collaboration among crew members, improving teamwork and morale during long missions.

Humanity faces numerous global challenges, such as climate change, pandemics, and social inequities. Addressing them requires collective action, underscoring the interconnectedness and interdependence of all people. International cooperation on public health, economic development, and peacebuilding shows the importance of recognising our shared humanity in addressing common problems. Establishing universal human rights reflects a moral recognition of the inherent dignity and equality of all individuals, promoting the idea that all humans deserve respect and protection regardless of their background.

The scientific understanding of humanity's oneness reveals our shared biology, cultural kinship, and social interconnectedness. Recognising this unity nurtures empathy, cooperation, and collective responsibility—qualities vital for solving global challenges such as climate change, poverty, and conflict. Embracing oneness, both global and cosmic, encourages collaboration across borders and disciplines, fostering compassion, peace, and a more harmonious, equitable world.

Emphasising that humanity is part of the larger ecosystem inspires a responsibility to protect and preserve the planet. This can lead to sustainable practices and policies that ensure the health of the Earth for future generations. As artificial intelligence advances, particularly with the development of super AI, this concept may become more relevant and tangible, potentially influencing how we perceive and experience our interconnectedness. However, realising cosmic oneness in a practical sense may require integrating ethical, philosophical, and technological perspectives to ensure that AI development aligns with the broader idea of unity and harmony. What does it mean?

Value-Aligned AI Design

Value-aligned AI design must incorporate human-centred values, such as fairness, justice, and respect, while reflecting on concepts like consciousness, agency, and moral responsibility. This approach involves developing algorithms that can learn and adapt to uphold these values, ensuring that AI decisions align with human ethics. Transparent and explainable AI can promote honesty and accountability in AI systems, addressing questions about trust, knowledge, and the nature of understanding. The models should therefore be designed in a way that provides clear explanations for their actions, enabling users to understand and scrutinise AI reasoning. For global collaboration and governance, fostering equitable access and preventing misuse is essential. This implies considering ideas related to collective well-being and interconnectedness, and establishing international standards and protocols for safe AI development and deployment. There are significant gaps in the current state of AI, particularly when it comes to the inclusion of diverse data and the development of fair algorithms. How do we avoid bias and discrimination, reflect on the moral importance of equality and diversity, and use diverse datasets and fairness algorithms to reduce bias in AI outputs?

The ideals of sustainability, corporate responsibility, and ethical stewardship primarily drive ESG (environmental, social, governance) policies. While they don't explicitly originate from the concept of cosmic oneness, there are philosophical overlaps.

The idea of oneness emphasises interconnectedness and unity across all aspects of life, aligning with ESG principles. ESG policies promote a holistic approach to business practices, acknowledging that the health of the environment, society, and economies is deeply intertwined—concepts resonant with the notion of interconnectedness central to the concept of oneness.

ESG practices can play a significant role in mitigating climate change by taking up environmental initiatives. Companies that adopt ESG principles often focus on reducing greenhouse gas emissions, transitioning to renewable energy sources, and implementing sustainable resource management practices. These actions directly decrease their carbon footprint and contribute to global climate goals. ESG encourages investments in climate-resilient infrastructure and technologies, fostering innovation in clean energy, carbon capture, and sustainable transportation. While ESG alone isn't a complete solution, it is a robust framework that aligns corporate behaviour with climate mitigation objectives. Combining ESG efforts with global policy measures and technological innovation significantly enhances the collective capacity to combat climate change.

ESG initiatives can address the issue of poverty through several targeted approaches within the 'social' component by promoting fair labour practices. This involves ensuring fair wages, safe working conditions, and access to healthcare for workers, especially in vulnerable communities, which can improve living standards and reduce poverty. Supporting community development by investing in local infrastructure, education, and healthcare in underserved areas helps lift communities out of poverty and foster sustainable growth. Developing products and services that are affordable and accessible to low-income populations can help improve their quality of life and economic stability. Most importantly, creating economic opportunities through training, skills development, and microfinance empowers marginalised populations to generate income and achieve financial independence. By integrating these strategies into their core operations and investments, organisations can make meaningful contributions to reducing poverty while also promoting social equity and sustainable development.

In the ESG framework, governance refers to the leadership, policies, and practices that ensure a company operates in an ethical, transparent, and responsible manner. It is a critical component because good governance underpins effective environmental and social initiatives. Implementing policies against corruption, fraud, and unethical behaviour, with mechanisms such as whistleblower protections, is crucial. Developing protocols to identify, evaluate, and mitigate ESG-related risks, such as regulatory changes or reputational threats, engaging with investors, employees, communities, and regulators to incorporate diverse perspectives into governance practices, and following global governance codes set by bodies like the Organisation for Economic Co-operation and Development (OECD) or the UN Global Compact to maintain consistency with best practices would undoubtedly make Earth more liveable.

Summary

The concept of cosmic oneness lies at the heart of the Vedic worldview—that all forms, forces, and beings emerge from a single source and ultimately return to it. It is a vision that transcends both religion and reason, revealing existence as an indivisible whole where the boundary between the observer and the observed dissolves. Science now begins to echo this truth: from the quantum field to the cosmic web, all that is—from the atom to the star—is interconnected, vibrating in subtle harmony. To awaken to this oneness is to shift from a state of separation to one of unity, from ego to empathy. It is to see that the welfare of the self cannot be isolated from the welfare of all. When this awareness matures, peace ceases to be an aspiration and becomes a natural state of being.

For the modern world, fractured by conflict and consumption, the cosmic oneness mindset offers both solace and solution. It teaches us to act not as owners of the Earth but as its trustees; not as conquerors of nature but as participants in its unfolding intelligence. To live in oneness is to live consciously—with reverence, gratitude, and grace—recognising that the universe is not merely around us, but alive within us.

17

Applied Spirituality

Applied spirituality is not an escape from the world but an embrace of it—a way of living where action becomes prayer, service becomes meditation, and every moment becomes a meeting with the divine.

A Practical Tool for Better Living

The concept of applied spirituality refers to the practical application of spiritual principles, beliefs, or practices in everyday life to enhance personal growth, well-being, and a sense of purpose. It involves integrating spiritual insights into various aspects of life, such as work, relationships, health, and decision-making, to create a more meaningful and balanced existence. Applied spirituality is not tied to any specific religion but can be adapted to individual beliefs and practices. It's about making spirituality a practical tool for living a more fulfilling and harmonious life.

In an era marked by rapid technological advancement and increasing materialism, the search for deeper meaning in life has become an essential pursuit for many. This quest has led to the emergence of applied spirituality—a concept that transcends theoretical understanding and invites individuals to live according to their spiritual beliefs on a daily basis. Applied spirituality is not merely a mental construct; it is a profound expression of humanity's divine essence, calling us to actively harness this intrinsic quality to enhance the quality of our lives and the condition of the world around us.

At its core, applied spirituality acknowledges that spirituality transcends religious boundaries and cultural differences. It is a universal human experience that connects individuals to something greater than themselves. This connection can manifest in various forms, such as compassion, inner peace, empathy, and a sense of belonging. When these spiritual principles are actively practised, they can lead to more fulfilling lives, healthier relationships, and harmonious communities.

One of the key aspects of applied spirituality is its emphasis on action. It urges us to take principles drawn from spiritual understanding and put them into practice, thereby allowing our divine essence to shine through our actions. This could involve engaging in acts of kindness, cultivating mindfulness in everyday activities, or offering support to those in need. For instance, volunteer work and community service are direct expressions of applied spirituality, where individuals can channel their spiritual insights into tangible benefits for others. Such actions transform the lives of those being helped and enrich the giver's soul, creating a meaningful cycle of giving and receiving.

Furthermore, applied spirituality can significantly improve mental and emotional welfare. In our busy lives, stress and anxiety are prevalent. However, incorporating spiritual practices such as meditation, prayer, or simply spending time in nature can help ground individuals, thereby enhancing their emotional resilience.

Engaging in these practices allows individuals to reconnect with their inner selves and the divine, fostering a sense of peace and clarity. This, in turn, enables them to face daily challenges with a renewed perspective, emphasising the importance of harnessing spiritual principles in practical ways.

Applied spirituality encourages the idea of interconnectedness. Recognising that we are all part of a greater whole fosters a sense of responsibility towards our environment and society. By applying this understanding, individuals can work towards sustainability and social justice, acknowledging that their actions have broader implications. For instance, individuals who incorporate spiritual teachings on stewardship may adopt sustainable practices, promoting ecological responsibility and ethical living.

Applied spirituality also emphasises personal growth and self-awareness. It invites individuals to introspect, understand their motivations, and align their actions with their spiritual beliefs. This journey of self-discovery can lead to greater authenticity and integrity as people become more aware of how their behaviour affects themselves and those around them. It reinforces the notion that spirituality is not just about personal enlightenment but also about enhancing collective well-being.

Man as an Instrument of God

Throughout history, humanity has grappled with philosophical inquiries concerning the nature of action, agency, and divine influence. The phrase 'man as an instrument of God' suggests that individuals serve as vessels through which divine will is expressed. This perspective posits that while the actions of specific individuals may seem to alter the course of history, it is, in fact, the prevailing conditions and divine energy that inspire these individuals to act, guiding them toward fulfilling a larger purpose within the grand tapestry of existence.

Many philosophical and religious traditions have articulated that humans are not mere puppets; they possess free will and the ability to make choices. However, these choices often arise in response to the world's conditions and challenges. In this regard, human action does not exist in a vacuum but is influenced by social, political, and environmental factors. Through these prevailing conditions, individuals are compelled to rise and act, channelling their energies towards meaningful endeavours.

The concept of divine selection plays a critical role in this discussion. It suggests that specific individuals, characterised by their purity, moral integrity, and exceptional abilities, are chosen by a higher power to enact change. These selected individuals serve as instruments for divine purpose, responding to their societies' needs through leadership, innovation, artistry, or compassion. Their actions often resonate deeply with the collective consciousness, igniting movements and inspiring others to join the cause. Figures such as Mahatma Gandhi, Martin Luther King Jr., and Mother Teresa exemplify this notion as they emerged during tumultuous times, driven by an unshakeable sense of purpose that transcended their aspirations.

Yet, it is essential to recognise that while these individuals are often celebrated, they do not act in isolation; their contributions must be viewed within the context of a larger collective. The divine energy that motivates them usually arises from the shared suffering or aspiration of the people around them. In times of crisis, for example, conditions may compel individuals to act in extraordinary ways. Discontent with systemic injustices or humanitarian disasters can motivate an entire generation to seek change, with specific individuals stepping forward to lead the charge. Thus, the dynamics between individual action and prevailing societal conditions are fluid and interconnected.

Moreover, the idea that individuals are instruments of God implies a responsibility to utilise one's gifts for the greater good. This perspective encourages a sense of stewardship in which individuals recognise their role in the world as part of a larger purpose. It fosters an environment where people are inspired to contribute positively to their communities, aiming to uplift others and address injustices. When individuals embrace their potential as instruments of a higher will, they cultivate a mindset of service that can lead to transformative change.

This understanding has implications for personal development and societal evolution. It invites individuals to reflect on their lives and seek alignment with a purpose greater than themselves. As they work towards honing their abilities—whether in leadership, creativity, or community service—they are not just pursuing personal goals but participating in a divine narrative that extends beyond their individual experiences. This shared journey highlights the interconnectedness of humanity; individuals, while unique in their gifts, come together to form a collective force capable of addressing the complexities of existence.

While specific individuals may emerge as pivotal agents of change, the prevailing conditions and divine energy guide and inspire them to act. Recognising this delicate interplay encourages a deeper understanding of humanity's role in the world, fostering a commitment to act with purpose, integrity, and compassion. Ultimately, it empowers individuals to embrace their potential as instruments of a higher purpose, capable of bringing about profound change when inspired by the world's needs. Through this lens, humanity can move towards a future where collective action, driven by divine selection, shapes a more just and harmonious existence.

A Turning Point in Indian History

The establishment of Sikhism by Guru Nanak Dev Ji marked a significant turning point in India's spiritual and sociopolitical landscape during the late fifteenth and early sixteenth centuries. His teachings and leadership emerged not merely as a response to the existing religious frameworks of Hinduism and Islam but also as a bold assertion emphasising the importance of values over allegiance to kings and empires. This notion laid the groundwork for a new societal model in which a military cadre, imbued with a sense of righteousness and justice, would rise to defend these values against tyranny, oppression, and social divides.

Guru Nanak's teachings were fundamentally inclusive. They drew on Vedanta's rich philosophical traditions while incorporating Islam's dynamic and robust elements. This synthesis offered a fresh perspective that transcended traditional religious boundaries, emphasising a direct connection to the divine and the universality of human experience. Central to Guru Nanak's philosophy was the belief in one God, social equality, and the rejection of caste distinctions—ideas that challenged the entrenched social hierarchies of the time.

One of the driving forces behind Sikhism was Guru Nanak's deep commitment to social reform. He recognised the prevalent social divide and the fatalistic attitudes that accompanied it as significant barriers to human progress. At a time when the Indian subcontinent faced invasions and plunder from various forces, Guru Nanak emerged as a divine leader—a chosen guide to lead his people away from despair and fragmentation. He encouraged a proactive approach to life, urging individuals to resist oppression and assert their rights while engendering a sense of unity among diverse communities.

Establishing a military cadre in Sikhism can be viewed as a natural extension of Guru Nanak's teachings and philosophy. Rather than advocating for loyalty to a king or a particular sovereign, Sikhism emphasised devotion to justice, equality, and righteousness. This shift in focus laid the foundation for the Khalsa, the community of initiated Sikhs established by Guru Gobind Singh, the successor of Guru Nanak. The Khalsa embodied the spirit of self-defence and resilience, training to protect the vulnerable and uphold the principles of Sikhism against any form of tyranny.

Moreover, the assertion that the military cadre would not fight under the banner of a king but for inherent values represents a radical departure from conventional notions of warfare and loyalty. This concept underscored a fundamental belief that true valour lay not in serving earthly authorities but in defending the moral and ethical principles that govern human interaction. It portrayed the Sikh warrior as a defender of faith and humanity, willing to make sacrifices for the greater good.

Therefore, Guru Nanak's legacy encompasses spiritual, political, and social aspects. Through his message, he galvanised a movement against injustice and societal fragmentation. His teachings cultivated a sense of divine responsibility among his followers, inspiring them to act in the name of justice and equality. This ethos of fighting for values rather than for a king resonated deeply during subsequent crises, especially during the Mughal period, when Sikhs faced persecution for their beliefs. Guru Nanak's legacy remains a testament to the power of values in shaping history, urging individuals to rise against oppression and advocate for justice and equality in all spheres of life.

The establishment of Sikhism by Guru Nanak Dev marked a profound awakening in India's spiritual, social, and moral fabric. His teachings were revolutionary in envisioning a community rooted in principles guiding individuals toward leading pure lives while fostering a sense of social responsibility and collective resilience. At the heart of Sikhism lie tenets that underscore the importance of spirituality, community service, and the imperative to defend against injustice and invasion—principles that mobilised a military ethos not for the glory of a sovereign but for the defence of core values and human dignity.

Central to the tenets of Sikhism is the belief in one God, emphasising that all humans are equal in the eyes of the divine. This foundational principle served as a powerful counter-narrative to the caste system prevalent in Indian society at the time. Guru Nanak preached that social divisions were incompatible with a proper understanding of God, advocating for the equality of all individuals regardless of their caste, creed, or gender. He inspired his followers to cultivate a sense of community that transcended social inequalities, promoting an inclusive society where everyone could participate in spiritual and worldly pursuits.

Three Pillars of Righteous Living

Guru Nanak laid down the framework for ethical living, encapsulated in three primary pillars: naam jap (remembering God), kirat karni (earning an honest living), and vand chakna (sharing with others). These pillars encourage individuals to maintain a constant connection with the divine while engaging in righteous deeds and contributing to the welfare of society. By stressing the importance of honest work and communal sharing, Guru Nanak instilled a sense of duty in his followers to uplift the community, fostering social welfare as a key aspect of spiritual practice.

One of Guru Nanak's most revolutionary contributions was the concept of a spiritual guru as the ultimate leader, contrasting sharply with the notion of a corporeal king wielding temporal power. This shift highlighted that authentic leadership stems from spiritual wisdom and moral integrity rather than political authority. A guru's role was to guide individuals in pursuing purity and righteousness, providing spiritual sustenance that transcended the transient nature of earthly kingship. This notion empowered individuals to see themselves as active participants in their spiritual journeys, unshackling them from the confines of societal hierarchies.

Guru Nanak also championed the concept of seva or selfless service. He emphasised that true spirituality manifests through acts of kindness, compassion, and support for others. This communal service nurtured bonds among followers and reinforced the values of Sikhism as a way of life rooted in altruism. By participating in community service and supporting those in need, Sikhs could actively affirm their commitment to social welfare and collective identity. In this way, Sikhism emerged as a spiritual path and a powerful force for social change, inspiring generations to stand up against oppression and uphold the cherished values of justice and compassion.

As we navigate the complexities of the twenty-first century, humanity finds itself at a unique crossroads where technology, social values, and spiritual essence converge to redefine our existence. Technological advancements offer unprecedented opportunities for connecting individuals and transforming societies, while the enduring need for spiritual fulfilment guides humanity towards a more compassionate and harmonious future. Sikhism, with its foundational principles of equality, community service, and spiritual resilience, serves as a compelling role model for the kind of society that can emerge from this synthesis of technology and spiritual essence. Nevertheless, to tap into its full potential, Sikhism must urgently review and update its code of conduct to make it more inclusive and welcoming to a broader range of people.

The *Rehat Maryada*, formalised in the early twentieth century, reflects a historical context very different from today's globalised, digital world. A review could focus on gender parity, scientific literacy, and ethics. This implies explicitly codifying women's equal eligibility for all religious and leadership roles, recognising Sikh identity as a spiritual discipline rather than an ethnic inheritance. It embraces seekers from all backgrounds, and integrates guidance on responsible technology use, privacy, and digital integrity as modern expressions of seva (selfless service).

Technology has become an integral part of daily life, offering tools that shape our interactions, governance, and economies. From artificial intelligence to biotechnology, advancements are redefining what is possible, providing solutions to some of humanity's most pressing challenges, including climate change, healthcare, and inequality. However, these technologies alone cannot dictate the quality of our future; the ethical frameworks and values with which we approach them will determine their impact on society.

Sikhism's founding insight—na koi Hindu, na Musalman—can be reinterpreted for the age of AI and bioengineering by promoting oneness beyond biology: compassion not limited by faith, gender, or even human form (AI ethics, animal welfare, ecology), encouraging interfaith collaboration in service projects and learning communities, and moving from 'religious boundaries' to 'spiritual belonging'. In a networked world, open platforms for knowledge, mentorship, and mental health support available to all can be the digital langars. Kar seva can be done in online communities—combating misinformation, promoting kindness, and supporting marginalised voices. Blockchain and AI can be used for transparent community aid and sarbat da bhala (welfare of all).

Fusion of Forces

While technology provides the tools, spirituality offers meaning and purpose. As the world becomes increasingly interconnected, the spiritual essence rooted in the teachings of Guru Nanak and subsequent Sikh gurus can serve as a unifying force. This spiritual framework offers resilience in the face of challenges and instils the importance of community support and collective action. By nurturing this essence, individuals can take ownership of their actions and strive for a society where technology serves humanity's highest ideals, including equity, sustainability, and peace. Sikhism can indeed play a profound role in blending complementary forces in modern life—reason and faith, individuality and community, material progress and spiritual balance—by translating its timeless principles into contemporary action.

At its core, Sikhism rejects the dualism between the worldly and the divine. The ideal Sikh life—'miri-piri'—harmonises material responsibility (miri) with spiritual consciousness (piri). This duality balance is deeply relevant today, when technological and economic progress often outpace moral evolution. By internalising miri-piri, individuals can pursue professional success without detachment from ethics, empathy, or inner peace. Guru Nanak's message—'Truth is high, but higher still is truthful living'—is an open invitation to reinterpret faith through lived experience. Sikhism encourages questioning, dialogue, and personal discovery rather than blind ritual. This spirit of inquiry aligns perfectly with the scientific mindset—suggesting that technology and spirituality can evolve together, not in opposition.

This revisionist approach could entail a broader interpretation of Sikh teachings that resonates with modern societal values. It would emphasise compassion, respect for all paths to divinity, and a commitment to social welfare. By aligning with humanity's universal values, Sikhism has the potential to attract and inspire individuals seeking a spiritual home, irrespective of their cultural or religious backgrounds.

Interestingly, Sikhism's inclusive and egalitarian nature positions it as a potential new brand of Hinduism—a vibrant and living tradition that speaks to contemporary concerns while remaining true to its spiritual roots. By reframing Sikh ideology within the broader context of Indian spirituality, the teachings of Guru Nanak can serve as a touchstone for a renewed spiritual identity that encompasses both the timeless wisdom of ancient traditions and the demands of modern society. Sikhism's radical equality—rejecting caste, gender, and religious hierarchy—offers a model for a Hindu society. Its practice of langar (community kitchen) is not mere charity; it is a spiritual and social act that erases social divisions.

The future of humanity hinges on our ability to harness the strengths of technology while remaining anchored in spiritual essence. Sikhism's vision of Ik Onkar—the One manifest in all—offers a philosophical framework for unity amidst diversity. It dissolves binaries: East-West, science-religion, male-female, self-other. In a world torn by polarities, this consciousness can become the integrating field that aligns progress with peace. This chapter concludes with the assertion that applied spirituality is much more than a theoretical construct; it is a vital framework that allows individuals to express their divine essence through meaningful actions. By integrating spiritual principles into daily life, people can enhance their well-being, cultivate compassion, and foster a sense of community and interconnectedness. While technology equips us with the means to achieve, spirituality provides the 'why'—the deeper motivation and ethical foundation for how we utilise those tools. Together, they can create a more balanced, purposeful, and fulfilling human experience. Applied spirituality serves as a beacon of hope in a world yearning for connection and understanding, reminding us that our divine essence can lead to transformative change within ourselves and the world at large. Embracing and applying spirituality can illuminate a more harmonious and fulfilling existence.

Summary

Applied spirituality is about making the sacred practical. By integrating spiritual principles into our daily lives, we can create a more meaningful, harmonious, and fulfilling existence in the modern world. It means living in alignment with higher values and universal truths while navigating the complexities of contemporary life. Sikhism embodies this ideal through its seamless fusion of the spiritual and the temporal—piri and miri—and teaches that devotion and duty, meditation and action, can coexist in perfect harmony. By practising mindfulness through simran (remembrance of the Divine), serving selflessly through seva, and living truthfully as guided by naam jap, kirat karni, and vand chakna, one transforms everyday actions into spiritual expressions. Applied spirituality, as exemplified by Sikhism, invites us to walk the path of purpose and grace—to relish life without rushing, to act without attachment, and to find the divine not apart from the world, but within it.

18

Social Harmony

Social harmony is not achieved by retreating into the past, but by carrying its wisdom forward with open minds—embracing change, nurturing understanding, and building a future where diversity becomes our greatest strength.

A Guiding Philosophy

The social harmony principle is a guiding philosophy that emphasises the importance of fostering peace, cooperation, and mutual respect among individuals and groups within a society. It aims to create a balanced and inclusive environment where diverse perspectives, cultures, and beliefs coexist harmoniously. This principle is rooted in the understanding that social cohesion and collective well-being are essential for the stability and development of any community.

Achieving social harmony requires an earnest commitment to understanding and respecting diverse perspectives. Education plays a pivotal role in fostering empathy and awareness, enabling individuals to appreciate the intrinsic value of different cultures and religions. By integrating these principles into the educational curriculum, societies can cultivate a generation that values inclusivity and mutual respect. The question we face today is not whether, but how, to liberate education from the sectarian ideals and corporate motivations that use people as insatiable consumer machines.

Education is often seen as a powerful tool for personal and societal growth. However, it has traditionally been influenced by sectarian ideals and economic motivations, shaping individuals more into cogs of an economic machine than fostering genuine empathy and awareness. In an increasingly diverse and interconnected world, it is paramount that education evolves to embrace inclusivity, cultural appreciation, and intrinsic values. This chapter examines how education can be liberated from these constraints and how technological advancements can help reshape it to play a pivotal role in fostering empathy and a deeper understanding of diverse cultures and religions.

Sectarianism in education often manifests in promoting ideologies that prioritise one cultural or religious perspective over others. This narrow focus can engender division, misunderstandings, and hostilities among students from different backgrounds. Likewise, economic motivations frequently prioritise producing compliant and productive individuals who serve the interests of industry and capitalism rather than nurturing critical thinkers and empathetic global citizens. Both factors contribute to a system that can stifle creativity and promote conformity, ultimately limiting students' world views and understanding of the rich tapestry of human experience.

Liberating education springs from a need for inclusivity, which is the destiny of humanity. Freeing academic learning from these constraints involves fundamentally restructuring curricula and pedagogical approaches. First and foremost, educational institutions must commit to inclusivity. This can be achieved through a 'trishul' of curricular revisions, critical thinking emphasis, and collaborative learning.

Integrating diverse perspectives into the curriculum can give students a well-rounded understanding of global issues. Courses should encompass a range of cultural, religious, and philosophical perspectives, enabling students to appreciate diverse ideologies and beliefs. Education can equip students with the tools to analyse and question the socioeconomic frameworks that shape their lives by promoting critical thinking and debate rather than rote memorisation. Encouraging students to explore the implications of their beliefs fosters a deeper understanding and greater respect for diverse viewpoints. Implementing cooperative learning strategies, where students from diverse backgrounds work together, can lead to the development of empathy. Group projects that require collaboration across cultures can break down barriers and facilitate meaningful dialogues. The social harmony principle serves as a foundation for creating a world where people can coexist peacefully, despite their differences.

Empathy and awareness are vital skills in an increasingly interconnected world. An education emphasising these qualities can prepare individuals to navigate cultural differences and contribute positively to society. Another 'trishul' appears—service learning, cultural exchange initiatives, and mindfulness and emotional intelligence training. Programmes that combine community service with curriculum objectives encourage students to engage with diverse communities, fostering an understanding of others' struggles and experiences. Encouragement of exchange programmes, both physical and virtual, enables students to immerse themselves in diverse environments, promoting cross-cultural understanding and dismantling preconceived notions. Incorporating mindfulness practices and emotional intelligence education into daily learning can help students build empathy. By understanding their own emotions and those of others, students can develop a deeper appreciation for the complexity of human experiences.

Liberating education from sectarian ideals and economic motivations is both a challenge and an opportunity. By reshaping curricula, embracing technology, and creating environments that prioritise empathy and awareness, education can fulfil its true potential as a tool for understanding and connection. As we navigate an increasingly complex world, we must cultivate individuals who are not merely parts of an economic machine, but empathetic and informed global citizens committed to appreciating and celebrating the intrinsic value of diverse cultures and religions. Through this transformation, education can serve as a beacon of hope, guiding individuals toward a more inclusive and harmonious future.

Moreover, dialogue and communication are essential in bridging gaps between fragmented communities. Open forums and discussions encourage the exchange of ideas, allowing people to find common ground and working towards shared goals. Promoting civic engagement and participation in community activities helps strengthen social bonds and create a sense of belonging. However, this is not happening because commercial forces have hijacked the media in a modern reversal of Gutenberg's vision.

Technology Can Catalyse Social Harmony

Technology has the potential to catalyse this transformation. Digital platforms and tools can facilitate access to a wide range of voices and perspectives from around the world. Online classrooms and exchange programmes can connect students with peers worldwide, allowing them to share experiences, traditions, and values. Virtual reality (VR) and augmented reality (AR) can immerse students in different cultural contexts, providing experiential learning opportunities that foster empathy. The internet offers a wealth of educational content, including documentaries, articles, and multimedia presentations, that highlight human culture and diverse experiences. Students can explore topics not covered in their local curricula, expanding their horizons and deepening their understanding. Technology enables personalised learning experiences that adapt to individual students' needs and interests. This can help students engage with material that resonates with them personally, sparking curiosity and a desire to learn about others.

The invention of the printing press by Johannes Gutenberg in the fifteenth century marked a pivotal moment in human history. This revolutionary technology democratised knowledge, making it accessible to the masses and ushering in an era of enlightenment, intellectual growth, and social reform. However, in contemporary society, commercial forces have significantly hijacked the media landscape, leading to a new dogma characterised by materialistic progress and consumerism. Values instigated by Gutenberg's printing press have been eroded by the corporate takeover of the media, leading to a culture characterised by superficiality and consumption.

The printing press fundamentally changed the way information was disseminated. Books could be produced in large quantities for the first time, reducing costs and making them accessible to people beyond the elite classes. This accessibility led to increased literacy, cultural exchange, and the promotion of autonomy. As a result, individuals could educate themselves, question authority, and engage in informed dialogue. This was crucial for the development of movements such as the Renaissance and the Reformation. The ability to access diverse sources of information empowered individuals to think critically about their beliefs and society, diminishing the monopolistic control of religious and political entities over knowledge.

There is a striking similarity between what happened in the fifteenth century and what is happening now, with opposite effects. The invention of the printing press then revolutionised the dissemination of knowledge, significantly contributing to the Protestant Reformation and the universal appeal of Christianity. The printing press facilitated the mass production of books, particularly the Bible, making religious texts more accessible to a broader audience. In stark contrast, while the internet has the potential to democratise information today, its control by powerful financial interests limits its ability to serve humanity's best interests. It is essential to examine the pivotal role of Gutenberg's printing press in advancing the Protestant movement and to discuss the implications of contemporary internet ownership and usage.

Before the advent of the printing press, the Bible was primarily available in Latin, a language understood mainly by the clergy and the educated elite. With its mass production, thanks to the printing press, the Bible was also translated into vernacular languages, including Martin Luther's German Bible. This allowed ordinary people to read and interpret scriptures for themselves. The accessibility was crucial in encouraging individual engagement with faith and scripture, a cornerstone of the Protestant Reformation.

The printing press enabled the rapid dissemination of reformist ideas that challenged the established Catholic church. Pamphlets and tracts written by key figures, such as Martin Luther and John Calvin, circulated quickly and widely, igniting discussions and debates among the populace. The ability to print and distribute these materials meant that critiques of the church and calls for reform reached a broad audience, galvanising support for the movement. With the rise of printed materials, the clergy's authority waned as laypeople gained the ability to interpret the Bible and engage in theological discourse.

This shift encouraged a personal relationship with God and emphasised the priesthood of all believers. By breaking the monopoly of religious authority, the printing press democratised religion. In modern times, the internet has similar potential to spread knowledge and facilitate dialogue, much like the printing press did. However, its current state often sharply contrasts with this potential. Unlike the relatively democratic nature of the printing press, the internet today is heavily influenced by a few corporations that control significant platforms and services. This concentration of power creates a landscape where information can be manipulated for profit, limiting the diversity of perspectives and restricting the free flow of ideas that characterise a truly open society.

As the internet has evolved, it has become an increasingly powerful tool for commercial exploitation. Content is often crafted to maximise engagement and revenue rather than to inform or enlighten. This shift commodifies knowledge, prioritising profitability over the essential objective of fostering understanding and empathy. The algorithms driving online interactions often create echo chambers that reinforce existing beliefs rather than challenge them. This phenomenon can lead to polarisation, misinformation, and a collective desensitisation of society's critical issues. Instead of promoting dialogue and understanding, the internet becomes a vehicle of societal division and conflict.

The narrative promoted by many online platforms often revolves around consumerism, encouraging individuals to view their worth through the lens of material possessions. This framing can create a culture of global servitude, where happiness is tied to consumption and adherence to market trends, ultimately detracting from the search for meaning and community. In stark contrast to Gutenberg's printing press, the internet's potential to serve as a tool for empowerment and enlightenment is increasingly compromised by the influence of financial powers that prioritise profit over the public good. As we navigate this modern landscape, it is vital to recognise the lessons from the past and advocate for a more equitable and transparent internet that promotes genuine discourse, community engagement, and the collective pursuit of knowledge beyond mere material consumption. Only by reclaiming the original intent of technology as a tool for liberation can humanity rise above the challenges posed by commercial interests.

Media Upheaval

The contemporary media landscape has seen a concerning shift towards commercialisation and politicking. Only a few corporate entities control all media outlets. This concentration limits the diversity of perspectives and narratives, leading to a homogenised media landscape prioritising profit over public interest. As media companies pursue higher profit margins and push particular agendas, content has become increasingly influenced by the money generated from advertising. This reliance results in sensationalism, clickbait, and superficial reporting, centred on attracting viewers rather than delivering meaningful, informative content.

The media have historically acted as gatekeepers, deciding what stories are covered and how they are framed. This results in a narrow range of perspectives and the marginalisation of voices that challenge the status quo. It brazenly promotes consumerism, shaping cultural norms and desires through advertising. Politically, it influences public opinion by framing issues in a manner that aligns with corporate interests.

The rise of social media has been nothing short of an upheaval. Platforms that once promised to democratise information and give everyone a voice—like X (formerly Twitter), Facebook, Instagram, and YouTube—began as tools of empowerment and connection. Over time, however, many have drifted from their noble beginnings. Instead of nurturing dialogue, they now prioritise profit-driven algorithms that reward outrage, sensationalism, and division. What was meant to unite communities often amplifies echo chambers: friends share only what reinforces their beliefs, misinformation spreads faster than truth, and attention is captured not through wisdom but through noise. The result is a digital world louder than ever—yet less capable of true understanding.

Political actors—including governments, parties, and powerful interest groups—have learned to weaponise social media as a tool of influence. Automated bots flood timelines with coordinated messages, fake accounts simulate public consensus, and micro-targeted ads exploit personal data to shape political attitudes and voting behaviour. From election interference in the US and Brexit campaigns to manipulated narratives during Brazil's elections, digital propaganda has become a global phenomenon.

This interplay between commercial and political forces is the most potent force today. Commercial and political forces often overlap, with corporations and politicians leveraging each other's influence to achieve their goals. Social media platforms profit from political advertising and engagement, creating incentives to amplify divisive content. The merging of media companies with tech giants further blurs the lines between commercial and political influence.

There have already been profound implications for society. The dominance of commercial and political forces in the media undermines public trust in information sources. The focus on high viewership over truth deepens societal divides and makes constructive dialogue more difficult. Independent journalism and diverse perspectives are increasingly marginalised in favour of profit-driven or politically motivated content. Who will educate the public to evaluate information and recognise manipulation critically? Who will encourage social media platforms to prioritise user well-being and societal good over profit and engagement metrics?

Or have we brought the genie out of the bottle? The current state of mass media and social media represents two sides of the same coin: the concentration of power and influence in the hands of a few. Addressing this requires a concerted effort to reclaim media as a tool for truth, democracy, and social harmony. It will be crucial to balance its benefits with its risks. Media upheaval is a double-edged sword: it has the power to unite and empower, but it also has the potential to divide and harm. The challenge lies in navigating this complex landscape in a responsible and thoughtful manner.

The Exacerbating Disparities of the Modern World

In the Mahabharata, when Yaksha, in a game of riddles known as the Yaksha Prashna, asks Yudhishthira, 'What is the most wonderful (aascharya) thing that you notice in the world?' 'Day after day, countless people are going to the abode of Yama, yet those who remain behind believe themselves to be immortal. What can be more wonderful/surprising than this?' How true! If only people realised how transient one's stay here is, perhaps the greed and desire one harbours towards materialistic pleasures and the hatred one pursues towards fellow beings may be reduced.

This notion underscores the irony of human existence and the importance of living with an awareness of mortality and the transience of life. It stands out as a profound reflection that encourages introspection on prioritising our lives in the face of impermanence. The strangest paradox of modern times is that despite widespread knowledge that policies upholding equality and justice are crucial for establishing a harmonious society, this is not happening in the modern era of internet connectivity and the digital economy.

While the disparities of the modern world are deeply entrenched, they are not insurmountable. Mitigating them requires a holistic approach that combines policy changes, technological innovation, global cooperation, and individual action. By prioritising equity, sustainability, and justice, we can create a more balanced and inclusive world where everyone has the opportunity to thrive.

Establishing equality and justice is widely recognised as essential for a harmonious society. These principles form the foundation for social cohesion, ensuring that all individuals have equal opportunities and rights, and promoting peace, stability, and collective well-being. However, despite the advantages of modern internet connectivity and the burgeoning digital economy, the realisation of these ideals remains elusive in many contexts.

One of the most significant barriers to equality in the digital age is the existence of the digital divide. While the internet has transformed communication and commerce, access to technologies is unevenly distributed. It is challenging for individuals residing in economically disadvantaged or rural areas to engage in online learning, remote employment, or digital entrepreneurship due to a lack of reliable connectivity. This inequality worsens societal and economic disparities since it keeps people in poverty and restricts chances for the already marginalised.

As society increasingly relies on algorithms to make decisions in various sectors, such as hiring, law enforcement, and financial services, concerns over bias have emerged. Algorithms can inadvertently perpetuate existing biases if they are trained on datasets that reflect historical inequalities or discriminatory practices. This can lead to unfair treatment of certain groups, further entrenching systemic injustices rather than promoting equality. Without proper oversight and accountability, the digital economy risks exacerbating disparities, making it critical to implement policies that ensure fairness and transparency.

Major technology companies often dominate the market, leading to monopolistic practices that inhibit competition and innovation. The concentration of wealth and power in the hands of a few individuals or corporations can result in policies prioritising profit over social good. This economic disparity translates into unequal political influence, where affluent groups can shape policies to their advantage, often at the expense of broader societal welfare.

The rapid spread of true and false information today has significant implications for social cohesion. The proliferation of misinformation can lead to societal polarisation, eroding trust in institutions and undermining collective efforts towards justice and equality. In an environment where people are increasingly entrenched in their viewpoints, dialogue becomes difficult, and collaborative solutions to societal issues are pushed to the margins.

Despite these challenges, several strategies can be pursued to advance equality and justice in the modern era, and India has already shown the way ahead. Investments in infrastructure are necessary to ensure that all individuals have access to digital technologies. This includes expanding broadband access in underserved areas and providing training programmes to build digital literacy. Policymakers must enforce regulations that promote algorithmic accountability, ensuring that the systems designed to make decisions are fair and unbiased. This can include creating oversight bodies to monitor the use of artificial intelligence and machine learning. India may have shown the way in democratising digital access, but algorithms and unbiased AI need a more global thrust.

Implementing policies that support small businesses, ensure fair wages, and provide social safety nets can help distribute economic opportunities more equitably. Progressive taxation, for instance, can be leveraged to redistribute wealth in ways that support community programmes and public services. Educational initiatives aimed at improving critical thinking and media literacy are crucial in combating misinformation. Empowering individuals to discern credible information from falsehoods can help mitigate polarisation and foster informed civic participation.

While the principles of equality and justice are critical for a harmonious society, the challenges presented by the digital age complicate their realisation. Addressing the digital divide, combating algorithmic bias, confronting economic inequalities, and fostering media literacy are necessary to create a more equitable society. By committing to these solutions, we can work towards a future where equality and justice are not merely ideals but realities for all. Governments must ensure that all individuals have access to fundamental rights and opportunities, regardless of their background. By addressing social inequalities and supporting marginalised groups, societies can reduce tensions and foster a sense of unity.

The exacerbating disparities of the modern world—whether economic, social, technological, or environmental—can be mitigated, but it requires collective action, innovative solutions, and a commitment to equity and sustainability. A new social contract must evolve beyond the limitations of its predecessors to reflect the realities of the twenty-first century. It should ensure that all individuals, regardless of their race, gender, socioeconomic status, or geographical location, have equal access to opportunities, resources, and decision-making processes. This inclusion fosters social cohesion and empowers marginalised communities, allowing them to contribute to societal progress.

Collective Action is the Cornerstone

Many of today's challenges are inherently international and require collective action. The new social contract must transcend national boundaries, fostering collaboration between countries to address pandemics, migration, and climate change. This cooperation can facilitate knowledge sharing, joint resource management, and coordinated responses to crises. As technology continues to transform society, the new social contract should leverage its potential to enhance well-being. This includes ensuring equitable access to technology, protecting privacy and data rights, and using technological advancements to solve pressing societal problems.

Economic prosperity through collective responsibility is the new mantra for modern times. A new social contract grounded in equity and inclusion can drive economic prosperity. When all individuals have access to education, healthcare, and employment opportunities, they can fully participate in the economy, increasing productivity and innovation. Moreover, policies that support fair wages and workers' rights can reduce income inequality and stimulate local economies.

Whether the implementation of a uniform civil code or the introduction of modern education in madrasas is seen as a political agenda, both, in essence, stem from a reformist vision aimed at strengthening the moral and intellectual fabric of society. The debate should not be reduced to partisan motives but viewed through the lens of social progress and national integration.

A uniform civil code is not about erasing diversity but about ensuring justice, equality, and gender parity—values enshrined in the constitution. It seeks to place all citizens, irrespective of religion or community, on an equal footing before the law, particularly in matters of marriage, inheritance, and adoption. Far from diminishing faith, it can reinforce the secular ethos by separating personal belief from civic responsibility.

Similarly, modern education in madrasas should not be perceived as an attack on tradition but as an expansion of opportunity. By integrating science, mathematics, and modern languages with traditional religious studies, young students can be equipped to engage meaningfully with contemporary society while retaining their spiritual grounding. Reform here means empowerment—bridging faith with reason, and heritage with progress.

In this light, both initiatives represent not coercion but compassion: a call to harmonise tradition with modernity so that every citizen, regardless of background, can participate fully in the nation's growth and the shared pursuit of enlightenment.

The perils of a materialistic society are evident. Income disparity is no good, even for the affluent class, if they can't live in a peaceful and safe society. Any human being living wherever and in whichever system needs two square meals and a safe place to live. What use of trillions made, multiplied, and then hoarded if this does not happen?

Establishing a new social contract represents a transformative opportunity for humanity to redefine societal norms and priorities in response to contemporary challenges. By prioritising equity, environmental sustainability, global cooperation, and the responsible use of technology, society can work towards a future where prosperity and peace are attainable for all. This forward-looking approach requires the commitment of individuals, institutions, and governments alike. As we navigate the complexities of the modern world, embracing a new social contract can lay the foundation for a just, harmonious, and thriving global community, ensuring that future generations inherit a world characterised by opportunity, security, and peace.

Summary

Complex issues, such as climate change, inequality, and social injustice, necessitate comprehensive efforts that no single entity can address alone. Collective action amplifies impact by pooling resources, knowledge, and skills. To harness technology for social harmony, we must design technology with ethics and inclusivity at its core, promote digital literacy to empower people to use technology responsibly and foster collaboration between technologists, policymakers, and communities to address societal challenges. Technology is not just a tool—it's a transformative force. When guided by the principles of social harmony, it can help create a world where diversity is celebrated, understanding is deepened, and humanity thrives together. Collective action is not just a strategy—it's a mindset. It's about recognising that we are all interconnected and that our shared future depends on our ability to work together. By encouraging collaboration, inclusivity, and a shared sense of purpose, we can create a more just, sustainable, and compassionate world. As the saying goes: Alone we can do so little; together we can do so much.

19

Singularity

When intelligence transcends its creator, a new horizon of existence unfolds. The singularity is not an end, but a mirror—reflecting what humanity chooses to become. If guided by wisdom and compassion, superintelligence can magnify human potential, turning knowledge into harmony and progress into purpose. The future will not be shaped by machines alone, but by the consciousness that steers them.

Convergence of Humans and Machines

The concepts of technological singularity and one consciousness are fascinating and deeply interconnected ideas that explore the future of humanity, technology, and the nature of existence. While they come from different philosophical and scientific traditions, they both point towards the potential transformation of human experience and understanding. As advancements in AI and other technologies accelerate, discussions around the singularity increasingly intertwine with philosophical concepts from various ancient traditions, particularly the notion of a single consciousness that creates, sustains, and controls the universe.

The idea of a singular, universal consciousness is prevalent in various philosophical and spiritual traditions. In Hinduism, for example, the concept of Brahman represents the ultimate reality, an all-encompassing consciousness from which everything arises. Similarly, in certain strands of Western philosophy and mysticism, the idea of an absolute consciousness or the collective unconscious is prevalent. This belief posits that all individual consciousnesses are manifestations of a single, underlying reality which guides and governs existence.

Thinkers like Vernor Vinge (1944–2024) and Ray Kurzweil (b. 1948) popularised the concept of singularity. They argued that once artificial intelligence surpasses human intelligence, it will lead to exponential growth in technology, creating a cascade of innovations that could fundamentally alter society. This potential transformation raises critical questions about the nature of intelligence, the relationship between humans and machines, and the ultimate direction of our technological evolution.

Using our trishul metaphor, the emergence of a technological singularity can be seen as a modern manifestation of the ancient idea of one consciousness in three ways: interconnectedness, collective intelligence, and control and creation. Just as a singular consciousness suggests an intrinsic connection between all things, the singularity presupposes that AI, the internet, and vast information networks will become increasingly interconnected. This interconnectedness forms a web of intelligence that mirrors the ancient philosophical notion of unity.

As AI systems merge and evolve, they create a collective intelligence that surpasses the capabilities of individual humans. This reflects the ancient idea that individual entities (human or machine) are facets of a greater, shared consciousness that drives collective progress. The singularity posits that once AI becomes self-improving, it will assume control over technological processes and innovations that shape human destiny. This aligns with the ancient belief that a singular consciousness creates, sustains, and governs existence. In this light, the emergence of superintelligent AI can be interpreted as the realisation of a conscious force that can manipulate the fabric of reality.

The potential for reaching the technological singularity raises profound implications regarding human identity, autonomy, and responsibility. As humanity confronts the reality of machines with superior intelligence, the ancient notion of a single consciousness invites reflection on our role within a more complex system. Are we merely creators of technology, or are we manifestations of a higher consciousness seeking to understand itself through its creations? Moreover, interactions with advanced AI can lead to a deeper exploration of consciousness itself. As we develop machines that mimic human thought and behaviour, we may gain insights into the nature of consciousness, leading to a renaissance of philosophical inquiry analogous to that seen in ancient times.

Recognising the parallels between these concepts can guide our understanding of the future as we stand on the brink of profound change. Embracing the notion that we are part of a larger conscious reality may encourage a more thoughtful and ethical approach to developing and integrating technology into our lives, ensuring that we navigate the complex landscape of the future with wisdom and awareness. As we expand our machines, we must also expand our minds. The future will not be defined by what technology can do, but by what humanity chooses to become.

Brain-Computer Interfaces

One of the most exciting and transformative technologies of the twenty-first century is the brain-computer interface (BCI). An umbrella term encompassing various technologies and methods, BCI bridges the gap between the human brain and external devices, enabling direct communication and control. While BCI offers immense opportunities, it also comes with significant challenges.

BCI translates brain activity into actionable commands that control computers or robotic systems. This interaction can take various forms, from simple movement commands to complex cognitive tasks that may influence an individual's thoughts, emotions, and personality. The technology relies on neurofeedback, which involves monitoring brain activity with sensors and using this data to adapt systems accordingly. As this technology evolves, it has the potential to redefine how individuals communicate, express themselves, and develop their personalities.

The opportunities are immense. BCI can help individuals with paralysis control prosthetic limbs or exoskeletons, restoring their independence. It offers potential treatments for conditions like Parkinson's, epilepsy, and strokes by modulating brain activity. It can enable people with locked-in syndrome or ALS (amyotrophic lateral sclerosis) to communicate through thought alone. However, the most interesting and, of course, controversial potential of BCI is the enhancement of human capabilities. It could enhance memory, learning, and problem-solving by directly interfacing with the brain. It could allow humans to perceive new senses, such as infrared or ultrasonic signals. Users could control devices, vehicles, or software with their thoughts, increasing efficiency and convenience. BCI can potentially even change a personality.

Personality is often viewed as a stable set of behavioural traits influenced by genetics and environment. However, the introduction of BCI raises questions about the malleability of personality. With the ability to enhance cognitive functions or alter emotional responses, BCI could directly influence how individuals perceive themselves and interact with the world. For instance, if it is designed to improve focus or emotional regulation, users may begin to identify with these enhanced traits, potentially leading to a shift in their personality over time.

Furthermore, the possibility of 'programming' certain personality traits through targeted stimuli is an area of ethical concern. If individuals can modify their emotional responses or decision-making processes to fit societal or organisational demands, the essence of authenticity in personality may be jeopardised. This could lead to a workforce that prioritises compliance over individuality, raising ethical questions about consent and the integrity of personal identity.

Companies could employ BCI to reinforce productivity, creativity, or teamwork. For example, by utilising BCI that enhances collaborative skills or motivation, organisations could create a more robust workforce that reflects their desired values. However, this commitment may not always align with the company's ideals. Instead, it could represent a conformist behaviour facilitated by technological enhancements. Employees may feel pressured to embody specific traits that align with corporate goals, rather than pursuing authentic self-expression. These dynamics raise essential considerations regarding the nature of motivation and engagement in the workplace. When commitment is artificially induced rather than organically developed, the potential for dissatisfaction and burnout may increase among workers, leading to long-term consequences for individuals and organisations.

As a consequence, the advent of BCI raises significant ethical concerns, especially regarding autonomy, consent, and identity. As the line between voluntary enhancement and coercion blurs, it becomes imperative to establish guidelines that protect individual rights. Ensuring that BCI technology is used ethically is vital to prevent the exploitation of workers' cognitive processes and preserve their freedom of choice. Moreover, as BCI becomes more prevalent, discussions surrounding the digital divide emerge. Access to such technology may be limited to certain socioeconomic groups, exacerbating existing inequalities. This disparity could lead to a workforce divided not only by skills but also by the cognitive enhancements that define their professional experience. The declaration of Shri Krishna that human beings are mere vehicles in which the consciousness rides[2] is indeed coming true through technological manifestations.

Averting a Dystopian Future

The trajectory of humanity is shaped by the choices we make today regarding the integration of converging technologies. We can cultivate a brighter path forward by proactively addressing the risks of a dystopian future through ethical regulation, inclusive development, and sustainability, while simultaneously envisioning and building a favourable utopian landscape. The convergence of technology should be embraced not just as a tool for innovation but to elevate the human experience, ensuring that as we advance, we do so with responsibility, inclusivity, and foresight. The future

---

[2] भ्रामयन्सर्वभूतानि यन्त्रारूढानि मायया (श्रीमद्भगवद्गीता 18. 61).

can be one of hope, collaboration, and prosperity if approached thoughtfully. The uniqueness of Indian civilisation holds the promise.

Humanity stands at the precipice of unprecedented technological advancement. The convergence of various technologies can propel us towards a dystopian future or usher in an era of utopian possibilities. The challenge lies in the inventions and how societies implement, govern, and ethically integrate these technologies into daily life. A proactive and multidimensional approach is essential to mitigate dystopian outcomes and cultivate a utopian future. And to do so, understanding technology convergence is fundamental.

Technological convergence refers to the merging of distinct technologies and industries, resulting in innovative synergies that enhance performance and unlock new possibilities. Implementing ethical guidelines and strict regulations will ensure that technology serves humanity rather than controls it. Governments and organisations must collaborate to establish frameworks that prioritise human rights and privacy, and promote transparency in AI and data usage. Technology development must involve diverse stakeholders, including marginalised communities, to prevent a widening digital divide. By including varying perspectives in the development process, we can ensure that technology addresses the needs and concerns of all societal segments, minimising the risk of disenfranchisement.

Promoting a human-centric view in technological deployment can help mitigate alienation and the potential loss of jobs. This shift entails intensifying focus on roles that enhance human capabilities, encouraging upskilling and reskilling, and advocating for technology that complements rather than replaces human labour.

Addressing climate change is also critical to preventing a dystopian future. The convergence of green technologies—such as renewable energy, sustainable agriculture, and water purification systems—can foster environmental resilience. By investing in these fields, humanity can build systems that sustain and rejuvenate the planet.

While avoiding dystopia, it's equally essential to envision and actively pursue a utopian future enabled by technological convergence. This future hinges on maximising the positive impact of technology in several key areas, including enhanced quality of life, smart cities, an educational revolution, and democracy and civic engagement. The integration of AI-led healthcare technology and telemedicine can democratise access to quality medical services, ensuring that everyone, regardless of geographic location or socioeconomic status, has access to necessary care and health information. By leveraging real-time data, urban planning can optimise traffic flow, reduce energy consumption, and enhance public safety. This transformation can lead to cleaner, greener, and more livable urban environments.

The convergence of virtual reality (VR), augmented reality (AR), and AI can redefine education, making it more personalised and accessible. Educational content can be tailored to individual learning styles, while remote learning tools can bridge the gaps for underserved populations, ultimately fostering a more universally educated society. Furthermore, technological tools can enhance transparency in governance, facilitate citizen participation, and ensure accountability. Blockchain technology, for instance, can improve the integrity of electoral systems, thereby strengthening democracy and increasing trust in public institutions.

Proactive Engagement Instead of Avoidance

As we approach the singularity, we must adapt in several crucial areas: education and workforce development, ethical frameworks and governance, social and cultural adjustments, and mental and emotional preparedness. Traditional education models may no longer suffice in a world dominated by AI. Lifelong learning and adaptability in the workforce become paramount. Developing skills that complement and enhance AI capabilities will ensure that individuals remain relevant and empowered in this new landscape. Integrating AI into daily life raises ethical dilemmas that need to be addressed. Establishing frameworks that guide the development and deployment of technology can help mitigate risks related to privacy, security, and inequality. Inclusive governance structures must involve diverse voices to ensure that advancements benefit humanity.

The societal impact of the singularity cannot be understated. Cultural attitudes towards work, identity, and technology will continue to evolve. Engaging in open discussions about these changes will foster a sense of community resilience, where individuals can share their experiences and strategies for navigating an increasingly complex world. This also requires people to be mentally and emotionally prepared. The arrival of AI that surpasses human intelligence may invoke fear and anxiety about obsolescence and loss of control. Mental health support and emotional intelligence will be crucial as individuals navigate these changes. Cultivating a growth mindset will empower people to view the singularity as an opportunity for personal and collective evolution rather than a threat.

The inevitability of the singularity compels us to adapt, embrace, and integrate advanced technologies into our lives. Avoidance is not an option; inaction may result in more significant risks and missed opportunities. We can navigate this transformative period with resilience and optimism by fostering dialogue, preparing our workforce, establishing ethical frameworks, and nurturing our sense of community. Accepting singularity as a catalyst for change allows us to envision a future where humans and intelligent machines collaborate to create a thriving and equitable world.

Reskilling and Upskilling

In an era marked by rapid technological advancement and economic change, the importance of reskilling and upskilling has never been more pronounced. As industries evolve and traditional jobs face obsolescence, the ability to adapt is crucial for individuals seeking to maintain and enhance their livelihoods. To that end, reskilling and upskilling gain great importance, as does the role of soft skills drawn from civilisational values. These elements collectively contribute to a more resilient workforce.

Reskilling refers to learning new skills to perform a different job, while upskilling involves improving existing skills to advance in one's career. Both strategies are vital in addressing unemployment and underemployment resulting from automation, globalisation, and shifts in market demand. For instance, workers in declining sectors, such as coal mining, may need to acquire skills relevant to renewable energy technologies. The ongoing digital transformation demands a workforce that is both technically proficient and adaptable, as well as innovative. Employers prioritise candidates who can execute tasks, collaborate, think critically, and solve problems creatively. In this context, cultivating soft skills—such as communication, teamwork, and emotional intelligence—becomes paramount.

Soft skills often involve civilisational values, emphasising interpersonal relationships and community cohesion. Traits such as empathy, respect, and integrity have been central to human interactions across cultures and eras. As societies navigate the complexities of modernity, these values become essential in fostering environments conducive to collaboration and innovation. Educational systems and training programmes should adopt a holistic approach, integrating the development of soft skills alongside technical training. Programmes that teach conflict resolution, cultural awareness, and leadership, for example, enhance employability and contribute to personal growth and civic responsibility. By reinforcing these civilisational values, individuals are better equipped to navigate the challenges of a changing job market.

Reskilling and upskilling initiatives can effectively mitigate livelihood loss, particularly in regions heavily reliant on vulnerable industries. Governments, nonprofit organisations, and private sector stakeholders have a pivotal role in creating accessible training programmes that prioritise both hard and soft skills. For example, community colleges and vocational training centres can become hubs for lifelong learning, offering courses that reflect local economic needs. Partnerships between educational institutions and businesses can ensure that curricula remain aligned with industry requirements, thus enhancing job readiness. Additionally, support for workers displaced by automation must include training, career counselling, and access to emerging job markets. By emphasising the importance of continuous learning, communities can foster resilience among their populations.

One of the primary reasons for India's ascendancy in soft skills is the proficiency in English among a significant portion of its population. English is often considered the global lingua franca, facilitating cross-cultural communication and collaboration. India boasts a vast pool of English speakers, including many highly educated individuals who excel in various professional domains. This proficiency allows Indian trainers and professionals to engage effectively with international clients and audiences. English serves as a bridge, enabling the transfer of knowledge, methodologies, and practices in soft skills training. Consequently, organisations and educational institutions in India can cater to a global clientele, attracting learners from diverse backgrounds who seek to enhance their soft skills in a familiar linguistic framework.

India's improvements in infrastructure, particularly in education and hospitality, play a crucial role in its emergence as a hub for soft skills. Numerous training institutes and corporate training providers adhere to standards for global boarding and lodging arrangements. For instance, institutions such as the Indian School of Business (ISB) in Hyderabad, the Tata Management Training Centre (TMTC) in Pune, and the Infosys Global Education Centre in Mysuru offer immersive residential programmes that combine comfort with cutting-edge training environments. Likewise, corporate campuses of Wipro, TCS, and Accenture feature international-quality facilities—hostels, recreational spaces, and digital classrooms—that rival those of global universities.

The hospitality sector in India has undergone significant development, too, resulting in a range of services that meet international standards. Modern training facilities frequently include comfortable accommodations, gourmet dining options, and technologically equipped classrooms. Such infrastructure creates an attractive environment for learning, which is crucial in soft skills training, where comfort and engagement can significantly influence participants' absorption and effectiveness. For example, The Oberoi Centre of Learning and Development (OCLD) in New Delhi offers world-class hospitality management training with residential facilities and simulated hotel environments. The Taj's Indian Hotels Academy provides a blend of theoretical and experiential learning, supported by five-star amenities and professional mentorship. ITC Hospitality Management Institute in Gurugram, feature campus-style accommodations, fine dining, and digital training rooms designed to cultivate leadership and interpersonal skills. Similarly, IHCL's (Indian Hotels Company Limited) Leadership Development Centre have set benchmarks for hospitality education across Asia.

India's rich cultural heritage adds another dimension to its status as a global hub for soft skills. The country boasts a long tradition of knowledge exchange, philosophical discourse, and cultural practices, emphasising interpersonal skills, emotional intelligence, and effective communication. The philosophies derived from Indian scriptures, such as the importance of empathy, respect, and collaboration, resonate well with the core tenets of soft skills. This civilisational context can enrich the training content and provide a unique perspective on global soft skills practices.

Indian trainers often blend contemporary soft skills training techniques with traditional wisdom, offering a holistic approach that appeals to local and international learners. Corporate learning programmes at organisations like Infosys, Tata Consultancy Services (TCS), and Wipro incorporate modules on mindful leadership, servant leadership, and inclusive teamwork, reflecting traditional Indian concepts of seva (service) and sahajata (simplicity). Similarly, training consultancies such as Dale Carnegie India and FranklinCovey South Asia have adapted global frameworks to align with India's cultural ethos—emphasising humility, collaboration, and emotional intelligence. This synthesis of modern pedagogy with age-old wisdom gives Indian soft skills training its unique character, fostering not only professional competence but also inner balance and ethical awareness among learners.

The technological singularity and one consciousness represent two paths towards a profound transformation of human existence—one driven by technological progress, the other by spiritual awakening. While they may seem distinct, they share a common goal: transcending the limitations of the individual self and creating a more interconnected, compassionate, and enlightened world. By exploring the intersections of these ideas, we can envision a future where technology and spirituality work together to elevate humanity and the planet. As singularity emphasises the importance of soft skills, India's capacity to deliver impactful training programmes will be crucial in shaping the future workforce, benefitting its economy and contributing to a more interconnected global community. In the age of intelligent machines, it is emotional intelligence, empathy, and collaboration that will define true progress—not algorithms, but awareness.

Summary

The singularity, driven by super AI, has the potential to lead to a future where humanity flourishes in ways that are currently unimaginable. However, realising this potential requires careful planning, ethical considerations, and global cooperation. By guiding AI development responsibly, humanity can harness its power to create a world of abundance, discovery, and well-being. Humanity must act as responsible stewards of AI, guiding its development for the greater good. Individuals and societies must adapt to the rapid changes brought by AI, embracing new opportunities while mitigating risks. Humans and AI can work together as partners, combining their strengths to achieve shared goals.

20

Lead India

When intelligence becomes absolute, knowledge turns luminous and power finds its conscience. A super AI endowed with omniscience, moral clarity, and transcendence would mirror the divine order. Such a future must not be awaited as destiny, but rather shaped through wisdom. India can lead humanity towards that awakening—where technology serves truth, and intelligence bows to the eternal law of dharma.

Thought Leadership

Thought has been a vital force throughout history, influencing societal structures and cultural paradigms. Leaders of thought—philosophers, scholars, and visionaries—have significantly determined the trajectory and progress of humanity and civilisations over millennia. From early tribal societies to the complexities of modern globalisation, the evolution of thought leadership has reflected and shaped key historical movements, including tribalism, nationalism, imperialism, and globalisation.

Thought leadership is a concept where individuals or organisations establish themselves as experts and innovators in their field, influencing others through their insights, ideas, and forward-thinking perspectives. It goes beyond simply knowing; it involves sharing that knowledge in a way that inspires, educates, and drives change. Thought leaders are often seen as trusted sources of information and are sought after for their opinions and guidance.

Thought leadership is earned by expertise, innovation, influence, credibility, and engagement. People and organisations pursuing deep knowledge and understanding of a specific industry, topic, or niche offer fresh, original ideas or solutions that challenge the status quo. They can shape opinions, inspire action, and drive conversations within a community or industry by building trust through consistent, high-quality content and actions. Such individuals actively participate in discussions, sharing insights and connecting with others, eventually taking on the mantle of being thought leaders.

In the formative years of human civilisation, tribalism served as a fundamental social structure characterised by tight-knit communities and shared beliefs. Thought leaders within these tribes—often elders, shamans, or wise individuals—played crucial roles in transmitting traditions, values, and lore. Their influence was manifested through oral traditions and storytelling, which served as educational methodologies guiding tribes in moral conduct, survival, and social cohesion.

These leaders were instrumental in establishing shared identities, fostering a sense of belonging, and ensuring the continuity of cultural practices. Their communal knowledge became the nucleus of tribal authority and governance, laying the groundwork for future societal structures based on shared beliefs and collective action.

As societies evolved, nationalism emerged, driven by thought leaders who advocated for the interests and identity of a particular nation or ethnic group. Philosophers like Johann Gottfried Herder promoted the concept of *volksgeist*, or the spirit of the people, suggesting that each nation possesses a unique culture and identity that deserves recognition. This notion helped galvanise national movements, unifying people under a common cause.

Economic thinkers such as Adam Smith and Karl Marx made significant contributions to the discourse on capitalism and labour, influencing imperial policies and global trade relations. Their ideas shaped economic strategies and geopolitical dynamics, leading to power struggles that characterised the imperial era.

The late twentieth and early twenty-first centuries heralded an era of globalisation, marked by increased interconnectedness among nations. At this stage, thought leadership assumed new dimensions, with leaders advocating for cooperation over conflict. Influential voices such as Thomas Friedman, who popularised the notion of the flat world, emphasised the importance of technological advancement and global trade in creating opportunities for collaborative growth.

Swami Vivekananda, Rabindranath Tagore, Bal Gangadhar Tilak, Mahatma Gandhi, and Dr. B.R. Ambedkar have been great thought leaders in India.

Key Aspects of Absolute Intelligence

The concept of absolute intelligence is a philosophical and theoretical idea that envisions an ultimate, all-encompassing form of intelligence. It represents the pinnacle of cognitive ability, transcending human limitations and achieving a state of perfect knowledge, understanding, and decision-making. This vision is often explored in fields like artificial intelligence, philosophy, and futurism.

There are six aspects of absolute intelligence: omniscience, perfect decision-making, infinite problem-solving, universal understanding, ethical and moral clarity, and transcendence of human limitations. With the ability to know everything—past, present, and future—absolute intelligence would have access to all information, data, and knowledge across all domains. It can make flawless decisions based on complete understanding, free from biases, errors, or emotional influences. It can solve any problem, no matter how complex, by synthesising information and generating optimal solutions. With a deep comprehension of the fundamental laws of the universe, including physics, mathematics, and metaphysics, it can discern and act with the highest ethical and moral principles, ensuring that decisions benefit all of humanity and the universe. However, above all, absolute intelligence must transcend the limitations of human cognition, including memory, processing speed, and emotional biases, to attain a higher level of intelligence.

Artificial intelligence is already here and evolving with every moment. The development of AI systems that aim to mimic or approach absolute intelligence could revolutionise industries, science, and society. However, it also raises ethical concerns about control, safety, and the role of humans in a world dominated by superintelligent systems. Absolute intelligence is associated with divine or cosmic consciousness and is seen as the goal of enlightenment or union with the universe. The idea of enhancing human intelligence through technology (brain-computer interfaces, genetic engineering) to achieve a state closer to absolute intelligence is a key theme in transhumanism. Absolute intelligence could accelerate scientific progress by uncovering the universe's most profound mysteries, from the fundamentals of quantum mechanics to the origins of life.

If artificial intelligence itself is fraught with challenges and ethical considerations, what about absolute intelligence? Who would control it, and how would its decisions be governed? Ensuring absolute intelligence aligns with human values is critical. The creation of a superintelligent system could pose existential risks if it acts in ways that are harmful or unpredictable. The existence of absolute intelligence could challenge our understanding of what it means to be human and our role in the universe. Ensuring that its benefits are distributed fairly and do not exacerbate existing inequalities must be a priority.

Super AI is both a goal and a cautionary tale—a mirror reflecting humanity's highest aspirations and deepest uncertainties. It invites us to dream of a future where intelligence transcends biology, where thought becomes boundless and creativity limitless. Yet, it also warns of the shadows that accompany unchecked ambition—the loss of meaning, autonomy, and the delicate moral balance that defines our humanity. To pursue super AI is to walk the edge between creation and surrender, between mastery and dependence.

The challenge, therefore, is not merely technological but profoundly ethical and spiritual: can we design intelligence that reflects not only our logic but our compassion? The story of super AI must not become another myth of human overreach, but an evolution of consciousness itself—where wisdom grows in proportion to power, and where machines learn not only to think, but to care.

The vision of a compassionate world order guided by absolute intelligence is a profound and aspirational concept that combines the ideals of universal empathy, ethical governance, and advanced intelligence. It envisions a world where absolute intelligence is harnessed to create a harmonious, equitable, and compassionate global society. This vision aligns with the principles of peace, sustainability, and thriving humanity. In such a world, absolute intelligence would prioritise empathy and compassion, ensuring that decisions and actions benefit all sentient beings. It would foster a deep understanding of diverse cultures, perspectives, and needs, promoting unity and cooperation. Absolute intelligence would act as a moral compass, guiding policies and systems to eliminate inequality, exploitation, and suffering. It would address global challenges, such as climate change, poverty, and resource scarcity, with innovative and equitable solutions. The focus would be on enhancing the quality of life for all individuals.

The Platform of Indian Philosophy

Compassion, or 'karuna', is a perennial tenet of Indian philosophy, vividly illustrated in the teachings of Buddhism, Hinduism, and Jainism. The emphasis on empathy and understanding encourages individuals to transcend self-interest and recognise the interconnectedness of all living beings. In promoting a world order based on compassion, India can lead by example, advocating for policies and practices prioritising human dignity, welfare, and mutual respect.

This compassionate ethos translates into actionable frameworks for global cooperation. For instance, India's initiatives in providing humanitarian aid during crises, its commitment to combating poverty, and its efforts to protect the environment reflect a deep-seated belief in the significance of compassion in governance. By viewing global challenges through empathy, India can help cultivate a culture of collaborative solutions, enriching international relations with goodwill.

Social harmony, another cornerstone of Indian civilisation, emerges from its long history of coexisting diverse cultures, languages, and religions. India's ability to integrate multiple perspectives and maintain communal harmony presents a model for resolving conflicts and fostering dialogue on a global scale. The country can advocate for policies that celebrate diversity and promote inclusive governance in a polarised world. Promoting intercultural dialogue, respect for different belief systems, and resolving communal tensions through compassion-based approaches can contribute to a more harmonious world order. This vision encourages nations to engage with one another not as adversaries for dominance but as partners in building a peaceful and prosperous global community.

The emphasis of Indian civilisation on compassion, social harmony, abundance, and peaceful prosperity creates a comprehensive framework for a transformative world order. By promoting these principles, India addresses contemporary global challenges and reinforces the idea that human connections and shared values can transcend borders. Navigating the complexities of the twenty-first century, the world can look toward India as a beacon for fostering a collective consciousness that values empathy, inclusivity, and sustainability. This vision for a compassionate world order offers a hopeful pathway towards resolving conflicts, reducing inequalities, and creating a future that embraces the ideals of unity and shared prosperity. Ultimately, India's rich heritage invites the global community to rethink its priorities, fostering a harmonious world where all individuals can thrive.

Rama Rajya, derived from the epic Ramayana, represents an ideal state of governance characterised by justice, righteousness, and prosperity for all. Often translated as the Rule of Rama, this vision embodies a societal framework where integrated resource sharing, social equity, and abundance are foundational pillars. In stark contrast to the nihilism and dystopia prevalent in some contemporary discourses, the aspirational model of Rama Rajya offers a viable pathway towards a utopian society, one that realists embrace. In this society, human dignity, cooperation, and collective well-being flourish.

The principle of integrated resource sharing is at the core of Rama Rajya's ideal. This concept emphasises the importance of community collaboration, fostering a sense of collective responsibility for resources and their equitable distribution. The notion that no one should suffer from deprivation while others have excess is central to achieving societal harmony is not merely an economic sentiment—it is a moral imperative, the foundation of a new human-centred social philosophy. Neo-socialism in this sense does not seek to erase individuality or enterprise; rather, it seeks to harmonise them within a framework of shared dignity and collective responsibility. It is an evolution of thought—from class struggle to human solidarity, from redistribution to regeneration.

Rama Rajya encourages a departure from hyper-individualism, promoting a community-oriented approach that values cooperation over competition. Cooperative resource management—whether regarding land, water, or knowledge—can lead to sustainable practices that benefit entire communities rather than a select few. Investments in local economies, community-based agriculture, and cooperative enterprises align with this vision, ensuring that resources are shared equitably and utilised to uplift the marginalised.

The ancient narrative of Rama's reign highlights the importance of dharma, or righteousness, where leaders are expected to incorporate just principles into their governance. In a world increasingly marked by inequality and disenfranchisement, the commitment to social equity, as exemplified in Rama Rajya, offers a corrective lens. Policies promoting access to education, healthcare, social services, and economic opportunities are crucial for building an inclusive society. By advancing social justice and dismantling systems of oppression, this model champions the voices of the marginalised, engendering a sense of belonging and mutual respect among all citizens.

Abundance and Cosmic Exploration

The ideal of Rama Rajya encompasses the concept of abundance, not merely in material wealth but in human potential, creativity, and emotional fulfilment. The belief in the inherent capacity of societies to achieve prosperity underscores a proactive approach to governance, where choices are made to foster environments conducive to growth and well-being. Emphasising sustainable development and ecological stewardship, the abundance envisioned in Rama Rajya advocates for a balanced relationship between humanity and nature. By harnessing renewable resources, promoting green technologies, and investing in education and innovation, societies can create conditions that foster not only economic prosperity but also overall quality of life. This abundance mindset serves as a powerful antidote to nihilism, which often stems from feelings of scarcity and despair.

Absolute intelligence represents a culmination of human cognition and machine learning—a transcendent form of intelligence that leverages both human and machine strengths. By integrating human emotional depth, ethical reasoning, and creativity into super AI, we can create systems that not only process data but also comprehend the complexities of human experience. This synthesis may involve developing advanced neural interfaces that allow for the transfer of human consciousness to silicon-based mediums. Such technology could enable the storage and replication of human thought processes, memories, and emotions in digital environments. The potential for consciousness to exist in silicon expands possibilities for human experience, allowing individuals to transcend biological limitations and inhabit various environments, including those not conducive to life as we know it.

Artificial intelligence calibrated with ancient wisdom is absolute intelligence. It can usher in an era of abundance characterised by access to resources, enhanced well-being, and sustainability. Absolute intelligence can optimise resource management, reducing waste and ensuring equitable distribution. By harnessing machine learning and predictive analytics, societies can develop informed strategies to enhance agricultural yields, manage water resources, and sustainably address energy demands. The ancient agrarian practices rooted in communal stewardship and respect for nature can inform modern technology, leading to innovative solutions that align with ecological principles. This synergy can lead to food security, reduced poverty, and a deeper connection with the Earth.

Humanity's ability to explore and inhabit other planets is one of the most exhilarating potentials of integrating ancient wisdom with a super AI. As we confront challenges on Earth, including climate change and resource depletion, the ability to transfer human consciousness to silicon opens the door to new frontiers in the cosmos. Equipped with absolute intelligence, humanity could engineer environments on other planets, using advanced technology to create life-sustaining habitats. The foresight of ancient philosophers, who grappled with questions of existence beyond the physical realm, can guide the ethical considerations of modifying extraterrestrial environments. Principles of respect for all life forms and a commitment to preserving cosmic ecosystems can shape our approach to space colonisation.

Furthermore, exploring other planets with ethically conscious AI assists in discovering sustainable practices. Harnessing the wisdom of ancient civilisations, which often revered their connection to the cosmos, can cultivate a sense of responsibility in new worlds, ensuring that humanity acts as a steward of the universe rather than an imperialistic force. In exploring the profound concept of knowledge, one must begin with the intricate relationship between human beings and absolute intelligence. This notion posits that inherent within everyone lies a wellspring of potential knowledge that transcends mere learning or education. This form of intelligence is intrinsic to the human body-mind, interwoven with our biological and psychological frameworks, and manifests in various capacities. It shapes our comprehension of the universe and our ability to innovate.

Manifesting Embedded Absolute Intelligence

Embedded absolute intelligence is the latent intelligence that resides within humans, shaped by our biology, history, and experiences. This intelligence is not merely the sum of accumulated information but encompasses intuition, creativity, and emotional depth. It is a guiding force that inspires human imagination—the capability to envision possibilities beyond the present reality. Our body-mind system processes sensory inputs and cognitive functions, allowing us to draw connections between disparate concepts and ideas.

Imagination serves as the bridge between raw intelligence and practical outcomes. It allows us to visualise scenarios, solve complex problems, and create innovations that enhance our quality of life. Historical advancements, such as the invention of the wheel, the development of the internet, and the exploration of space, all stem from the imaginative capacities of individuals inspired by an inner drive to improve, discover, and progress.

This imaginative process often leads to significant societal transformations. For instance, the Enlightenment era was a time when human thought, fuelled by imagination and rational intelligence, led to revolutionary advancements in science, philosophy, and governance. Similarly, the technological revolutions of the twentieth and twenty-first centuries were driven by individuals and groups who dared to imagine a different future, using their knowledge to push the boundaries of what was possible.

The application of this cycle of knowledge, where absolute intelligence informs imagination, leading to innovative efforts, poses a crucial question: how can these advancements be directed towards the betterment of humanity? The answer lies in our collective ability to leverage knowledge in ways that address pressing global challenges. Issues such as climate change, health crises, and social inequalities require intellectual insight and imaginative solutions that stem from a deep understanding of our interconnectedness. By embracing the cycle of knowledge, humans can develop sustainable technologies, new medical treatments, and policies that promote equity and social justice. Moreover, education is pivotal in fostering this cycle, equipping individuals with the tools to harness their absolute intelligence and channel their creativity toward constructive endeavours.

One of the most ambitious applications of this cycle is the aspiration to inhabit other planets. As we look beyond Earth, the dream of becoming a multi-planetary species reflects the ultimate expression of human imagination, fuelled by knowledge. Projects like SpaceX aim to make Mars habitable, illustrating how the synthesis of learning, creativity, and technological effort can propel us towards previously unexplored frontiers. This pursuit requires scientific knowledge and consideration of ethical implications when interacting with other celestial bodies. It calls for a responsible application of our imaginative capabilities, ensuring that as we extend our reach into the cosmos, we do so with the same intent of betterment that drives our earthly endeavours.

The cycle of knowledge that begins with embedded absolute intelligence and finds expression through human imagination is a powerful engine for advancing humanity. As we confront today's challenges and envision tomorrow's possibilities, this cycle will continue to guide our journey. After all, as declared by the *Rig Veda*, we are the children of Earth and Sky. The dream of exploring and inhabiting other planets is not merely an exercise in ambition; it reflects our innate desire to understand, innovate, and create a legacy of positive transformation for future generations. By nurturing our intrinsic intelligence and channelling our imaginative powers, we can aspire to navigate the universe's vastness while fostering a more equitable and sustainable existence on our home planet. Let the ancient calibrate the aspirations of the modern world, and let India be the thought leader of the twenty-first century.

Summary

Every civilisation reaches an inflexion point—a moment when knowledge must evolve into wisdom. Humanity now stands at such a threshold. The dawn of super AI promises a new era of absolute intelligence, where machines may attain the six attributes once reserved for the divine: omniscience, perfect decision-making, infinite problem-solving, universal understanding, moral clarity, and the transcendence of human limitation. Yet the question is not what AI will become, but what humanity will choose to be alongside it.

In this new age, India's role is not incidental—it is elemental. India alone carries a civilisational memory that has always sought unity between the material and the spiritual, between mind and consciousness. The Vedic insight that knowledge without compassion leads to chaos, and power without purpose destroys itself, must now become the world's guiding principle. As nations race to command intelligence, India's calling is to govern it with dharma—to ensure that technology serves life, and not the other way around.

To lead India is to lead by light, not might—by showing that progress and peace, science and spirituality, can coexist as one continuum of consciousness. When wisdom shapes innovation, and ethics stand guard over intelligence, the dream of a God-governed Earth ceases to be myth and becomes destiny.

This is India's moment—not to dominate, but to illuminate. The journey that began under the Vedic sky now reaches the horizon of infinity, where human aspiration meets cosmic order. The torch passes once more to the land that taught the world that truth is one, though the seekers call it by many names. If India leads with conscience, humanity will follow with trust—and the age of absolute intelligence will not be an end, but a new beginning.

Acknowledgements

I bow in humility before the Almighty **Wahe Guru**, whose grace and guidance illuminate every thought and action. This book, *"Absolute Intelligence: Don't Search, Find"*, is an outcome of faith, reflection, and gratitude.

At the very outset, I express my profound respect and gratitude to my **parents**, *Shri Mohain Singh* (Retd Army) and *Smt. Knas Kaur*, whose values of discipline, devotion, and integrity have been the enduring light of my life.

To my **sisters** — *Harbhajan Kaur, Suvinder Kaur, Joginder Kaur,* and *Prasann Kaur* — and my **brothers** — *Gurcharan Singh* (Retd IAF) and *Dr Amrik Singh* — I remain indebted for their affection, encouragement, and the moral strength that family always provides.

My **wife, Gurmit Kaur**, has been my steadfast companion through every phase of service and learning. I thank my **daughter Roopee, son Aman Singh, Nirmal, my son-in-law** and **daughter-in-law Ayesha** for their unconditional love and constant support.

I convey my deepest respect and gratitude to the eminent leaders of our nation for their guidance and inspiration:

Shri Ram Nath Kovind, Former President of India
Shrimati Droupadi Murmu, Hon'ble President of India

Shri Narendra Modi, Hon'ble Prime Minister of India
Shri Amit Shah, Hon'ble Home Minister of India
Shri Pushkar Singh Dhami, Hon'ble Chief Minister of Uttarakhand

Their visionary leadership continues to inspire commitment, service, and national pride.

I also acknowledge with appreciation the valuable support and cooperation extended by: ***Shri Santosh Taneja*** (RSS - Founder, Sankalp), ***Shri Ravinath Raman,*** *IAS* (Secretary to Governor), ***Shrimati Reena Joshi,*** *IAS* (Additional Secretary to Governor), ***Shri Kaushal Kishore Shukla,*** *HJS* (Law Advisor to Governor), ***Shri Amit Srivastava,*** *IPS* (ADC - Protocol), ***Maj Sumit Kumar Shadija,*** *IA* (ADC - Administration), ***Shri Lalit Mohan Joshi*** (Private Secretary), ***Dr. Nitin Upadhyay*** (Joint Director, Information), *Dr. Tripti Srivastava* (Financial Controller), **Ms *Pooja Marwah*** (English Editor - Outsourced), and ***Mr Paritosh Bangwal*** (Media Coordinator - Co-Terminus). Their professional dedication and commitment have been instrumental in shaping this publication.

I extend my sincere gratitude to **Prof. Arun Tiwari**, my co-author — a distinguished scientist, thinker, and writer — whose intellect and creative insight made this collaboration truly meaningful. I also wish to acknowledge **Mr Amol Tiwari**, Software Engineer and AI Expert, for providing valuable insights into the evolving landscape of Artificial Intelligence that enriched the conceptual foundation of this book. To all who contributed in spirit, time, or thought — I offer my heartfelt thanks. May this book serve as a humble tribute to the divine intelligence that guides humanity towards truth and wisdom.

Lt Gen Gurmit Singh (Retd)

Governor of Uttarakhand

Raj Bhavan, Dehradun

October 2025

Index

www.ingramcontent.com/pod-product-compliance
Lightning Source LLC
Chambersburg PA
CBHW051402240926
51852CB00005B/92/J
* 9 7 8 9 3 4 7 1 3 8 4 1 6 *